THE IRISH TIMES

BOOK

of the

YEAR

2011

EDITED BY

PETER MURTAGH

Gill & Macmillan

Gill & Macmillan
Hume Avenue
Park West
Dublin 12
with associated companies throughout the world
www.gillmacmillan.ie

© 2011 *The Irish Times*
978 07171 4809 7
Design by Identikit Design Consultants, Dublin
Print origination by Carole Lynch
Index compiled by Cliff Murphy
Printed and bound in Italy by Printer Trento S.r.l.

The paper used in this book is made from the wood pulp
of managed forests. For every tree felled, at least one tree
is planted, thereby renewing natural resources.

A CIP catalogue record is available for this book
from the British Library.

5 4 3 2 1

Contents

Introduction

The past 12 months have been among the most traumatic in this small island's history – certainly its post-independence history.

In November 2010, Ireland lost economic sovereignty when the then Fianna Fáil-led government applied for assistance to the European Central Bank and the International Monetary Fund. Never before in the history of the State has a regime performed so ineptly or discharged its public duties with such a degree of incompetence and abject failure that others have had to come to our rescue. At the time of writing, Ireland's various systems of governance (across politics, the law and business) have singularly failed to bring to account anyone responsible for any of what has unfolded. No national politician has been charged, let alone convicted, of abuse of office or fraudulent use of facilities or expenses. As far as is known, no public official has been brought to book within the civil service for failing to discharge their duties competently. On the contrary, many in both politics and the public sector have retired, laden with six-figure severance payments and pensions – pensions linked not to their final salaries but to future rates of pay.

While there has been a general election and Fianna Fáil has been reduced to a squabbling and poorly led rump within the Oireachtas, the electorate has had to sit back and watch as, not for the first time, political dishonesty and fraud is dealt with speedily within the justice systems of other nations, notably the United Kingdom and United States.

Within business – in banking, financial services, accountancy and construction in particular – no one has been called to account before the law for the fraud, false accounting, market manipulation and lying to shareholders that has been revealed since the banking and property bubble collapse. Compared to other jurisdictions, Ireland seems unwilling, or unable, to deal with wrongdoing.

Much about this sorry saga is detailed in the pages that follow. In one of his last columns for the newspaper before the end of his long and well-lived life, much of it devoted to public service, Garret FitzGerald sought to analyse *why* things are the way they are in Ireland. 'The civic morality that underlies the social cohesion of many democratic societies, especially in northern Europe, has been absent in Ireland for some time,' he wrote. His words reward re-reading. It would be nice to think that, in perhaps 10 or 20 years' time, what he identifies would appear alien to the reader of the future. Sadly, there is no reason to believe, as of now, that anything will change.

For the first time in an *Irish Times Book of The Year*, a speech by a serving Taoiseach is reproduced, having been published in full on our Opinion and Analysis pages. Enda Kenny's address to the Dail in July in response to the Cloyne report on the failure of Bishop John McGee and others in his diocese to protect children struck a chord with people like few others in recent years. His comments were widely interpreted as representing a marked change in relations between this State and the Vatican. The power of Kenny's words was not what was said but the fact that he, as Taoiseach, said them. As such, he angered hard-line conservatives but pleased liberals.

Two visitors to Ireland, US President Barack Obama and Queen Elizabeth II of Great Britain, lifted spirits – markedly so in the case of the Queen. Her dignified visits to the Garden of Remembrance in central Dublin and the National War Memorial at Islandbridge, and her speech at the State banquet in Dublin Castle, were occasions of historic significance, as well as considerable emotional pleasure for many … and also relief that it all went so well. The warmth of the greeting she received from people in Cork capped a State visit that began laden with anxiety but which ended joyously.

The royal visit pleased to a degree equalled perhaps only by Irish success in sport – notably in golf where two Ulstermen, Rory McIlroy and Darren Clarke, scooped two majors respectively, the US Open and the British Open. And the whole country watched in admiration as Dublin goalie Stephen Cluxton coolly trotted up Croke Park and slotted the winning free kick, from 35 metres out, between the Kerry uprights to win the All-Ireland senior football final. And as the final whistle blew, he retired unruffled to the changing rooms. Job done.

My thanks, as always, to my colleagues for writing about and capturing images of these and other events, at home and abroad, with authority, passion, style and wit during the past 12 months. The pages here are simply too few to get everyone in. My thanks also to everyone at Gill & Macmillan, especially my editor Catherine Gough, for indulging me this year more than is better for both of us.

Peter Murtagh
September 2011

Contributors

David Adams is an *Irish Times* columnist.

Eileen Battersby is Literary Correspondent.

Maeve Binchy is a novelist, and was for many years a columnist and feature writer with *The Irish Times*.

Rosita Boland is a feature writer.

Brian Boyd is a music journalist.

Tara Brady is a film critic.

Elaine Byrne is Adjunct Lecturer in Politics in Trinity College Dublin.

Simon Carswell is Finance Correspondent

Donald Clarke is *Irish Times* Film Critic and a columnist.

Tony Clayton-Lea is a music journalist.

Catherine Cleary is Restaurant Critic.

Denis Coghlan is a former Chief Political Correspondent.

Stephen Collins is Political Editor.

Isabel Conway is a freelance reporter based in the Netherlands.

Paul Cullen is a political reporter.

Keith Duggan is a sports journalist and a feature writer.

Editorials are unsigned but are published in the name of the Editor.

Newton Emerson writes a weekly satirical column, Newton's Optic.

Mary Fitzgerald is Foreign Affairs Correspondent.

Garret FitzGerald, who died in May 2011, was a columnist in Saturday's edition of the newspaper.

Simon Fitzmaurice is a man, a husband and a father coping with motor neurone disease.

Seán Flynn is Education Editor.

Karen Fricker is a freelance journalist and Eurovision aficionado.

Michael Harding is a playwright and columnist.

Shane Hegarty is Arts Editor and writes a weekly column in Saturday's Weekend Review supplement.

Mark Hennessy is London Editor.

Tom Hennigan is South America Correspondent.

Ann Marie Hourihane is an *Irish Times* columnist.

Róisín Ingle is a feature writer and also writes Up Front, a personal column in the Magazine, which is part of Saturday's edition of the newspaper.

Michael Jansen is a Middle East analyst and reporter.

Sara Keating is a theatre critic.

Colm Keena is Public Affairs Correspondent.

Morgan Kelly is Professor of Economics in University College Dublin.

Karlin Lillington writes on new technology and the internet.

Miriam Lord is a political sketch writer.

Damian Mac Con Uladh reports from Athens.

Patsy McGarry is Religious Affairs Correspondent.

Ronan McGreevy is an *Irish Times* reporter.

Daniel McLaughlin is based in Budapest from where he reports on Eastern Europe, Russia, the Balkans and the Caucasus.

John McManus is Business Editor.

Frank McNally writes An Irishman's Diary.

David McNeill is Tokyo Correspondent.

Lara Marlowe is Washington Correspondent.

Mary Minihan is a political reporter.

Seán Moran is Gaelic Games Correspondent.

Gerry Moriarty is Northern Editor.

Maurice Neligan, who died in October 2010, was a retired surgeon and columnist for HEALTHplus, a supplement with Tuesday's edition of the newspaper.

Carl O'Brien is Chief Reporter.

Dan O'Brien is Economics Editor.

Ross O'Carroll-Kelly is the alter ego of writer Paul Howard.

Enda O'Doherty is an Assistant Foreign Editor.

Michael O'Regan is a political reporter.

Ian O'Riordan is a sports journalist.

Fintan O'Toole is an *Irish Times* columnist.

Michael Parsons is a correspondent based in Kilkenny specialising in auctions.

Jane Powers is Gardening Correspondent.

Philip Reid is Golf Correspondent.

Emmet Riordan is Cricket Correspondent.

Barry Roche is Cork Correspondent.

Derek Scally is Berlin Correspondent.

Kathy Sheridan is a feature writer.

Gerry Thornley is Rugby Correspondent.

Cian Traynor is an intern reporter with the *Irish Times*.

Michael Viney writes Another Life about him and his wife Eithne's life at their small holding on the edge of the Atlantic in Co. Mayo.

Caroline Walsh is Literary Editor.

John Waters is an *Irish Times* columnist.

Photographers and illustrators whose work features in this year's edition include *Irish Times* staff members and external contributors Alan Betson, Cyril Byrne, Brenda Fitzsimons, Matt Kavanagh, Eric Luke, Dara Mac Dónaill, Frank Miller, Bryan O'Brien, David Sleator, Martyn Turner and Michael Viney.

The Irish Times Book of the Year 2011 also features the work of freelance photographers attached to Irish and international photo agencies, whose names appear in the photograph captions.

Jacket cover photographs were taken by Billy Stickland/Inpho, Brenda Fitzsimons, Chris Ison/PA, Conor Healy, David Sleator, Dylan Martinez/Reuters, Eric Luke, Eric Luke, Frank Miller, Graham Crouch/Getty Images, Leon Farrell/Photocall Ireland, Mari Sarai, Matt Kavanagh, Maxwell Photography, Pier Paolo Cito/AP, Reuters and Wolfgang Rattay/Reuters.

FRIDAY, 1 OCTOBER 2010

A Historic Day but No One Knows what is Yet to Come

Dan O'Brien

Yesterday was an extraordinary day. The Government removed all doubt that an even harsher budget than planned will be introduced in the coming months. New, even more staggering figures for bailing out the banks were announced. AIB was all but nationalised. Some of that bank's senior management were finally and very belatedly shown the door. The Government's borrowing agency unexpectedly cancelled scheduled fundraising efforts over the rest of 2010.

The news caused bewilderment, shock, fear, anger and other emotions besides. When will it all end and where? Not soon and no one knows for sure are the respective answers to those questions.

If there was some good news yesterday, it was that the usually hypersensitive herd of bond market traders did not stampede in blind panic. If they had rushed to ditch their remaining holdings of Irish Government bonds, the State would have been driven closer to the cliff edge.

In the event, interest rates on those bonds fell slightly, suggesting the Government was judged to be a safer bet to lend to yesterday than the day before, despite the blizzard of hardly auspicious news. The avoidance of panic was all the more remarkable given the downgrading of Spanish government debt yesterday morning by a credit rating agency, an occasion that has in the recent past triggered continent-wide selling off of weak government debt.

Be thankful for small mercies. There was not much else to give relief yesterday.

The announcements on the banks do not draw a line under the financial crisis. They do not do so

Cartoon by Martyn Turner.

because that simply cannot be done at this juncture. As long as property prices continue to fall, nothing will be certain in the world of Irish banking. And the property market does not look like bottoming out until next year, at the earliest.

Most of the talk was of loans to property developers. There was little about loans to households and non-property businesses. The number of mortgages under water is surging. Many companies are clinging on by their fingertips. The percentage of loans to households and non-property companies destined to go bad is rising. They will rise even more sharply if Frankfurt starts to raise interest rates before an Irish recovery is well under way. Banks would then need even more capital.

The bottoming-out of the property slump and much else besides will depend on the economy recovering. Here again the past days have brought little reason for optimism. According to figures released last Thursday week, economic growth was feebler than previously thought in the first quarter of 2010. It went into reverse in the second. In the third, there was no sign of real recovery. It may come, possibly soon, but it hasn't come yet.

The announcement yesterday of an estimated budget deficit this year – a mind-blowing 32 per cent of GDP – is higher than officials were indicating only weeks ago. This one-year imbalance is larger than the entire accumulated national debt as recently as 2007. Nothing approaching it has ever been recorded since the State's founding. Around the world, such deficits have historically only been run up in times of major war or devastating natural disaster.

Irish red setter Anny with her 18 pups, owned by Gerd and Marita Holey from Neverin in Mecklenburg-Vorpommern, Germany. Photograph: Sebastian Haerter.

The underlying budget deficit – excluding the costs of bailing out the banks – is smaller than the headline figure, but is massive nonetheless and all but certain to be the largest in the developed world yet again this year. As is frequently pointed out, the running of massive deficits each year will end up accounting for much more of the public debt tax-payers will ultimately be lumbered with than the cost of incompetent bankers' lending.

Because those losses have already been incurred, there is infuriatingly little to be done, short of the nuclear option of defaulting on bank liabilities. Future deficits have not yet been racked up and there is, therefore, much more that can be done about them.

This, correctly, is what the Government has committed to doing. As the size of budgetary imbalance has grown, so must its adjustment efforts if it is to remain on track to arrive at the destination of a deficit one-tenth the size of 2010's by 2014. It may well be that this announcement was the crucial factor yesterday in preventing bond market panic.

It certainly wasn't because the National Treasury Management Agency (NTMA) announced that it would cancel further debt issuance for the remainder of the year. This was a very hard call. It may prove to be correct, but the timing was surely wrong. Having put out so much bad news, it would have been better for the agency to sit tight and watch the market reaction. The next auction was three weeks away. If the market didn't calm, it could have cancelled. If it had, the agency could have claimed all was well and stuck to its plan.

That the NTMA made the decision – despite maintaining all along that regular bond auctions are vital to retaining the faith of its purchasers – gives an indication of the gravity of the situation in which Ireland finds itself.

Although the situation is very serious, it is still just about manageable. But as the probability of the State having to resort to external assistance is rising towards 50 per cent, it is worth beginning to consider what would happen in the event of a bailout.

In May, a mechanism was established to rescue countries in the euro zone suffering severe economic crisis. It is co-funded and co-managed by the EU and the International Monetary Fund (IMF). It is cast-iron proof that default – in any form – is not an option for states in the euro area. Any debate on the wisdom or otherwise of default as a way out of the crisis is irrelevant in the face of the political fact that European leaders have put their resources and credibility behind a 'no default' position.

If Ireland's budgetary and economic position continues to weaken, the country will be forced to activate this mechanism. The consequences of so doing would be multiple.

From a funding perspective, a three-year rescue plan would likely be put in place, as has already happened in Greece. During that time, Ireland would no longer depend on the international bond market to fund its deficits. Instead, money would be borrowed from other countries and the IMF at somewhat lower but much more stable rates of interest.

In return, those throwing the lifeline would demand changes in how Ireland manages its affairs. Officials from Brussels and Washington, with close involvement from those in other euro zone capitals, would come to Dublin to draw up a programme. Such a programme would be unlikely to attempt to cut the deficit by much more than is planned, but it would very probably target the measures differently.

The involuntary loss of sovereignty necessarily accompanying a bailout is to be avoided for many reasons. It could have serious and unpredictable political and social consequences and the reputational damage of being lumped in with Greece would be appalling, and far more serious for Ireland than for the Mediterranean country (as Greece is the most closed economy in the EU, it matters much less how it is perceived abroad than for Ireland, which is among the most open economies in the world).

Everything possible must be done to avoid the last resort of a bailout. Thankfully, it remains only a possibility at this point and the Government's good cash position allows time and space to consider all options carefully and without panic.

SATURDAY, 2 OCTOBER 2010

Hotel on Wheels from Istanbul to Budapest

Michael Parsons

The Danube isn't blue. Bulgaria grows the world's most precious roses. And Dracula had halitosis. Doesn't travel broaden the mind? And there is no more agreeable – or stress-free – way to see the world than by rail. Especially from the window of a private touring train.

The British-owned Danube Express has re-invented elegant rail travel and even trumped the Orient Express by providing passengers with the luxury of showers on board. The train, designed for 42 passengers, is based in Budapest and travels on selected routes through central and eastern Europe – from the Baltic to the Bosphorus.

The company tailor-makes holidays for independent travellers and also offers a range of escorted tours, which combine a rail trip with hotel stays in chosen cities. I joined the 'Transylvanian Return', a tour which began in Istanbul, included sightseeing stops in Bulgaria and Romania and ended in Budapest.

**Day One
Turkish Delight**

Istanbul's Sirkeci Station looks like it hasn't changed much since its grand opening 110 years ago. Built in a style known as European Orientalism, the

The Casa Sfatului (Council House) in Piata Sfatului, the centre of medieval Brasov in Transylvania. Photograph: Gavin Hellier.

Bran Castle – 'Dracula's Castle' – perched atop a 60 m peak in the centre of Bran in Transylvania.
Photograph: Robert Harding/Getty.

sumptuous edifice provides a suitably atmospheric starting point for a great rail journey.

The surrounding streets teem with life, friendly cafes and gloriously kitsch shops selling products as diverse as pots of 'Natural Viagra' (conveniently priced for tourists at €8) and fabulously hued conical towers of dusted Turkish delight.

The megacity of 12 million people is home to some of the world's greatest sights, but not even the Blue Mosque or the Topkapi Palace could quite compete with the alluring prospect of strangers on a train, preparing for dinner, as old Constantinople glides past. It was time to board.

Uniformed staff on the platform assisted guests onto the navy-blue and cream liveried Danube Express carriages. A 'deluxe' air-conditioned sleeping compartment, the size of a compact bedroom in a Parisian hotel, was equipped with a surprisingly

comfortable bed, seating area, excellent lighting, a mini-safe, ample storage including a wardrobe, a full-length mirror, a picture window and – the ultimate rail luxury – an en suite bathroom with shower and toilet.

The passengers were mainly British and American; the dress code informal. This was a holiday for people who enjoy the adventure of travel rather than faux-Edwardian dressing up. Aperitifs were served in the lounge car where a pianist tinkled out Sinatra.

Dinner – like all meals on board – had a central European flavour, and a *table d'hôte* menu of mushroom soup, venison goulash and apple and sour cherry strudel was served at a single sitting. While passengers dined, staff discreetly made up beds in the sleeping cars.

At midnight, the train stopped in Kapikule for

customs formalities before reaching the Bulgarian border. There was time for the few smokers on board (the non-smoking train) to hop off for a last puff on Turkish soil.

Day Two
Guns and Roses
As requested, at 7 a.m. the sleeping car attendant knocked with a gentle wake-up call and coffee on a silver tray. The minarets of Turkey's mosques had been replaced by the onion-shaped domes of Orthodox churches. Ah, mysterious Bulgaria: land of poison-tipped umbrellas, Olympian weightlifters and, improbably, Irish property investors. After breakfast (cooked to order), the train arrived at Kazanlak for the morning's guided excursion.

An informative guide explained that the town was once renowned for Kalashnikov machine gun production, but is more happily known as one of the world's great centres of rose oil production. From guns to roses.

In the nearby Valley of the Roses, flowers are harvested in late May/early June and distilled to yield a precious oil widely used by international manufacturers of cosmetics and perfume. A distinctly Soviet-looking Research Institute for Roses, Aromatic and Medicinal Plants housed a little museum devoted to the history of the industry, but the gift shop – which could be a gold-mine – was reminiscent of Moscow's GUM department store in the bad old days with dim lighting, grumpy staff and poorly presented products.

The day's unexpected highlight was a visit to a 5,000-year-old tumulus where the tomb of an ancient king of Thrace was unearthed. The discovery, with its fabulous gold hoard, created an international sensation. Budding archaeologists who dream of emulating Howard Carter should take heart. Bulgaria still has over 4,000 such burial mounds yet to be excavated.

After lunch back on board the train, it was time for an afternoon stop at the city of Veliko Turnovo, the mediaeval capital of Bulgaria, on the Yantra River. The city – a curious architectural mix of old and the hideously concrete recent Communist – is gradually being 'westernised'. Twenty minutes into a guided tour and a narcoleptic commentary about the intricacies of Bulgarian history inevitably resulted in a breakaway group seeking a caffeine fix.

Cyrillic street signage was challenging, but the shaded tables outside Coffee House Stratilat looked appealing – despite being overlooked by a hulking statue of local-boy-made-good, one-time prime minister Stefan Stambolov. Some passengers had bought fistfuls of lev, the local currency, but the euro was also accepted. Honey-drenched chocolate cake provided just the right energy boost ahead of a visit to the 'folkloric' village of Arbanassi, with its wealthy merchant house examples of Bulgarian National Revival architecture. Desultory street traders attempted to flog 'authentic' lace and embroidery, which looked like it had just arrived from factory No. 34 in Guangdong province.

Later, as the train rolled on, the Bulgarian countryside appeared curiously deserted. A legacy of the disastrous farm collectivisation of the 1960s, perhaps? After a dinner of succulent roast goose, the waiter cheekily pre-empted a response by asking: 'Was it delicious?' Well, yes, it was. A nightcap of Zwack apricot brandy, combined with the train's rocking motion, helped to cure lingering first-night insomnia. At midnight, a Romanian border guard knocked on the doors of sleeping compartments to check passports. Another frontier crossed.

Day Three
Romanian Romance
If it's Tuesday, it must be Transylvania. It was heart-warming to discover that the late, crazed, former dictator Ceauşescu hadn't quite succeeded in entirely destroying Romania.

Brasov has a lovely central square, Piata Sfatului, surrounded by red-roofed mediaeval houses and unexpectedly impressive baroque buildings. The city is close to the Carpathian Mountains and the international ski resort at Poiana, but tourists make a beeline for Castelul Bran – popularly known as Dracula's Castle.

The vampire myth is largely the invention of Dublin-born novelist Bram Stoker, who based the character on Dracul, a local tyrant who suffered from bad breath and earned the nickname Vlad the Impaler for inflicting unspeakable cruelties on his enemies.

Although the tour guide wearily, but gamely, indulged tourists' fascination with the blood-sucking creature, the castle is quite unlike the spooky, sinister creation of Hollywood's imagination.

In fact, Bran Castle is more a Transylvanian Balmoral and was a favourite summer retreat for the old Romanian royal family during the early 20th century. The only caped vamp on display was Queen Marie gazing from sepia-tinted photographs.

Outside the castle gates, though, a lively and rather shambolic street market has evolved selling a motley selection of tacky Dracula merchandise. Despite the inexplicable worldwide popularity of the vampire legend and the pernicious influence of America's ghastly Halloween festival, the Romanian authorities, to their credit, have not approved plans for a theme park. Yet.

An afternoon excursion to Sighisoara revealed a Brothers Grimm fairy-tale town with a 14th-century clock tower that could have been home to Rapunzel. But there was no escape from the dreaded fangs. A marble plaque outside a cafe recorded Vlad Dracul's residency from 1431 to 1435.

The perfect antidote was to follow in the footsteps of Prince Charles (who is quite a Transylvania enthusiast) and adjourn to Casa cu Cerb, a restaurant decorated with his photograph and a stag's antlers, where charming staff served walnut cake and coffee.

Back aboard the train, there was a final chance to observe the Romanian countryside, which was reminiscent of John Hinde images of a lost rural Ireland. Haystacks dotted the landscape; horses and carts plodded along traffic-free roads; and women and children hoed fields with not a tractor in sight. As the light faded, the train headed towards yet another border.

Day Four
Hungarian Rhapsody

After a journey of some 1,200 miles, the Danube Express turned morning commuters' heads as it arrived into Budapest's Nyugati Station. The train's courteous, friendly and efficient staff had arranged a farewell champagne reception in the old imperial waiting room, where Franz Joseph and his Empress Sissi once awaited the royal train as they gadded about their Austro-Hungarian empire. It was a fittingly elegant way to disembark. But once the heavy, gilded doors closed on that lost world it was back to reality with a jolt.

On the bustling streets of central Budapest, there are few reminders that this was a Soviet bloc city just 20 years ago. The Hungarian capital, on the not-so-blue Danube, has regained much of its former glory and offers a wealth of cultural and architectural attractions. A perfect place from which to plan the day's itinerary – or simply watch the world go by – is the terrace of Cafe Gerbeaud, one of the world's greatest confectioners. A slice of the house specialty, a Valrhona chocolate 'torta' served with whipped cream and apricot sauce, washed down by pungent espresso, is one of Europe's most distinctive culinary experiences.

But if you're tired of sightseeing, can't listen to another word of a guide's commentary, have seen one mediaeval citadel too many, or are just suffering from a dose of over-Balkanisation, you may succumb to a 'Kerrygold moment' and seek refuge in one of Budapest's Irish bars. The Longford, which according to its non-Irish staff has 'Serbian proprietors', displayed a menu touting dishes such as 'fried totters with fried onions and smashed potatoes' and a 'mixed grill' called, appropriately, the 'Longford Fatál'. It was time to go home.

Traditional musician and accordionist Máirtín O'Connor playing a tune at NUI Galway where he was conferred with a Master of Music degree. Photograph: Joe O'Shaughnessy.

Danube Express

Danube Express offers a range of rail trips and fully escorted holidays on routes through Poland, Hungary, Slovakia, Romania, Bulgaria and Turkey.

A four-day Transylvanian journey on the Danube Express between Istanbul and Budapest (via Bulgaria and Romania) costs £2,790 (about €3,262) per person, based on two sharing a deluxe twin en suite compartment or in a 'classic' single compartment. It includes three nights on the Danube Express full board with complimentary wine, beer and soft drinks, and all scheduled sightseeing.

In addition, the Transylvanian trip is available as a nine-day fully escorted holiday from £3,690 (about €4,315) per person, including BA flights from/to the UK, two nights in Istanbul and three nights in Budapest, half board in four-star hotels with a full sightseeing programme and free time.

SATURDAY, 9 OCTOBER 2010

Could Try Harder

Catherine Cleary

The smell of diesel and beef fat wafts around the dark empty streets, where waiting burger stands sit in separate puddles of generator light. There's a roar from the stadium. Some black-clad drink-promotion girls are getting their gear from a man in a jeep. He's handing them harnesses. Maybe they're going to scale the outside and drop on to the pitch, Mission Impossible-style.

I'm late for the match at Dublin's Aviva Stadium and on a mission to see if the food inside can live up to its surroundings. Friends who have experienced the posh seats say the food is great. The stadium website promises 'innovative, creative and varied' food. On match nights, it says it will serve 2,000 portions of fish and chips, 4,000 speciality gourmet burgers and 5,000 hot beef sandwiches.

I'm clutching a ticket to steerage, and somewhere inside this bowl of light and Leinster fans is a gourmet fast-food experience with my name on it.

It starts with a promising sign on the grey concrete wall beyond the turnstile directing staff towards the kitchen. It turns out there are many kitchens in the Aviva, most of them the serving-hatch sort where the heat lamps make the wearing of a Guinness fleece seem like a punishment for the pleasant young servers. I'm on the fifth floor of the East Stand and our burger joint is recovering from the pre-match feeding frenzy and preparing for half time.

'Food' is spelled out in brushed steel letters over the hatch. The word gourmet is used in the brief menu and the fish and chips are said to be in a 'tempura' batter. So far, so pleasant. A good burger is a guilty pleasure, the heat of the meat softening the bap, juices soaking into the bread, maybe some soft, browned onions and just a bit of ketchup. Fist food, designed to be eaten with one hand and no dignity.

And so to the game. The first glimpse of the pitch and the capacity crowd is jaw-dropping. My friend, an American in Ireland who has taken rugby to her heart, is wearing her Leinster scarf and a wide grin. There is a touch of *Breakfast at Tiffany's* about the place. Above us there's a perfect velvet-black sky and the floodlights are making the turf and everyone on it look box fresh. It's easy to forget the tumbleweed blowing around NAMA hotel suites outside. Holly Golightly would have liked 'the proud look of it', and that feeling that 'nothing very bad could happen to you there'.

But it does and it comes in white cardboard cartons. At half-time we make it to the hatch and place our order. There are queues seven and eight deep. We order a plain burger and the 'tempura' fish and chips, with two bottles of water. It comes to €17.80. The young man asks if I'd mind waiting for the fish and chips. That's fine. A white cardboard box with a 'P' on it is pushed forward. Seconds later the fish and chips follow. So that constitutes a wait when you're feeding thousands.

Next comes the jostle to the ketchup table and the realisation that a pint of beer would have been a much better drinks order. You can't balance a cardboard carton of food on top of a water bottle. And they confiscate the lids (no Axl Rose attacks here). So you can't grip it under your arm. We put the open bottles between our feet to free up a hand to eat.

'I've never seen anything quite so plain as that,' the friend says, lifting the bap lid off her burger. It's a diagram of a meal. The pattie appears to be without meat juices, as if it's sealed in an invisible membrane. It needs ketchup, if only to add a bit of moisture. The 'tempura' batter on my fish is about as fluffy and crisp as a damp sock. The watery white fish tastes like it was blast-frozen as soon as it flopped out of the sea. The chips are okay, potato-y in a competent sort of way. But there are no tables, not even the standing sort, to let you balance the food and rip open a vinegar sachet. The ketchup station is as busy as a petrol pump on Budget Day morning. And I draw the line at putting my food on the floor. I struggle to finish before chucking the component parts into separate recycling bins.

Back in our seats I ask the friend's friend his opinion of the burgers. His thumb goes emphatically down. 'Like chewing on a scrum cap,' he adds later. Walking away with the *Irish Times* photographer, we see the stadium shooting wands of laser light into the clouds above the pretty rooftops of Havelock Square, the mothership sending messages to her people. Food encounters of a very ordinary kind await you here. Pedestrian mass catering at a sports stadium? It's hardly a surprise, just a bit disappointing, when the rest of it rises above that to the spectacular.

TUESDAY, 12 OCTOBER 2010

One Health Vision that Must Become a Reality

Maurice Neligan

I was not cut out to be a psychiatrist. The surgical vocation requires clearer diagnoses and treatment pathways in so far as are possible. My early and, indeed, woefully short exposure to psychiatry was the mandated course before we faced final medical exams. This consisted of a series of lectures and visits to a clinical setting. In my case, this was to Grangegorman, which later became St Brendan's Hospital.

I have always had the impression that changing the name of a hospital is often an attempt to leave negative connotations behind. In my time, psychiatry was a Cinderella specialty, overshadowed by the cutting-edge disciplines of medicine and surgery. I learned enough of the subject to pass my exams, but I now think far more tuition and experience would have stood me in good stead in later practice.

There was a tendency to quickly refer such patients to the appropriate colleague lest the order of your practice was dislocated and your beds occupied by problems deeper than those cured by the knife. Walter Lincoln Palmer, distinguished physician, adjured colleagues, 'Don't send a patient to a psychiatrist as if you were telling him to go to hell.' There was, and to some degree remains, an 'out of sight, out of mind' approach to such patients. The medical student's superficial conclusion that the subject concerned the 'care of the id by the odd' was not conducive to considering the very real issues involved.

In medicine, luckily, there are always bigger and better minds than your own. The great pioneering surgeon John Hunter wrote, 'Perhaps there is nothing in nature more pleasing than the study of the human mind.' More tellingly, the equally distinguished physician Sir William Osler, in his classic *Principles and Practice of Medicine*, said, 'Everywhere the old order changes and happy they are who can change with it.' There was a lot to change in the treatment of those with diseases of the mind; there remains a lot to improve.

It has been a long and arduous road to the incorporation of psychiatry fully into the body of mainstream medicine. Such illnesses are like most others: a mixture of genetic, social, biological and psychological functions. The genesis of many psychiatric conditions is as yet poorly understood, but we must ensure that the treatment of those with such conditions is not allowed to be dealt with once more on the 'out of sight, out of mind' principle. Society has for too long turned its back on these patients.

In earlier days, some patients with epilepsy and other neurological and psychiatric conditions were associated with demonic possession and witchcraft, and many perished cruelly because of our fears of the unknown. Others were banished from society or incarcerated so that the rest of us could remain secure in our ignorance.

The Bethlehem, or Bedlam, Hospital established in London in 1330 is a case in point. There were held a mixture of the 'mentally disabled, the criminally insane, epileptics and indigent poor' and one might be tempted to add 'other inconvenient persons'.

The Pitié-Salpêtrière Hospital in Paris served the same function and was also a prison for the flotsam and jetsam of the lower classes. It was stormed during the French Revolution and while incarcerated prostitutes were freed by the mob, many shackled 'lunatics' were murdered in cold blood. With the dawn of enlightenment, this great hospital grew into the world-class institution it is today.

Pierre Janet, writing about the Paris of the time, pointed out the class distinctions of psychiatric practice: 'If a patient is poor, he is committed to a public hospital as "psychotic", if he can afford the luxury of a private sanatorium, he is diagnosed as "neurasthenic", if he can afford to be nursed at home with attending physicians, the diagnosis is "eccentric".' In some respects, *plus ça change*.

In our little island, the great Dean Swift wrote of his own death:

He gave the little wealth he had
To build a house for fools and mad,
And showed by one satiric touch
No nation needed it so much.

Now we talk the talk with our *Vision for Change* document for the mental health services here. Will we walk the walk, or will these vulnerable patients be sacrificed with so many more of our people for the failures of others?

Maurice Neligan died suddenly on 8 October, shortly after dispatching this, his final, column to The Irish Times.

SATURDAY, 16 OCTOBER 2010

A Miner Triumph for Chile

Tom Hennigan at the San José Mine, Chile

The postcard from Ireland is at first barely noticeable. It is tucked in discreetly at the foot of a Mother Teresa statue at the makeshift shrine erected by relatives of the 33 miners during the long vigil they held while their men remained trapped underground.

But there it is, a line of cows on an Irish country road, incongruous amid the Virgin Mary figures, Pope John Paul II prayer cards, goodwill messages and signed miners' helmets. Addressed to 'The Chilean Miners', it was posted by a family in Oldcastle, Co. Meath. It reads: 'Dear Miners. You are in our thoughts and prayers each day. Very best wishes from Ireland. God bless.'

The card is another small reminder of the extent to which the very human drama that played out on this remote and rocky hillside over the past 10 weeks gripped people across five continents. It is the story of 33 men trapped deep in their copper and gold mine by a cave-in on 5 August and how, against the odds, they were contacted alive 17 days later to the amazement of a watching world that had given them up for dead.

It is those first 17 days that were the darkest for the men, surviving on spoonfuls of tuna every two days and drinking polluted water, all the while waiting for any sign of their rescuers. For the families on the surface this period was also the hardest. 'Until that first contact it was very difficult. There were just the families here and we were praying but knew others didn't think they were still alive. So when they found them, well, that was the most emotionally intense moment of all,' says Margaritta Rojo, mother of Dario Segovia Rojo.

When all the men were finally brought up to the surface over 22 emotional hours on Wednesday, it was not just the religiously inclined who were talking about the men's resurrection.

Chileans have taken huge pride in the professionalism of the rescue and the fortitude shown by the men. In sweltering conditions they survived underground longer than any previous group of miners, and their rescuers got them out sooner than was thought possible; when they were first located, on 22 August, estimates about how long they would have to wait underground stretched as far as Christmas.

The country's unlimited respect for the miners and their families is also tinged with guilt. 'The truth is, most people thought they were already dead,' says a local bus driver, Luis Godoy. 'After that amount of time with no contact everyone assumed the worst. Only the families kept on believing they would be found. Then, when after

17 days they were found alive and well and all together, patiently waiting for their rescuers, people felt a kind of private shame that they had not shared the families' faith.'

Chile is a country well versed in the risks of mining. Its increasing prosperity might be based on stable politics and sound economic management, but much of the cash comes from exporting the huge mineral wealth found in the Atacama Desert. Mining is a dangerous occupation, and Chileans know tragedies are inevitable: 35 miners died at work last year.

Chile's mining communities are known for their intense faith; it acts as a shield against the inherent dangers of their work. The country's mining minister, Laurence Golborne, broke down in tears two days after the accident as he told family members that an attempt to reach the men through a ventilation shaft had failed; he was publicly upbraided by the men's mothers, brothers and colleagues, who told him not to become disheartened so easily.

Golborne had been ordered to take charge of the rescue operation by Chile's president, Sebastián Piñera, who ignored the counsel of political advisers to distance himself from what they feared would be a tragedy. Instead he went to the mine and ordered the state-owned mining giant Codelco to take over the rescue operation from the pit's beleaguered private bosses.

Though his minister managed the day-to-day operation, Piñera left no one in doubt: he was running the show, driving on his team and providing regular bulletins to his countrymen on progress. He was there on Wednesday to personally greet every miner as he emerged from the ground.

Chilean miner Osman Araya (29) is hugged by a relative as he becomes the sixth miner to exit the Phoenix rescue capsule at the San José mine near Copiapó, Chile. Photograph: Hugo Infante/Chilean Government.

Piñera is a billionaire businessman famous for his hands-on management style. Only his most cynical political opponents have suggested that he led from the front for any reason other than to try to do all he could to free the men alive. But he has benefited politically from his management of the crisis, and he has sought to use the outcome to overcome the blow to national confidence inflicted by the earthquake earlier this year.

Piñera was sworn in less than two weeks after the huge quake – 8.8 on the Richter scale – in February. In the immediate aftermath, Chile received widespread international praise for its earthquake preparedness, which meant that, although the earthquake was stronger than the devastating one that hit Haiti a month before, just over 500 people lost their lives.

But for Chileans the earthquake provoked a bout of national introspection and doubt in what was meant to be a year filled with celebrations to mark the country's bicentenary. Though Chile's infrastructure held up remarkably well against the sudden shift in Earth's tectonic plates, the country was shocked at the outbreaks of looting that followed in the days afterwards.

Some blamed a society where the social bonds were weaker than many suspected after two peaceful and prosperous decades following the return of democracy in 1990. Others simply blamed the Government's slow response in getting help to the affected areas, leaving quake victims desperate. Either way, footage of shops in the country's second city being looted shook Chile's image of itself as a society on the verge of First World status.

Now the government wants the national questioning that followed the earthquake to be transformed into pride in the performance of all involved in the events at the San José mine: the miners and their families for their dignity and solidarity, and the rescuers for their professionalism. The technical expertise displayed by the rescue crews fits in with the idea of a Chile that Piñera

Trapped miner José Henríquez waves as he emerges from the Phoenix rescue capsule after reaching the surface to become the 24th miner rescued from the San José mine near Copiapó, Chile. Photograph: Ivan Alvarado/Reuters.

says can be ready to join the developed club of nations by 2018, in time to celebrate the 200th anniversary of the final defeat of Spain's armies in the war of independence.

'Chile is not the same country as it was 69 days ago. We are more respected,' he said on Wednesday. He meant by the countries abroad whose leaders have rushed to congratulate it on the successful conclusion of the rescue. But he could just as easily have been speaking about his fellow citizens, who, after the confused days of late February and early March, once again have reason to view their country as the continent's sober, can-do nation. Even Golborne recovered from his shaky start, and his sure performance in subsequent weeks has transformed him from the most obscure member of Piñera's cabinet into a politician with an 87 per cent approval rating who is talked about as a possible future presidential candidate.

The miners' rescue has even sparked hopes of helping to improve Chile's rocky relationship with neighbouring Bolivia. The two countries have not maintained full diplomatic ties with each other since the 1879–1883 War of the Pacific, when Chile conquered and annexed Bolivia's only access to the sea. Bolivia's demand for an outlet on the Pacific has proved a block to normal relations ever since.

On Wednesday, the Bolivian president, Evo Morales, came to the San José mine to stand along-side his Chilean counterpart and greet the fourth man lifted to the surface, his compatriot Carlos Mamani, the only foreigner among the group. In thanking the Chilean authorities for rescuing the 23-year-old, he said the events at the mine 'bind us together, they strengthen us . . . Bolivia will never forget the efforts of the Chilean Government . . . and of the Chilean people.'

It is too early to say if the outpouring of goodwill that has followed the miners' rescue can help resolve a historical dispute well into its second century. But it must surely help that the two presidents now share a personal bond as they seek to negotiate a tough 13-point agenda agreed by both countries in 2006 as a road map to resolving their impasse.

A more pressing matter for Morales to resolve is the reported rebuff his offer of a gift of land back home received from Mamani. The miner has agreed to visit Bolivia next week. But his family says he wants to remain in Chile – a setback to Morales, who promised to bring Bolivia's most famous miner home with him.

Piñera should take note: the Chilean miners might also not be as willing to take up the roles of national heroes that he has assigned them. They have got new lives to get on with.

SATURDAY, 16 OCTOBER 2010

You Don't Need to go to Journalism College to be a Journalist

Shane Hegarty

Hot Press is putting its name to a diploma in music journalism. Its sessions will include 'music and society', 'music and popular culture' and 'popular culture and music in Ireland since independence'.

Leaping Lester Bangs! I suppose you've got to find a way to fill one night a week for 12 weeks at a cost of €895. Nevertheless, here's lesson one from the Present Tense correspondence course in music journalism (free with this newspaper): if you have a burning ambition to be a music journalist, then you will already have done your course in 'music and society'.

And you would have paid that cash already in downloads and CDs and gigs and magazines and maybe even the odd copy of *Hot Press*. It was called your youth. You earned a master's in it.

Actually, *Hot Press*'s course already has a rival: a free course in music journalism, over just four weeks, announced this week by the *Sunday*

A surfer gets to grips with some big waves at a surfing session in Mullaghmore, Co. Sligo. Photograph: Gary McCall.

Tribune's Una Mullally during a Phantom Radio chat with *Hot Press's* Stuart Clark.

The rival course is called Dancing About Architecture. The name says it all: immediately self-deprecating and knowing. Because, of all areas of writing (with the notable exception of the linguistic torture chamber that is the world of visual arts), music journalism has already been summed up quite perfectly by Miles Davis/Elvis Costello/Frank Zappa/Whoever, when they quipped, 'Writing about music is like dancing about architecture'.

The *Irish Times* writer and blogger Jim Carroll – also involved in the free course – explained it on his blog: 'Dancing About Architecture is about showing that you don't have to pay €900 and get a diploma to be a music hack. All you have to do is start writing. Heck, you don't even have to go to a course like Dancing About Architecture but, if you have questions to ask and you're curious about the trade, it may be a good place to start. And, like we said, it's free.'

The 50 places were booked up almost immediately.

Which brings us to lesson two: you don't need to go to journalism college to be a journalist. You don't need a three-year degree or a 12-week course. Certainly not to be a music or features journalist.

The truth is that over a decade or more during which journalism courses have spread like an Asian flu, from the perspective of editors one thing is clear: you could scoop any six journalists at random off the street, ask them to pitch and write and do it to length and on time, and you would still not be able to tell which ones had a bit of paper saying they're a journalist.

It is not to suggest that courses are pointless. They are no doubt helpful for learning elements of libel law, shorthand and subediting. They may well be good for the more technical aspects of radio and television. They are definitely good for getting work placements – and that can be a crucial opportunity for those who get it. But if that is the chief benefit some graduates get from their courses, their colleges are little but expensive recruitment companies.

When it comes to writing – or even knowing how to pitch an idea – many college courses appear to have delivered little that a bit of life experience, talent and self-motivation won't already give a person.

And that is lesson three: those are the key qualities for a freelance life, when there are many graduates but jobs are few and far between.

If your ambition is to be a music writer, you're probably either able to do it already or you're not. You can either put the words together in the right order, with some flair and insight, and the chutz-pah needed to explain a medium that defeats language, or you can't.

Those who are decent and reliable at it would always have been, and were probably identified by their tutors within a week of their courses beginning.

In my experience, some of the best journalists are those who have avoided that path, whose writ-ing, eye, curiosity and personality were developed through experience, whose tutors were the writers they read.

Which brings us to the fourth and final lesson: always write to the word length, or else the editor may have to cut your

SATURDAY, 16 OCTOBER 2010

Apocalypse may yet Spark the Rebirth of Civic Morality

Garret FitzGerald

While – understandably – we all blame individuals in government, in parts of the public service, in property development and in the banks for the collapse of our economy, no one so far seems to have reflected on just why there has been such a simultaneous collective collapse in public responsibility in all these areas. Surely there must be some common element in this simultane-ous emergence of deep fissures in so many areas of our society?

A factor common to this whole range of fail-ures seems to me to have been a striking absence of any sense of civic responsibility throughout our society. The civic morality that underlies the social cohesion of so many democratic societies seems to me to have been absent in Ireland in recent decades.

Protestants, and especially Anglicans, had a strong civic sense, a loyalty to what had been their State. Despite the disproportionate role accorded to them initially in the Senate of the new State, thereafter they opted out of playing a significant role in its governance.

As for the Catholic majority, a society under alien rule cannot be expected to develop a sense of civic responsibility. And a popular church, identifying with its flock, first in opposition to the dominance of a ruling minority of another faith and then to aspects of an alien government, could not be expected to instil much respect for public authority.

One might have expected that all this would change with independence, and in one (in retro-spect perhaps unfortunate) respect it did: when in 1922 the hierarchy denounced violent republican opposition to the new Irish Free State government.

But, having done what it conceived to be its duty in this respect, thereafter it sought to dominate the State by relying upon the strong personal faith of members of successive governments to secure its objectives. It succeeded – up to a point. But when, in 1929, the Catholic hierarchy challenged the non-denominational provisions of our constitution by attempting to persuade the government to limit the appointment of dispensary doctors to Roman Catholics, it was outwitted by W.T. Cosgrave, who, as I understand it, told them that while as a Catholic he would have to obey their edict, he would of course also have to resign as president of the Executive Council (i.e. Taoiseach) in defence of our non-denominational Constitution, which would not permit such discrimination. The bishops promptly climbed down!

Again they were blocked by de Valera in 1937 when, in drawing up his new Constitution, he refused to make Ireland a Catholic state. This underlying stand-off between Church and State – the subtleties of which are little understood by the present generation – seems to have inhibited the Irish Catholic Church from advocating civic responsibility or from addressing issues of civic morality. Instead, all its energies were concentrated on aspects of sexual morality – an area where (as a recent *Irish Times* poll showed) it has since lost credibility not only with the younger generation, but with the older one as well.

The consequences of all this have been that a society whose education has been almost exclusively in the hands of the Catholic Church was left with virtually no training in civic morality or civic responsibility. This has been particularly noticeable in the failure of the Church to preach about the evils of tax evasion for the additional taxes that have to be imposed to offset this shortfall.

But why has this defect become fatal to our economy only in quite recent times?

The problem was postponed, I believe, by the remarkably unselfish patriotism of our two sets of national revolutionaries, who, after the post-independence civil war, challenged each other for power through the democratic system.

Some of these revolutionary leaders remained in politics for 43 years thereafter – one indeed for 47 years following independence – disagreeing about many things, but all deeply committed to personal integrity in public life.

Even though from the 1930s onwards, tolerant of political appointments within the very narrow range of areas in respect of which the first government had not imposed a meritocratic appointments system, they got rid of financial corruption in local government, guarded against its emergence within national government and lived frugally on their £1,500 salary, reduced by de Valera to £1,000 a year (about €70,000 in today's terms) with, I believe, no expense allowances.

In the 1970s, the surviving Fianna Fáil ex-ministers were horrified at the prospect of the emergence of a very different kind of Fianna Fáil. It was only with great difficulty that Frank Aiken, because of his concerns for the party and the country, was persuaded to stand again for election in 1973. Later, President de Valera confided his deep fears for the country to a minister in whose integrity he had confidence. And when he was dying, Seán MacEntee asked to see me to confide his deep concern for the future of the State because of what had happened to his party, Fianna Fáil. The truth is that because of the widespread lack of a tradition of civic responsibility or a sense of civic morality, for which I fear the Catholic Church must bear some of the blame, the disappearance of the revolutionary generation from government in the 1960s removed the only barrier to the spread to politics of the socially inadequate value system that we, as a people, had inherited from our colonial past.

Unhappily, that value system undervalued integrity in public life, to such a degree that it has seen tax evasion by a minister as grounds for repeatedly re-electing him to parliament.

There can be little doubt that a decline in standards has been at least partly – perhaps even largely – responsible for the collapse of our financial system and of our economy.

I do not think that this collapse could have occurred on such a dramatic scale during the first half of our State's existence. Certainly many mistakes were made by governments during that period, but because our political system then upheld high standards, I do not think it would have permitted the simultaneous collapse of so many aspects of our economic system. However, the disaster we are currently experiencing may have belatedly started to re-moralise our society – if we are to judge by the recent *Irish Times* poll which showed the emergence of huge public concern for integrity – a virtue that in recent decades had become grossly undervalued by our electorate.

MONDAY, 18 OCTOBER 2010

It is Hard to See What the Taxpayer Got out of Statutory Bank Audits

John McManus

If you raise the issue of the dominance of the 'big four' accountancy firms – or indeed the 'big five' Dublin law firms – with business-people, it will be greeted with a knowing look, a shrug of the shoulders, eye-rolling or a combination of all three. This is often followed by a reference to Chinese walls, implying that the person you are talking to thinks their existence is slightly less probable than that of the tooth fairy.

But still these firms get the lion's share of the high-value corporate work going in Ireland and are – it must be said – the firms of choice of the vast majority of decision-makers.

The situation would appear to be that most businesspeople do not consider themselves to be so naive as to think these firms don't have a serious issue with conflicts of interest, but on balance they believe they have the best people working for them. The firms themselves would no doubt add that they expend a great deal of effort in trying to manage conflicts.

This was certainly the situation that pertained before the current crisis and it looks like the one that continues to exist based on the way that the big legal and accountancy firms are feeding off the National Asset Management Agency (NAMA), despite being advisers to the banks and property developers who are primarily responsible for the

€50 billion catastrophe that NAMA is meant to try to resolve.

According to the Auditor Comptroller General, PricewaterhouseCoopers – the auditor of Bank of Ireland and Quinn Insurance – has received €5.5 million in fees for services rendered to the Government as it grappled with the banking crisis. This, no doubt, includes the 2008 PwC report saying the banks were all adequately capitalised. KPMG (auditor to AIB and Irish Nationwide) got €2 million, while Ernst & Young (the former Anglo Irish Bank auditor) got €240,000. Deloitte, the last of the big four and current Anglo Irish auditor, got €420,000.

It would appear that the big professional firms have managed to weather the crisis without any external – or, it would seem, internal – questioning as to whether the way they go about business means they must shoulder some responsibility for what happened. It's a can of worms that nobody wants to open. Nobody, apart from the European Commission, which once again looks like forcing us to face up to things we would rather brush under the carpet.

Last week, the internal markets commissioner Michel Barnier published a Green Paper called *Audit Policy: Lessons from the Crisis*. It is based on the premise that there is probably something wrong with a system in which banks across Europe got clean audit reports one year, only to collapse under massive unseen losses the next. It's a simple premise, but not one that very many seem keen to accept in this corner of Europe.

Pretty much everything is up for review in the Green Paper, right down to the question of whether audit firms truly understand their social mandate. There must be some good reason why the State has passed a law that guarantees them work – the requirement for limited liability companies to make audited accounts publicly available. But when you look at the current state of the Irish banks, which were subject to years and years of highly lucrative statutory audits, you would be hard-pressed to see what the taxpayer got out of it.

But even if this sort of Euro-socialism is not to your taste, there are plenty of other issues raised in the Green Paper which Irish people might like to hear the big four firms respond to. The commission wants to know whether it might not make sense for a third party to decide who audits a bank and how much they should be paid to do it rather than leave it to the bank itself.

It also suggests the mandatory rotation of audit firms, 'with a view to instilling and maintaining objectivity and dynamism in the audit market'.

Another issue is the provision of non-audit services by auditors to clients they audit. The logic is blisteringly simple: how can you give an independent opinion on the financial health of a company you have a business interest in?

They also want joint audits of large companies as a way of upskilling second-tier audit firms and breaking the loop by which only four firms get big company audits because only four firms have the ability to audit them.

This has become such a problem, the commission argues, that should one of them collapse it could seriously disrupt the flow of information to shareholders and investors about a large number of companies. The big four firms may themselves be 'too big to fail'.

It's impossible to argue in the wake of the biggest financial crisis in history that these are not important issues. It's even harder to argue that, in the country that has experienced the most ruinous banking collapse, they are not doubly important. But plenty are still willing to try.

Minister for Science, Technology and Innovation, Conor Lenihan, with Science Foundation Ireland's Prof. Frank Gannon at a 3-D digital interactive museum exhibition. Photograph: Jason Clarke.

Upfront

Róisín Ingle

It's not as though my friend thought he was The One, but at least The Spark was there. As long as I've known let's-call-her-Cathy, she has been going on about The Spark. Cathy says anybody who starts a relationship in the absence of The Spark is only fooling themselves.

She might be 30-something, but she is not one for settling. 'I'd rather grow old in a bedsit full of Siamese cats,' she says.

There has been a series of unfortunate incidents regarding men. Ones who never call. Ones who send drunken texts at 3 a.m. looking for company. Ones who have too much undeclared baggage.

Then she meets let's-call-him-Matt, and never mind The Spark this is The Glow, The Simmer and The Smoulder all rolled into one. 'Wait until you meet him,' she says. When I meet him, I know what she means. He ticks all of her boxes – as well as a few she doesn't know she has. Good-looking, intelligent and fun: tick, tick, tick. He can even play the guitar and sing. Mostly Def Leppard, but still. Talented boy. Tick.

When I meet him I know he isn't The One. Scratch the surface and his good looks and confident demeanour are only barely masking a crippling insecurity. There is too much eye contact, too much conversation and he makes too much effort to charm every single person in the room.

He can't relax. Can't stop talking. We try to have a sing-song, but when one of the group turns out to be a better singer than him he refuses to perform and goes into a schoolboy sulk, which Cathy, under the myopic influence of The Spark, considers 'endearing'.

I say nothing. Well you don't. Imagine it: 'Er, Cathy, I know you have finally found someone you actually fancy, someone who returns your calls and takes you away for weekends and out for dinner – which he sometimes pays for – but it's all going to end in tears, not sure whose as yet, just thought I'd mention it.'

'What do you think?' she asks. 'What do you think, more importantly?' I answer. This buys me time and allows her to talk at length about The Spark and his eyes and the way he sings to her late at night, even if they are dodgy soft metal songs and even if he isn't so much singing to her as to himself. And I go, 'Yes, that sounds great', and then I wait for the phonecall, which comes a couple of months later.

She says when they go out he is always disappearing. Sometimes she finds him outside in the smoking area, even though he doesn't smoke, just talking to random groups of strangers.

It's as though she is never enough for him. He needs attention from everybody. Sometimes she thinks he won't be satisfied until he has tried to make friends with the whole world. And sometimes he gets into terrible rows with his new friends. Or he goes off with them to parties, leaving her behind. One night, left to make her way home alone, she gives him the push. She says she doesn't care how brightly The Spark burns. It is over. She is moving on.

The thing Cathy wants to know is: 'What's wrong with me?' She says it a few times; she says it after every eejit fella tells her he thinks her eyes are the most amazing things he has ever seen and then disappears into the ether or blanks her in a nightclub. I tell her the truth – that there is nothing wrong with her. She is beautiful, smart, caring and fun. She is what I would call a catch. Maybe it's the search for what I've taken to calling The Infernal Spark that is holding her back.

Those of us in long-term relationships know, although we don't really like to admit, that The Infernal Spark doesn't always last and often mutates into a Warm and Cosy Ember, which sounds a bit depressing and sexless but doesn't have to be, not necessarily. Maybe The Warm and Cosy Ember can turn into The Spark. Cathy doesn't buy it, and to be honest I'm not sure I do either.

There is some hope. Recently she encountered a nice policeman who helped her out at a time of need and she couldn't help noticing The Spark between them. Cathy is conflicted. He could be The One, but she doesn't have the nerve to call up to the station to find out if he feels the same. It's a long shot, she says – but could I write about it here so that he might read about it and discover that the smart, caring, fun blonde with amazing eyes he helped out recently has a little crush on him?

And I'm happy to oblige, if not (sorry, Cathy) hugely hopeful that we'll get our man.

TUESDAY, 26 OCTOBER 2010

Entrants Run Whole Gamut of Emotions as Streets of Dublin Prove Mighty Leveller

Keith Duggan

Everyone who finished the marathon looked to be in the grip of simultaneous agony and euphoria.

What possesses them? What mad spirit is it that gets hold of people and convinces them that they want to run 26 miles? Twenty-six miles no matter what.

Thirteen thousand people showed up in the refrigerated shade of Fitzwilliam Street early yesterday morning and could have offered 13,000 different reasons for putting themselves through this ancient race, this battle with oneself. By the end, most were too tired to remember the answers.

Few gatherings are as wilfully delusional as the mass field that forms a marathon race. All over Dublin, the city had that particular quietness peculiar to bank holidays. But the streets near the race start point were different. Along Baggot Street, couples hugged as if one of them held a one-way ticket for an ocean liner and not an entry number for a road race. Some wrapped their arms around themselves and jumped up and down. Others remained as still as Stoics. The sun shone and the leaves were golden and in the distance, at the top of Fitzwilliam Street, the big arch was covered in balloons, as if it were the gateway to a frivolous party and not a portal to anything between two and five hours of guaranteed pain and loneliness.

Under that arch the elite runners – the omnipotent few who seem to glide these 26 miles – gathered, and over the swelling field of runners drifted the sounds of the Garda Band playing Neil Diamond.

The runners sang cheerfully to the chorus of 'Sweet Caroline' and it was obvious that everyone there felt somewhere between nervous and terrified.

A marathon race is wonderfully democratic. You cannot tell the millionaires from the dispossessed. Age does not matter: it is not a race which offers any dispensation to youth. There is no glamour and no vanity. There is nothing but a collective will to get to the other end.

And as usual, it attracts all kinds. And so there was a guy who figured the only appropriate attire with which to run through Dublin included a baby's nappy, a pink leopard-skin tank top and a blonde wig. There was a guy running with an army pack strapped to his back. A guy painted like a tiger. And a guy who juggled three tennis balls for the entire course.

'Dropped them about four or five times in the last three miles,' Diarmuid Collins would lament some four hours later. 'My left wrist just went stiff and it was like throwing a plank of wood. But the people cheering kept me going.'

He had been training for this October day since June and like many people it was a cause – the World Society for the Protection of Animals – that kept him going.

Even among the marathon field, he caught the eye. On his solitary training runs, which were always completed with the tennis balls, he drew a lot of searching looks.

The Dublin Marathon 2010 gets under way at Fitzwilliam Place in the city centre, with a record 13,000 athletes taking part. Photograph: Dara Mac Dónaill.

'I had the cows staring at me. Dogs chasing me. I would pass pubs and people would be looking out thinking they had had a few too many.'

The strangest period of a marathon race happens about 11 minutes after the starting gun. By then, all of the runners have passed through the start line and shuffled out of sight. The band put their instruments away and the intense bank holiday quietness returned. Fitzwilliam Street was littered with thousands of discarded sweat shirts. There was no traffic. The place felt abandoned. One steward said cheerfully: 'That's it for another year.'

Except that it wasn't; not quite. On Merrion Street, volunteers were organising finishing packs for the heroes. They looked as surprised as anyone when two guys came trotting up past them. It was

clear they were looking for the marathon. Equally clear was that they had got their times confused. Badly. They had, presumably, trained for this, prepared for this.

And yet with a casualness which could surely only happen at an Irish marathon, they got their time wrong. The phone conversation must have gone something like this:

'What time is this thing tomorrow?'

'Nineish. Half, I think. Nine would be mad early.'

'Sure I'll meet ya at quarter past or so.'

It was twenty-five to 10 when they ran under the arch, not a sinner around. By then, Moses Kibbet, the eventual winner, must have had six or seven miles down. And so they ran a race of 13,000 people all by themselves.

But, of course, everyone is alone. Families, friends, charity organisations: they show up radiating a kind of invincible togetherness but at some mile or another comes the inescapable fact that they are on their own.

'You go light in the head,' gasped Owen Gahan (2 hrs 37 mins) thinking back to mile 18 when the real world began to fall away.

'My calves, my legs, everything went and I desperately wanted to walk,' said Trevor Hunt (2 hrs 59 mins). 'But I just kept going, one step after the other.'

And these are the runners at the choice end of the field. It makes no difference. The marathon punishes everyone in different ways. The best keel over the railings and get sick just like the novices do. They too turn punch-drunk once they cross the line and hobble away, broken and ecstatic.

Others finish the race wearing the kind of beatific looks last seen when the statues jogged in Ballinspittle.

As the clock ticked remorselessly to the four-hour mark, the runners began to sprint for home. To get through that line even seconds under four hours was to achieve something profound, some private victory.

And so one runner leaped and touched the clock as he finished with seconds to spare. Behind

Sisters Katie Mae (5) and Ellie (3) O'Sullivan from Kilmainham in Dublin get in the mood for Halloween with their carved pumpkin. Photograph: Marc O'Sullivan.

him, another pointed at those ticking seconds and pointed at it like it was a sworn enemy.

He laughed as he beat the four-hour watermark and shouted a delighted 'F★★★ you' at Time itself and then his race was over. Many held their arms aloft like Gebrselassie.

Others seemed to be in a trance. Everyone looked to be in the grip of simultaneous agony and euphoria.

'Ahhh, felt great,' said Dave Brady from Kildare, who has run 164 of these days. Yesterday was his 27th marathon of the year. This was 25 years after his first Dublin marathon. He ran 3:11 then. He ran 3:24 yesterday. He is 60 years of age.

'Vegas and then on to Clonakilty,' he said dreamily of his next appointments with road-racing hell.

Vegas to Clonakilty might be a useful summary of what happens to people's minds over the course of a marathon. Most seem altered in some way when they finally finish.

And it is a kind of magical thing to see what happens on this day. To walk along Trinity and see people applauding the runners, jaded and beat-up looking now, just for keeping going.

One spectator bought jellies and some energy drinks in a shop and held them out for the needy and the weak. He wasn't a volunteer. He just wanted to help. That mood seldom visits any city but all along the route yesterday was a feeling of shared triumph.

After four and a half hours, thousands had come home, limping away with their sky-blue sweatshirts for promised baths or pints or whatever. Others were still racing to that magical line. Some looked like they felt they would never see it.

Standing on the steps of the Mont Clare Hotel, a little girl marvelled, 'They are still running, Nana.'

And she was right. Their race is never run.

Women Want Romance More Than Sex – What's so Controversial about That?

Eileen Battersby

Before a lynch party of outraged women – and men – ride off to hang Stephen Fry – writer, wit and now commentator on female sexuality – perhaps we should concede that there is some truth in his remarks.

The controversy arose after an article appeared in a British newspaper, quoting Fry as saying: 'I feel sorry for straight men. The only reason women will have sex with them is that sex is the price they are willing to pay for a relationship with a man, which is what they want.'

I don't think it is exactly earth shattering to discover that women are not as interested in sex as men are. Libraries of scientific data exist confirming exactly that. Men have a much stronger chemical response to sexual stimuli.

But to be basic, well, as basic as the original interview, which was published in *Attitude*, a gay magazine, there is a simple explanation: women prefer romance. The idea of a romantic encounter, a walk through the woods on a summer's day, the sight of Mr Darcy on a horse – women need to fall in love whereas a man may well do with falling into bed.

For most women, sex is only part of a relationship; for many men, it is central. Women like men with a sense of humour; men like beautiful, unobtainable women. Sympathetic-looking women are rarely used in advertising campaigns; instead models tend to be ultra-cool, sexually intimidating and very tall – too tall, and thin, for most men. Sympathetic-looking men, be they five foot or six foot, have no trouble in attracting women.

Powerful new surfing waves far out in the Atlantic have been dubbed 'Prowlers' by Irish, British and South African surfers. They break on an undersea reef about 2 km (1.2 miles) off the west coast. The surfers, who include Andrew Cotton, seen here, have refused to disclose its exact location and say they have been waiting five years for the conditions required to surf it. These materialised when the massive swell generated by Hurricane Tomas slammed into Ireland, creating intensely heavy, tubing waves with 12–15 m (40–50 ft) faces. Photograph: Aaron Pierce.

A dishevelled eccentric man incapable of changing a plug and given to wearing odd socks may appeal to a woman because she wants to mother him and shape him into her ideal man and the father of her future children. On the other hand, that eccentric male's female physical equivalent – a messy-looking, plaid-shirt clad woman who can service an automobile single-handed in a few hours and then rewire an entire house in an evening – is not all that likely to have hordes of male suitors. Her skills will never compensate in the relationship stakes for a lack of physical allure. She is destined to remain every guy's favourite kid brother. It's that unfair. Let us not diminish the universal empathy we felt for

Bridget Jones, caught between wanton cad and gorgeous nerd.

Women enjoy romance; it is an industry in itself. For women it is more sigh than grapple.

So Stephen Fry, the wonderful voice of all the Harry Potter audio tapes, says straight men feel they 'disgust' women. Many women may well fear men, but the word 'disgust' is bound to bewilder and provoke men and women. Why did Fry use 'disgust' but not the word 'romance'?

The 19th-century novel resounds with the imbalances in sexual needs dividing men and women. History records that kings and kingdoms pivoted on sex and its logical outcome – heirs, not necessarily romance – as much as Fry suggests women view sex as the price to be paid for a relationship. This notion of barter is not that daring a thesis; woman wakes the morning after a romantic tryst with man and thinks, 'We're a couple.' Same man may well wake and wonder, (a) 'What have I done?' or (b) 'What time is the match on at?'

Women prioritise – for all the love of romance, there is the practicality: the laundry waiting to be ironed; a meal to be cooked; children to be collected. Fry's comments may have been taken out of context, but for general readers, his interview was taken out of context. Do straight men and straight women actively 'cruise'? Is not all social interaction between men and women a variation of cruising? Flirtation is enjoyable and uplifting and need not always end in sex. The gay male sexual experience appears heightened because it has to confront taboos.

No heterosexual writer has captured the sheer agony of sexual desire and its attendant loneliness as brilliantly as the US writer Edmund White in novels such as *The Farewell Symphony*. Fry's comments are shaped not only by his observations of heterosexual relationships but also from his experience of the dynamics of many gay sexual encounters. One of the most affecting ever studies of a woman's capacity to love was written by Pushkin in his characterisation of Tatyana, a young country woman, in *Eugene Onegin*. She decides she loves the bored Onegin, he rejects her. Years later he meets her after she has become a successful salon hostess. She still loves Onegin but will not leave her husband. How more romantic can you get? Unless you mention the movie *Brief Encounter*.

Sex as a recreational exercise is more common among men, although some women, no doubt far more than Fry imagines, may also view it as casually.

If Stephen Fry were a doctor or a recognised sex expert, or even heterosexual, far fewer would be angered by his comments. But he is a comedian, a wit, an Establishment English man and an openly gay celebrity who has written about his depression. I interviewed him before the release of *Wilde*, in which he played Oscar Wilde. He is charming, witty, sympathetic, immensely appealing, obviously hugely intellectual, vulnerable, great company and exactly the kind of man most women would love to be the father of their children.

MONDAY, 8 NOVEMBER 2010

Some Cold Comfort for Weary GAA Dual Agent

Seán Moran

It was as nostalgic for me as for the other elderly people who attended Saturday night's Horslips concert in Dublin, although maybe for different reasons. As an impecunious young man I was retained by the British Government to keep an eye on anything smacking of ultra nationalism and from an early stage had formed the view that closely monitoring the pioneers of Celtic rock would be a relatively undemanding way of fulfilling that brief.

In time, it was an obvious step to insinuate myself into the world of Gaelic games with a view to discrediting them.

Much has been written in these pages by my dear, dear comrade Tom Humphries about the Sports Editor. Being in possession of certain facts, I have so far avoided doing this. But I came to Dublin after a 'source' had apprised me of the fact that 'Malachy' had been forced to re-locate here, having exploited insider knowledge as a low-level CIA operative and expectantly moved a black market operation to Havana the week before the Bay of Pigs.

Anyway, I was fortunate to find employment with this newspaper, which has helped temper the unreliability of the revenue stream from MI6 and my other – if it's not too absurd a description – paymasters.

It was the late former Taoiseach Charles Haughey who wisely observed if you wanted to know what British intelligence services were up to, best ask the Russians. That was certainly the case with me and it was my 'contacts' in the KGB that initially got me the work when I moved here. Of course, I had a history in the old days during my time at Cambridge, where I mingled with a motley collection of aesthetes and unpublished poets. My heedless socialising led to a poor degree and premature episodes of gout.

It wasn't, however, entirely wasted and the time I spent hanging around the Cavendish Laboratory trying to bribe brilliant physicians opened my mind to the infinite possibilities of the intellect, which enabled me in later years to ingratiate myself with the Comhairle Árd Oideachais by helping to draw up the rules on eligibility for third-level competitions.

During the war I had found favour as a writer of propaganda leaflets designed to demoralise the Germans in occupied Europe and ended up, like so many idealists at the time, being recruited by the Soviet Union along with Philby, Burgess and Maclean, but due to unfair allegations of poor organisational skills, laziness and unreliability I was cut from the payroll (mercifully) before all of the unpleasantness came out.

Needless to say, I got no awards or any luxury dacha. I suppose in that austere old-style communist way my controllers disapproved of my 'lifestyle', although I did receive the occasional lump sum to pay off gambling debts and blackmail demands.

Russia has changed and not entirely for the better. I've tried to reactivate old contacts as a double agent (or 'dual player'), but many have found themselves out of favour with the new regime. Too often my visits, under cover of All Stars tours or to investigate whether intercounty teams on

Cartoon by Martyn Turner.

'winter wonderland' holidays were in fact training, ended up in drunken reminiscence. I benefited to no greater extent than the free consumption of inhuman amounts of rather corrosive vodka and the occasional company of women bored beyond even the civility of pretending to listen to my views on the qualifiers and illicit payments to managers. I'm afraid the Official Secrets Act comes into play here – given this newspaper circulates in Britain – as does, to be fair, a rather welcome lump sum to help me see the importance of keeping quiet about the circumstances of my recruitment by an MI6 puppet master, Nigel someone or other but known to us as 'Nancy'. Not, you understand, that I would compromise myself but the safety of any state is the safety of ordinary people.

My old contacts have been of assistance to me in undermining the GAA and vice versa. For instance, I sent studies of Frank Murphy and his 'Cork model' of democratic centralism to the politburo, but by then I had become regarded as erratic and untrustworthy and the dossier was forwarded to North Korea.

My work continued with humdrum schemes such as planting people with firm backbones and logical instincts on the GAA's various disciplinary committees but ensuring both of those qualities were rarely possessed by the same individual. During the summer, a long-standing project to use the techniques of the *Manchurian Candidate* to brainwash someone who one day would be in a position to do what club full forwards call 'a bit of damage' to the GAA was dropped.

Having reviewed what a duly appointed but unprogrammed referee managed to do in the Leinster final and the social unrest it fermented in Co. Louth or somewhere like that, my handlers in London came to the conclusion there was no need to retain my services at as handsome a rate as previously.

It's been an agonising decision for me to decide to come in from the cold. I suppose I'm weary of the whole thing and the economic melt-

down has persuaded the wretched security service bean counters, who put a price on everything regardless of its beauty, to humiliate me, but most of all I no longer have confidence in the purpose of what I'm doing.

Some call me a fantasist, a charge I have strenuously disputed since tipping Cork on the weekend of the 2007 All-Ireland football final, but I should say if anyone's actually reading this and they notice I've disappeared in the weeks ahead, just cut out the article and bring it to the Gardaí. At this juncture, with so much pessimism and despair abroad, it would be easy to say the state we have found ourselves in might convince us in future to scrutinise more rigorously those who we elect to govern.

I could say that like the Cork footballers, we'll eventually get there. I could say that, like Tipperary hurlers, we'll some day no longer need to look enviously down the road at wealthier neighbours. I could say all of those things. But who'd believe me?

FRIDAY, 12 NOVEMBER 2010

Swift Sales Show that 'Enemy of Feminism' Taylor Means Business

Brian Boyd

I t's the biggest story of the year in terms of music sales and no one wants to know: Taylor Swift's *Speak Now* album sold more than a million copies in the US alone in the first week of its release at the end of October.

Post-Napster, those sorts of figures weren't supposed to happen any more. One in every five albums bought in the US that week was *Speak Now*. Swift outsold the next 62 albums on the chart put together – something else that has never happened before.

The album was only on release for 58 minutes before it topped the iTunes chart. Swift has sold 2½

Forty-three headstones in Glasnevin Cemetery in Dublin at the hitherto unmarked graves of Irish servicemen and women who died in the two world wars. Photograph: Cyril Byrne.

million individual downloads from the album, which means that each of the 14 tracks are in the singles charts. Factor in her age – she's only 20 – and the fact that she wrote the entire album herself and you're looking at popular music records that have stood since Elvis, The Beatles and Michael Jackson being shattered all over the place.

And this is no one-off. Her last album, 2008's *Fearless* won four Grammys, including the biggest prize in music: the Grammy for album of the year. And she's getting some decent reviews as well, with two publications not known for their endorsement of mainstream country-pop (*Rolling Stone* and the *New York Times*) both going into superlative speak. The latter noting, rather curiously, that Swift is 'a country-pop Jane Austen'.

In Ireland, the new album has already gone gold, the last one went a few times platinum and her show at the 02 next March sold out in minutes.

A 20-year-old female who writes her own material and is reshaping the popular music history books – it's quite something. But for the 'male gaze' of the media she's the wrong sort of female.

Swift can't be corralled into the nymph/whore boxes. And, gasp, she's 'an enemy of feminism'. In a world gone Gaga, Swift is pilloried for letting the side down. She's not 'complex', 'damaged' and doesn't score too highly on the 'subversion' index.

'The rush to exalt Swift is, I believe, a desperate attempt to infuse our . . . country with a palatable conservative ideology in the form of a complacent, repressed feminine ideal. [She is not] an established/evolved talent (Beyoncé) or a revolutionary (Lady Gaga). According to her lyrics, she has spent her entire life waiting for phone calls and dreaming about horses and sunsets,' runs one of the many negative online opinions.

Elsewhere, Swift gets compared to Bristol

Palin (whatever that's supposed to imply) and derided for being a 'celebuteen'. Her runaway commercial success attributed to 'good marketing'.

And where once-concerned parents pored over the lyrics of metal bands or gangsta rappers to find proof of society coming apart at the seams, now their mirror counterparts are poring over Swift's lyrics to uncover their 'hidden meaning'. Yes, Swift's entire lyrical reach might not extend past 'walking in the rain with my boyfriend' but to put her beside Janis Joplin for a compare/contrast rant seems harsh, to say the least.

The core problem here appears to be that her Dan Brown/JK Rowling-like sales are putting her up into a pretty exalted position in the music world and that she's just a bit too much of a wide-eyed, know-nothing, uncool *ingénue* to warrant that elevation. For an Amy or a Gaga that's all fine – there's a whiff of cordite there – but for someone who makes The Jonas Brothers look like Megadeth, it's just dreadfully untweetable.

But at the business end of the argument you're looking at a situation where a number of big-name acts are deliberately releasing their albums in the immediate wake of Swift's *Speak Now* just so they can take advantage of the footfall in record shops.

She may well be 'a feminist nightmare', but Taylor Swift is still a 20-year-old woman who writes all her own material, breaking new ground, raising the bar and leaving the musically correct wringing their hands in anguish.

Pupils from Our Lady of Good Counsel College NS in Ferrybank in Waterford watching a monitor lizard from Dave's Jungle, Carlow. Photograph: Patrick Browne.

Gardening in the Wild

Jane Powers

In the middle of the 19th century, the face of gardening changed completely on these islands. Strangely, one of the things that prompted this revamp was the removal of the glass tax in 1845, as this allowed vast greenhouses to be built on wealthy estates. The protected buildings were used to raise tender bedding plants by the thousand, which were then planted out in regimented blocks and bands of colour.

In the heyday of bedding, the amount of plants that a person displayed was a gauge of their wealth and status. According to the head gardener at the Rothschild estate at Halton in Buckinghamshire, it was 10,000 plants for a squire, 20,000 for a baronet, 30,000 for an earl and 40,000 for a duke.

Around this time, a lonely and cantankerous voice could be heard making a plea for a more sensible approach to gardening: a way that was more natural, more appropriate to the climate, less labour-intensive and less wasteful. In other words, this was a voice that was advocating what we now think of as modern concepts of sustainable and ecological planting. Yet, it was only 1870. The voice (or pen, rather) was that of 32-year-old Irish-born William Robinson, who had arrived in England as a young gardener and who had transformed himself into a prolific and opinionated writer. It was his fifth book, *The Wild Garden*, that proffered the ideas that ran counter to the contemporary vogue for 'beds filled with vast quantities of flowers, covering the ground frequently in a showy way, and not unfrequently in a repulsively gaudy manner'.

Robinson didn't advise the sweeping away of bedding (he was canny enough not to antagonise his readers); rather, he suggested that the areas further away from the house could be cultivated in a more relaxed fashion. His proposed wild garden, he was at pains to explain, was 'not a garden run wild'; it was, instead, a way of 'placing plants of other countries, as hardy as our hardiest wild flowers, in places where they will flourish without further care or cost'. The species that he recommended were those that were resilient and unfussy, and that required no staking or tying in – exactly the same sorts of plants that are used in today's naturalistic perennial schemes. In his long and flowery introduction to *The Wild Garden*, he offers six reasons for adopting this way of planting and all are either aesthetic or ecological – or a combination.

Much of his advice elsewhere in the book is still germane today: suit the planting to the existing soil and conditions, use perennial plants as ground-cover under shrubs and trees, allow bulbs and wild-flowers to naturalise in grass that is managed as meadow. Others of his suggestions will bring a shudder to our 21st-century biodiversity-aware selves. He eagerly advocates collecting plants from the wild and swapping with similarly-minded gardeners, exchanging, for example, 'Orchids of the Surrey hills for the Alpines of the higher Scotch mountains'. He also refers to himself throwing seeds of plants out the window of the train, to beautify the margins of the railway. In Victorian times there was little consciousness, even among sophisticated gardeners, of conserving species or the landscape. Instead, collecting one and embellishing the other were considered worthy pastimes.

The Wild Garden, although written when he was still a young man, was probably Robinson's most influential book, and it ran to many editions over many decades. It garnered him admirers, such as the plantswoman Gertrude Jekyll and the designer of New York's Central Park Frederick Law Olmsted.

The 'Robinsonian' method of gardening can still be seen in Irish gardens, with extensive areas of naturalised bulbs and perennials. Some of the better-known examples are Mount Usher in Co. Wicklow, Fernhill in Co. Dublin and Annes Grove in Co. Cork.

This year, 140 years after it first came out, two new editions of Robinson's revolutionary book have been published, with notes and additions by contemporary horticultural writers. In the first, American landscape design consultant and writer Rick Darke elegantly connects Robinson's philosophy to current thinking on sustainable landscape-making. He uses the fifth edition of *The Wild Garden* as the main text, together with the charming original engravings by Alfred Parsons. Darke's expansive introductory chapters and his own handsome photographs of well-planted gardens in the US and Europe illustrate Robinsonian principles in a way that present-day gardeners will be able to understand and appreciate.

The second new edition of *The Wild Garden* is a slightly more academic affair and is the work of Charles Nelson, the former taxonomist at the National Botanic Gardens in Glasnevin. He chooses Robinson's first edition as his text and augments it with his own photographs, notes and an introductory essay.

William Robinson himself would be pleased, no doubt, that 75 years after his death, his *Wild Garden* is still being propagated.

SATURDAY, 13 NOVEMBER 2010

Upfront

Róisín Ingle

I'm in a taxi. For budgetary reasons, I'm supposed to be reducing the number of taxis I take by roughly 100 per cent. I think I might be a taxiholic though, because the plan is not really working. I keep finding myself in taxis without really knowing what I'm doing or how I got there. Pesky painkillers mixed with alcohol.

The taxi driver I employ this morning is fiddling about with a laptop on the front of his passenger seat. I am not sure which I am less keen on: a taxi driver making calls on a mobile phone, or one who is updating his social network status while he drives me from A to B-loody hell, watch out for that Dublin Bike.

The scenario reminds me of that taxi driver a few years ago who put a boardgame he invented in the back seat of his car. The incongruous presence of the boardgame, Mentalogy it was called, was a smart move, both as a conversation starter and a marketing strategy. Most people, I imagine, if they got into a taxi to find they are sharing it with a boardgame would make a remark, something like: 'Somebody appears to have left a boardgame in your taxi, mister.' Not me. I knew what would happen if I mentioned the boardgame, so I kept quiet.

Bringing up the boardgame would have been exactly the opening he wanted. I knew his game. His other game. He wanted to regale me with tales of how he invented the boardgame and I'd have to listen politely, pretending I was interested and possibly feeling guilt-tripped into buying one of them. The thing is, I'd already learned everything I could possibly know about his boardgame from the newspapers, because as well as being an inventor, he was a genius marketeer. I sat in the back pretending that taxis were the natural home for boardgames while he glanced at the rearview mirror wondering why I wasn't asking him about it.

I feel a bit bad about ignoring his boardgame now. Would it have killed me to make small talk about the game, his cardboard-and-plastic pride and joy? I haven't seen him around lately. I really hope he gave up the taxi and became a boardgame millionaire.

This laptop in the passenger seat scenario reminds of the boardgame. I make a quick decision. I am not going to ask the taxi driver about the laptop. I am going to ignore it completely. I am going to act like it's perfectly natural to drive accompanied by a laptop. I start thinking up plausible explanations. It's probably his GPS system. Or he is expecting an urgent email from the taxi regulator. But most of all, I ignore the laptop all the while knowing that he is going to steer the conversation in that direction anyway.

It takes approximately 67 seconds. 'You've probably noticed the laptop,' he says. What I want to say is, 'No, what laptop? I can't see any laptop,' but that will only prolong the inevitable. He doesn't wait for me to answer. He just tells me that what he is doing is having some fun at the expense of internet scammers. You know, those people who pretend to be princes in Nigeria or Russian women with very sick mothers who email complete strangers to ask for hilarious amounts of money and bank details.

It turns out the taxi driver is what is known as a scam-baiter, a worldwide community trying to rid the internet of scammers. He has a few different people on the go at any one time. They contact him in bad English, 'with warm hearts in the name of Jesus hoping this letter meets you in good time', asking for the loan of a few thousand for their ailing mother or their orphaned family. He writes back, leading them up the garden path, posing as a victim, sending false bank account numbers or keeping them on the phone for ages so they run out of credit. He gives them false names, strikes up a relationship and makes them think he is going to pay out. All the while he is draining their time and energy, time and energy they could otherwise be using to scam others. He says, not surprisingly, the scammers don't take kindly to being scammed.

He is kind of heroic, this online vigilante taxi driver. He and people like him are the bane of internet scammers from Nigeria to Siberia desperate to make a dishonest buck from poor eejits around the world. 'I just got into it out of boredom, but I am really enjoying it now,' he says. As I write, he's probably dropping someone to Tallaght and emailing some 'farmer' in 'Zimbabwe' to pretend that he has just lodged ten grand into their bank account.

There may be a health and safety issue involved with driving while operating a laptop, but if this is the kind of stuff taxi drivers are up to these days, it just makes it all the harder for me to stop taking them.

'I wake up today free for a few moments of my daily horror: Michael is dead. Michael is dead.'

Carl O'Brien

It wasn't exactly love at first sight. 'He looked very peculiar,' Phyllis MacNamara says with a laugh. 'He was wearing a cardigan with suede insets. And I thought, Ugh, where did that come from?' She was 14; he was 15. Michael was over from England, visiting relatives in Galway. It was a few years later before they met again, in first year at Trinity College Dublin. This time it was the beginning of a friendship that would lead to an enduring romance.

A family photograph of Phyllis MacNamara and her late husband, Michael.

'I felt so lost there and was thrilled to see him. We became best friends. I was always going on, telling him how lonely I was. He'd tell me about who he had asked out. We had a very happy platonic friendship for the next four years.'

They both had boyfriends or girlfriends, but their parents could see they had developed a bond that reached much deeper than friendship. 'They're in love,' Michael's father said to his wife one day, 'and they don't even realise it – but they will. They'll marry and be very happy.'

A month later Michael's father died suddenly. Phyllis's desire to comfort Michael was so intense that it dawned on her she was in love with him. Michael's first thought was that he needed to be with Phyllis to get through the grief of his father's death. 'We both realised we were in love with each other on the day his father died, although we didn't say it at the time,' says Phyllis.

The following year she and Michael married. She says she almost ran up the aisle of Galway Cathedral. 'It was very strange, going from a platonic relationship to a married relationship with someone I knew very well. It was a kind of a slow climb, and I think that's what made us have such a fantastic marriage. I married my best friend. We adored each other.'

Michael was, she says, the most even-keeled of people. At college he was meticulous about studying and was always well prepared for exams. It extended to his professional life, where he became a successful and sought-after solicitor. He was known to be methodical and careful. During the madness of the Celtic Tiger years he didn't take silly risks.

Phyllis MacNamara in the garden of her home in Galway. Photograph: Joe O'Shaughnessy.

At home his big passion was the garden and antiques; he loved restoring old furniture and gilding picture frames. Phyllis's sister often said how lucky she and Michael were to have so many shared interests: going to auctions, cooking, books. He often helped her source antique jewellery for her business. 'We had more interests in common, I think, than most couples. He adored home life. Our home was our hobby and passion,' she says. 'It was amazing how we shared everything.'

Their restored house and garden became their pride and joy. It was the home of Phyllis's dreams, a run-down Georgian house that as a child she had hoped to live in one day. Michael created a garden with loving care and restored a Victorian greenhouse in the grounds. They had their first and only child, who went on to a successful career in London. Business flourished. They couldn't have been happier.

It's hard to say when the warning signs started. Leonie, a close friend of Phyllis, spotted them first. She noticed Michael had lost weight and wasn't getting pleasure from his hobbies. Looking back, Phyllis says, the change in his working environment appears to have been the catalyst for his growing anxiety. His workload was increasing and he was spending longer and longer in the office.

'I think he felt there were lots of young people doing their jobs, working on computers, doing their own typing. And he still had two secretaries. But he made no allowance for his own experience. It's heartbreaking to think of now, but he was there each evening when he came home, trying to teach himself to type.'

Although he had no money worries, he grew anxious about the extraordinary financial risks clients were willing to take. Signs of anxiety began to creep into his behaviour. He found it difficult to sleep, which added to his distress. He insisted it was the amount of work that was keeping him awake. Phyllis eventually persuaded him to get sleeping tablets, but the anxiety didn't go away. 'I thought I could fix him with care and love, but I was wrong,' she says.

Phyllis thought a holiday would help. Three months before he died they visited India. On the way back to the airport they passed a colourful spice market. 'I was saying, "Oh, Michael, look! I wish I could stop and take a picture. I wish I could smell all this. We have to return here one day." And he wasn't interested at all. It was the first time I really noticed him being terribly detached.'

After the holiday he began doubting himself at work, convinced he had made mistakes and was no longer up to the job.

The panic attacks started. He bought a book, *When Panic Attacks*, and underlined passages, trying to understand what was happening to him. His bookmark is still in it, a third of the way through.

A week before he died he was behaving very erratically. His driving was either too fast or too slow. In the final three days his speech deteriorated badly. His words were jumbled. His mind was confused. When he went to the supermarket he looked through a hand-written shopping list, came to the word 'rosemary' and stopped. He didn't understand what it meant.

Phyllis had taken to doing jigsaws with Michael to help occupy his mind. The puzzles were getting progressively easier. She remembers handing him a simple piece, with an obvious space for it. He couldn't figure out where it should go. 'That night, the night before he died, we were here in the sitting room. I was sitting in this chair, and he came over and sat in it with me. He said, "I'm so frightened." And I said, "What are you frightened about?" He said, "I don't know: I'm just so frightened."'

Phyllis didn't know what to do or where to go. She had called friends for advice. She knew her husband was having a breakdown and needed immediate help, but where? They visited the GP and had an appointment with a psychiatrist, but Michael was reluctant to seek help. 'The thought that he might kill himself never entered my head. This is Michael: I know every cell of his skin, every hair of his body, every bit of him. He's almost part of me. It just never entered my head.'

It was a Thursday morning in early April. Michael had brought Phyllis a cup of tea in bed; he sat down beside her. 'You know, I've made so many mistakes,' he said. 'I'm thinking of the mistakes I made that I can't even remember, or giving people the wrong advice.' Phyllis answered: 'You haven't: you feel like you have, but you haven't. You haven't made a mistake about me, have you?'

'No. You're the best wife any man could have. I love you completely,' Michael said.

'You're easy to love,' Phyllis replied.

He went down to the conservatory, where, he said, he would finish off a jigsaw. When Phyllis went to look for him a short time later there was no sign of him. She ran around upstairs, then downstairs. She felt suddenly that something horrific had happened. His car was still outside. Out across the yard the two red doors to the barn were open. She ran over and stopped at the entrance. He was hanging from the rafters. She knew immediately he was dead.

'The first thing that came into my head was the word "now" . . . "now" . . . "now" do you see how bad he was? I was in complete shock, shivering, shaking, looking down at my skirt and remembering every detail and pattern on it. I rang my friend Leonie, Michael's business partner Billy, my father, the police, and after that I don't remember who I phoned.'

The days afterwards were horrific, indescribable and inescapable. Her diary provides a graphic window into the waves of grief over the following weeks and months.

It's two and a half years since Michael died. The recovery process, Phyllis says, can be like a game of snakes and ladders. You're going up the ladder one minute and slipping back down it the next. But she has made progress. The bereavement group Console has helped her through the darkest days.

'It's been a place where I could go and scream and scream and cry and cry. And it's where I learned to deal with the most upsetting things, the triggers, sadness and misery. I can recognise the triggers now, and I have learned to avoid them. The people at Console have been marvellous.'

Those blackest of days, combined with the white heat of grief, have given Phyllis an insight into the kind of turmoil that Michael must have been going through when he died. In those dark times she even considered taking her own life. 'I'm grateful for that, because now I know how he felt. I didn't think about my beautiful son and the devastation it would cause him, I didn't think about my father, my sister, my friends, the devastation. The effect of my death would be so horrific to all of them, in the midst of their sorrow.

'I remember thinking, It will be so easy, I'll just go into the bathroom, put my head under water and it will be all over. I didn't think of anything else. And I am very grateful to have experienced that. Now I know there's a difference. You can have suicidal thoughts, and you can think about suicide,' she says.

'Anyone can end up doing it. It's like you're caught in a wave and you don't know whether you're coming up or going down; you're going round and round and round, but there is a force pulling you. And that's what it's like. I'm not imagining it: I know what it's like.'

Phyllis is now dedicated to opening up the topic of anxiety and depression and giving people the opportunity to talk about it. 'We need to create a space where people can talk openly about their feelings and look for help. There is lots of work to be done. We need to make it okay for people, especially men, to talk about negative feelings about themselves and know they won't be judged.

'Michael had a breakdown. He felt going to a doctor about a mental-health problem was the greatest disgrace. He actually couldn't live with it, so he took his own life. He shouldn't have felt like that. It's our society and environment which make people feel like that. A mental-health problem should be no different to an illness affecting any other organ of the body.'

Phyllis says there is an urgent need to ensure there are approachable support services for people in crisis. A fear of committal persists around mental-health services. 'I didn't know what to do when facing this crisis. I want to save people from these situations. I would die happily if other people know what to do when confronted with a crisis like this. I have a new vocation now. This is my calling: to open up, be honest, share my experiences and, hopefully, makes changes which can save others from Michael's fate.'

Phyllis is continuing to make progress, one day at a time. She also feels hopeful that as a society we can make progress in tackling the problem of suicide. 'After Michael died I would walk down the stairs and think, Another day, I'm not sure I can do it. Now I walk down the stairs and think, What can I do today? There is so much I have to do. I have been blessed with skills to aid my recovery. I have my gardening, reading, my business. I have a wonderful circle of family and friends who are there to listen and help me through.'

One of the most helpful pieces of advice she recalls hearing was from the abbot of Glenstal Abbey in Limerick. 'He told me: "You are in the darkest place, and there is no place darker than this. Put your hand up and scream for help, and help will come." And he was so right. It's a human condition that people like to be asked for help. It gives people a sense of being worthwhile, of being able to do something,' she says. 'So I put up my hand to God, to people around me, and said, "Please help me." And it has been the best thing.'

Suicide Stories by Carl O'Brien was a groundbreaking series that ran for a week, in which people affected by suicide expressed their feelings, very largely in their own words.

MONDAY, 15 NOVEMBER 2010

Ministers Deny State is on Brink of Seeking EU Aid

Mary Minihan and Michael O'Regan

Economic crisis: ministers have dismissed speculation that the State is on the brink of seeking emergency financial aid from the EU, and insisted talks on a bailout had not taken place.

Minister for Enterprise Batt O'Keeffe said he was 'absolutely unaware of any moves from Europe'. He insisted no such discussions had taken place at government level, and denied the Coalition was under pressure to apply for a bailout. 'It's been a very hard-won sovereignty for this country, and this Government is not going to give over this sovereignty to anyone else.

'As a country we have to inspire confidence. We have to be the people, and a Government and an Opposition, that can show clearly that Ireland can stand alone, and will stand alone, and that it's determined to get out of the financial difficulties that we're in.'

Mr O'Keeffe said Ireland was well-financed up until the middle of next year, and also had a National Pension Reserve Fund of €25 billion. He said during an interview on RTÉ Radio One's *This Week* programme that it was important the two main Opposition parties agreed with the target deficit of 3 per cent of gross domestic product by 2014.

'Even if there was a change of government there would be no change in the containment of the 3 per cent by 2014.'

Minister for Justice Dermot Ahern said reports that Ireland was close to seeking financial aid from Europe had no basis in fact.

'It is fiction because what we want to do is get on with the business of bringing forward the

Cartoon by Martyn Turner.

four-year plan. We obviously have to ignore a lot of this speculation because it is only speculation. We have not applied. There are no negotiations going on. If there were, Government would be aware of it, and we are not aware of it.'

Mr Ahern said he had confirmed this with Taoiseach Brian Cowen and Minister for Finance Brian Lenihan yesterday morning.

Asked if he would stake his political reputation and say that Ireland would not apply for funding, he said: 'Things are happening day by day. We obviously have to take them, events, as they happen day by day. But the one thing this Government is, it is going to be calm in relation to the issue.'

Minister for Tourism, Culture and Sport Mary Hanafin also denied Ireland was discussing a possible bailout. 'There is no question of it,' she said.

Ms Hanafin said international publicity was having a destabilising impact on our economy.

'I am just back from the United States, where I met our global Irish network, and they are very concerned about media stories which have no foundation. They said that coverage in the *Wall Street Journal* had been quite damaging to our reputation abroad.'

Labour leader Eamon Gilmore called on the Government to ensure Ireland retained its economic independence.

'We fought hard for our independence, and we should not hand it away. I would be very surprised if there were any behind-the-scene discussions between the Government and the European authorities on this.'

He said he accepted Mr Cowen's assurance that no such talks had taken place.

A spokesman for Fine Gael said the Government had not made available the details of its plan. 'While we agree broadly with the targets, we have an entirely different way of getting there.'

THURSDAY, 18 NOVEMBER 2010

Biffo Tells Gasping Dáil There's No Such Thing as a Bailout

Miriam Lord

The emu has landed. It's all about the euro, stupid. It's why the Men in Suits are arriving here today to run the rule over our books.

Not a bailout, so?

No such thing, bristles Biffo. That's what he told a gasping Dáil and two senior officials from the British embassy in the distinguished visitors' gallery who were taking notes with alarming speed.

Nor are there any negotiations going on with the Bailout Boys.

It's just 'technical' stuff, insisted the Taoiseach, as his own backbenchers scrunched up their faces in despair.

Anyway, it's the fault of 'the markets' for creating this difficult situation for the euro, and unfortunate that when a big economic squeeze is imminent the markets go in search of the choicest lemons.

No wonder our leaders looked so haunted yesterday.

They are now contriving to feel very hard done by. Throughout the day, in Leinster House and on the airwaves, our governing lemons, from the Taoiseach down, put out the message that their handling of the economy had been nothing short of impeccable since they banjaxed it.

If Brian Cowen's performance in the Dáil was jaw-dropping for its bloody-minded insistence that the Bailout Boys are merely dropping by for some 'engagement' and to conduct a routine check-up, Frank Fahey delivered a tour de force on radio.

As the government talks to the International Monetary Fund and the European Central Bank about a bailout for Ireland, with its consequent loss of economic sovereignty, Taoiseach Brian Cowen gives a speech at the annual Fianna Fáil Easter Rising 1916 Commemoration at Arbour Hill, Dublin. Photograph: Matt Kavanagh.

The Taoiseach's loyal lieutenant was in such an upbeat state of sunny denial we feared he might be removed to hospital to have the party line surgically removed from his toes.

Speaking on Newstalk's *Breakfast* show, Frank began: 'Well. I think we're in a pretty good position . . . the Government have handled this situation well in that we now have the various players coming to Ireland tomorrow to look at the structure of our banking situation . . .'

When the Government asks, the 'players' jump.

Fahey stressed that Ireland would play its part 'in ensuring the continuing strength of the euro . . . This is a euro issue.'

Or a ransom note.

Fianna Fáil's Frank couldn't speak highly enough of the lemons. 'For the last two and a half years Brian Cowen and Brian Lenihan have taken all the right actions . . . We've done all the right things.'

Off microphone, a guest seemed to be hyperventilating. Fine Gael's Brian Hayes. Mad as hell. 'It's a pile of shit, Frank,' he snorted, 'and you don't believe it.' All over the country, people drew closer to their radios and cheered.

The Greens went missing. Dan Boyle issued a plaintive tweet about trust and uncertainty. Nobody paid much attention.

Back in the Dáil, Biffo was getting very frustrated with the Opposition and their questioning of his non-bailout/non-negotiating mantra.

And we harked back to happier days when we had no such thing as a recession either. It took months and months for the Taoiseach to utter the R word. He's at it now with the B word.

Cabinet members drifted away – Hanafin, Martin among them – until the faithful four remained: Cowen, Coughlan, Dempsey and Ahern. Éamon Ó Cuív departed, in deep negotiations with Jackie Healy-Rae.

Pat Rabbitte exited the chamber in disgust. 'This is calamitous. I can't listen anymore. The banks are going to cannibalise the country.'

Have faith (even if some Fianna Fáil backbenchers, privately, have lost it). For if all goes to plan, those Europeans in denial will take their courage in both hands and allow plucky Ireland rescue their single currency.

Whether or not Gunther and Gaston like it, we will force Brussels to bow to our demands for 'financial assistance'. They may resist, but the money is there and by God we will force them to make us take it. We will emerge as heroes when Europe capitulates.

Brian has a cunning plan. Mess with the big boys at your peril, eurocrats. The Taoiseach played minor hurling for Offaly.

Meanwhile, the Minister for Finance was in Brussels seeking to spare his Government's blushes at this difficult time. It was encouraging to hear him concentrating on the good news (and buttering up the Brits, who are keen to give us a dig-out).

'The engagement now takes place,' declared Lenihan.

Yes indeed, wonderful news from Buckingham Palace. All the best to William and Kate in their forthcoming nuptials. They were so right to delay their marriage plans: housing is much more affordable for young couples now.

The Government plans to give them Louth as a wedding present. Just to spite Gerry Adams.

And it'll please the IMF, too.

THURSDAY, 18 NOVEMBER 2010

Ignominy of Bailout Compounded by Contemptuous Leaders

Dan O'Brien

And so it has come to pass. The spectre of bailout, which has loomed ever larger on the horizon over the past two years, is upon us. Ignominy heaped on catastrophe.

Today, officials from Brussels, Frankfurt and Washington land in Dublin. Their arrival heralds the beginning of discussions on the terms of a bailout. The type, scale and scope of the conditions to be imposed are far from clear at this point.

The shorter the timeframe for discussions, the more limited the scope of the conditions are likely to be.

The extent to which the terms of the Croke Park deal are contravened, if at all, will indicate how radical it will be.

Front and centre in the talks will be the bleeding sore that is the Irish banking system. The International Monetary Fund, the European Central Bank and the European Commission will all have their say on this.

The latter institution will be represented by Olli Rehn's economic and financial affairs directorate-general. Despite Rehn departing Dublin only eight days earlier, he said in Brussels yesterday that it would be 'premature' for him to discuss Ireland's banks because he did not have the 'full picture'.

His officials will be the only ones representing the commission. This is curious. The directorate-general for competition has been penalising all European banks in receipt of taxpayers' money.

In Ireland's case, his officials have been very busy over the past couple of years in relation to the State's banks, either setting down conditions for their restructuring or vetoing their plans for their own restructuring.

That they are not joining Rehn's people tomorrow is more than a little strange given the explicit focus on getting to the bottom of the banking fiasco.

Even more curious were Brian Lenihan's ramblings on RTÉ's *Morning Ireland* programme yesterday.

He said that there is 'no question of loading on to the Irish sovereign or Irish State some kind of unspecified burden'.

Cartoon by Martyn Turner.

He cannot believe that the outsiders are here to expose Ireland to more bank losses given that he long ago guaranteed the lot. Is he trying to portray himself as the protector of the Irish taxpayer against wicked foreigners who wish to bury them in even more debt?

His comments on the four-year budget plan were notable. On Monday, the Government position was that it would be published early next week.

By yesterday, Lenihan said in the same interview, 'I take it the [four-year] plan will be published by the end of the month' (my emphasis). Either the formulation of the plan is at sixes and sevens or the rowing back from the early-next-week date is at the behest of the commission-ECB-IMF troika because they want to have even more say in its drawing up.

No matter how important these issues are, they are mere details in the broader ignominy of having to be rescued by foreigners.

Honour demands that those at the helm who have failed to navigate away from this national humiliation should concede their failure and stand down.

Instead, they have no intention of doing so. Worse still, Government representatives display contempt for citizens with their bare-faced denials of a bailout when it is so patently happening.

A government of honourable people would hang its collective head in shame, concede that it had failed, call an election and immediately bring the Opposition in to talks with the troika so that all parties that might potentially form a government are involved.

That would bring political unity, leveraging what limited influence the State has in talks with those who are bailing it out. Not to do so, and after all that has happened, is to weaken further this State and add to the harm inflicted on its citizens. If ever there was a time to do what is right and honourable, this is it.

THURSDAY, 18 NOVEMBER 2010

Surrender of Sovereignty Highlights Political Failings

Stephen Collins

Taoiseach Brian Cowen may not have been prepared to admit it in the Dáil yesterday, but there is no way around the fact that control of the country's economic affairs has passed outside the hands of our elected politicians.

After close to 90 years of independence, it is a sad day for the country that it has squandered its sovereignty through sheer economic mismanagement. What makes it even worse is that this has happened at a time when we are still, on paper at least, one of the wealthiest nations in the world.

The profligacy of the boom years is the direct cause of the calamity, but the inability of the political system, the social partners and society in general to get to grips with the tough choices that were needed since the bubble burst two years ago has helped bring us to the pass.

The immediate trigger for the decision of our European Union partners to force Ireland into the EU/International Monetary Fund (IMF) bailout is the state of our banks, but the impact on the country is likely to be felt across all aspects of Government policy and at every level of society. On one level, intervention by the EU and the IMF is no bad thing. It means that rational decisions on how we can live within our means will now be forced down the throats of the competing interests who have stymied any genuine national response to the crisis.

That, however, does not mitigate the failure of those who were charged with running the country for the past decade. The electorate who kept putting them back despite mounting evidence of danger cannot be absolved of responsibility either.

The fact that we have simply not been able to deal adequately in a unified way with the consequences of our actions had compounded the problem as others lost confidence in the ability of our institutions to deal with our bad behaviour.

In the Dáil yesterday, Cowen took issue with the Opposition for using the word 'bailout' and repeatedly referred to the fund as a 'facility' that could be of benefit to Ireland and our partners in the euro zone.

He also insisted the Government did not mislead anyone at the weekend when Ministers kept insisting that no application had been made to the EU. While he did not get much of a hearing for his views, he was probably being truthful. The storm that developed at the weekend took most people by surprise and Ministers like Dermot Ahern simply did not know that the European Central Bank had decided that the game was up for Ireland.

In hindsight, a leak from Brussels of a conversation between ECB officials and the Central Bank in Dublin on Friday was a signal that the EU's patience had run out. At the time though, a game of poker was being played with our EU partners

Ajai Chopra (left), Deputy Director of the European Department of the International Monetary Fund, passes a beggar as he makes his way to the Central Bank for talks about a financial bailout. Photograph: Peter Morrison/ AP.

and Cowen and his colleagues were desperately trying to bluff their way through. Still, the episode only compounded the image of a government making another wrong call and being forced to swallow a bitter pill by our EU partners.

Fine Gael leader Enda Kenny was not in the mood for excuses and he lambasted the Taoiseach and his Ministers for not giving the full facts over the weekend. 'Well now we know the truth. The white flag has been raised, the towel has been thrown in and like the prowler waves off the west coast, they're coming on Thursday,' said Kenny.

Talks with the EU and IMF officials will begin in Dublin today and hopefully they will result in clarity being brought to the whole sorry mess in quick time. The knowledge that the core issues are being dealt with will at least give the people of the country some respite from the constant uncertainty, which has been so damaging for national morale.

The course of events has also reduced the level of political uncertainty about the budget which dominated Government thinking last week. The four-year plan and the budget will now simply have to be accepted by the Dáil because our democratic representatives are no longer in a position to reject them without making complete fools of themselves.

Olli Rehn and his officials have already had a serious input into the budget decisions that have to be taken between now and 2014. Our TDs no longer have the luxury of refusing to accept those decisions unless they want to draw attention to their own powerlessness.

The question of when the general election will take place and who is likely to emerge as the next government is of less relevance. With a four-year budgetary framework set in stone, whoever is in power will have little choice but to press ahead and implement decisions already taken over their heads. They may have some discretion about the precise detail of where the cuts should fall, but that is all.

The real danger is that some other EU states will try to tamper with major national policy issues like the 12.5 per cent corporate tax rate, so the sooner we get through the pain of the four-year plan and out the other side, the better. On a party political level, the events of recent days are a disaster for Fianna Fáil. The party, which always thought of itself as being a national movement rather than a mere political party, has presided over the surrender of Irish sovereignty as a direct result of its own mismanagement.

In the longer run, that is likely to be devastating for the party that has never spent more than one term out of office. The voters who rewarded it for being so irresponsible in the good times are likely to be merciless now that everything has gone so badly wrong.

THURSDAY, 18 NOVEMBER 2010

Was it for This?

Editorial

It may seem strange to some that *The Irish Times* would ask whether this is what the men of 1916 died for: a bailout from the German chancellor with a few shillings of sympathy from the British chancellor on the side. There is the shame of it all. Having obtained our political independence from Britain to be the masters of our own affairs, we have now surrendered our sovereignty to the European Commission, the European Central Bank and the International Monetary Fund. Their representatives ride into Merrion Street today.

Fianna Fáil has sometimes served Ireland very well, sometimes very badly. Even in its worst times, however, it retained some respect for its underlying commitment that the Irish should control their own destinies. It lists among its primary aims the commitment 'to maintain the status of Ireland as a sovereign State'. Its founder, Éamon de Valera, in his inaugural address to his new party in 1926, spoke of 'the inalienability of national sovereignty' as being fundamental to its beliefs. The Republican Party's ideals are in tatters now.

The Irish people do not need to be told that, especially for small nations, there is no such thing as absolute sovereignty. We know very well that we have made our independence more meaningful by sharing it with our European neighbours. We are not naive enough to think that this State ever can, or ever could, take large decisions in isolation from the rest of the world. What we do expect, however, is that those decisions will still be our own. A nation's independence is defined by the choices it can make for itself.

Irish history makes the loss of that sense of choice all the more shameful. The desire to be a sovereign people runs like a seam through all the struggles of the last 200 years. 'Self-determination' is a phrase that echoes from the United Irishmen to the Belfast Agreement. It continues to have a genuine resonance for most Irish people today.

The true ignominy of our current situation is not that our sovereignty has been taken away from us, it is that we ourselves have squandered it. Let us not seek to assuage our sense of shame in the comforting illusion that powerful nations in Europe are conspiring to become our masters. We are, after all, no great prize for any would-be overlord now. No rational European would willingly take on the task of cleaning up the mess we have made. It is the incompetence of the governments we ourselves elected that has so deeply compromised our capacity to make our own decisions.

They did so, let us recall, from a period when Irish sovereignty had never been stronger. Our national debt was negligible. The mass emigration that had mocked our claims to be a people in control of our own destiny was reversed. A genuine act of national self-determination had occurred in 1998 when both parts of the island voted to accept the Belfast Agreement. The sense of failure and inferiority had been banished, we thought, for good.

To drag this State down from those heights and make it again subject to the decisions of others is an achievement that will not soon be forgiven. It

must mark, surely, the ignominious end of a failed administration.

Another Leafy Suburb, Another Planning Problem for Dunne

Paul Cullen

Having done the State some service, the developers and speculators who rode the Celtic Tiger for all it was worth are now fleeing the bust in all directions.

The former Anglo Irish chief executive David Drumm has washed up in Boston, the financier Derek Quinlan has landed in Switzerland and now the biggest and best-known builder of them all, Sean Dunne, has moved his family to the leafiest part of Connecticut.

But having left behind a few planning controversies in Dublin, Dunne finds himself in a fresh planning limbo, this time involving what he hoped would be his new home.

The exclusive private community of Belle Haven houses numerous wealthy or famous personalities, including the singer Diana Ross, two billionaires and the former chief executives of IBM and Xerox. Its newest residents, Dunne, his wife, Gayle Killilea, and their three children, are renting locally until they finish renovating their new home on the estate, where the safety of residents is ensured by 24-hour-a-day security patrols.

Work on renovating the $2 million (€1.5 million) house, which was purchased last April, has been suspended after planning officials were alerted that most of the building had been demolished. Planning staff in the local town, Greenwich, say the owners have exceeded the scope of their permit.

Dunne and his family moved out of their home on Shrewsbury Road, in Dublin 4, this year

In more prosperous times . . . Sean Dunne (right) at home in Ballsbridge in 2008 with his wife, Gayle Killilea.
Photograph: Derek Spiers.

and were seeking to rent it out to an embassy. It emerged in the past month that he was scouting for a base in the US, apparently to pursue new business interests. Word leaked out that his family was renting in Belle Haven, but it wasn't known before now that he intended a more permanent stay.

You wouldn't know that 38 Bush Avenue was Sean Dunne's house from the official records. According to the assessor's office in Greenwich, the house was sold by Sally S. Johnson to Philip Teplen for $2 million last April. Teplen, a lawyer with offices on Fifth Avenue in New York, specialises in immigration issues. He is described as a trustee and only his name appears on planning documents.

According to his website, Teplen has 25 years' experience in 'guiding the way to America' for this clients. He is also involved in the construction industry. His name appears on the 'stop work'

notice currently in place at the site. He has not returned calls from this newspaper.

It was the sudden arrival of a number of Irish construction workers in the area over the summer that first set local tongues wagging. Some workers were US-based, but others had come over on the plane from Dublin and were relatively unfamiliar with local planning codes.

The house itself was described by estate agents as a 'classic Victorian with turn-of-the-century details' on three floors. Dating from 1896, it had seven bedrooms and five bathrooms over 427 sq. m. (4,600 sq. feet), according to an internet listing. It had a 'wonderful port-cochere entrance' (in other words, wide enough for a carriage) and 'gracious rooms of great scale with high ceilings'.

Permission was given to carry out internal restoration and add a new garage, family room and

The property at Bush Avenue in Belle Haven, Connecticut, of which Irish property developer Sean Dunne identified himself as owner to neighbours.

kitchen, according to the division of building inspection in Greenwich.

Dick Case, a retired IBM executive who lives next to the house, told *The Irish Times* this week that Dunne introduced himself as the owner of the property and invited him to view the renovation plans in the kitchen of the old house.

In late July, the planning and zoning board of appeals in Greenwich heard an application in the name of Teplen to permit additions to the house by varying the required side yard and permitted floor-area ratio.

Case said he supported the plans as he believed they represented an improvement to the neigh-bourhood. 'I was under the impression that things were going to be different from the way they are now. I had a misleading impression.' The application was granted on 9 August. The board found

that there was hardship due to 'lot shape' and to the fact that the house was built in compliance with earlier regulations that had since been changed. It noted that the proposed alteration would slightly reduce the nonconforming square footage.

Greenwich town hall became involved again after the house was substantially demolished. Officials ordered workers carrying out the work to stop. A notice to this effect, dated 20 October, was put up.

Tom Schupps of Schupps Landclearing, which carried out the demolition work, confirmed to *The Irish Times* last week that most of the structure had been levelled, although he added that 'parts of it' were still standing. Schupps said he didn't know who owned the house, but he provided the name of an Irishman who he said was the project manager. This person said he was over from Ireland to work

Snow ploughs, accompanied by a Garda escort, clear the M9 at Mullinavat in Co. Kilkenny.
Photograph: Dylan Vaughan.

short-term on a US project but denied he was working for Dunne.

An official in the Greenwich planning office told *The Irish Times* the owners of the house had exceeded the scope of their permit and were therefore ordered to stop work. A permit for additions and alterations had been issued, but what was now required was a demolition permit.

Nicknamed the 'squire of Ballsbridge', Dunne paid €53.7 million an acre for the Jurys site in Dublin 4 in 2005, and paid €207 million for the front blocks of AIB Bankcentre a year later. These and other investments are now worth a fraction of what he paid for them.

Dunne did not respond to attempts to contact him through his PA for this article.

According to Case, Dunne's new plans for the site are significantly different from his original proposal and appear to be bigger. 'However, I still think the property is being improved and its value increased, and that helps me.' No work had been done on the site over the past month, he said. 'We have a half-constructed building beside us and we don't know what's going to happen to it.'

SATURDAY, 4 DECEMBER 2010

Surviving the Cold Snap on a Wing and a Prayer

Michael Viney

Inside that little sphere of fluff clinging to the feeder is a body not much bigger than a ping-pong ball, its ratio of heat-leaking skin surface to volume of bird a distinctly dodgy fit for icy

After their wedding at St Patrick's Church in Johnstownbridge, Enfield, Co. Meath, Darren Murray, his bride Áine McLoughlin and her sister and bridesmaid Caitríona McLoughlin enjoy fun in the snow. Photograph: Brenda Fitzsimons.

weather: in the Arctic you get not blue tits but big snowy owls with bulky anoraks and feathered galoshes. And inside the soft weave of down under a tit's fluffed-up feathers is a tiny heart going bang-bang-bang 500 times a minute to pump some of the warmest blood of any animal: 40 degrees compared with our 37. All that need for energy, that racing metabolism, and still it has to fight for a place at the nuts.

There are probably many more blue tits around than there would be without garden feeders. And before peanuts and fancy seeds there were (at least where I grew up) doorstep milk bottles with tops of foil or cardboard.

The tits spread the word across Europe about the feed of cream inside – all of them had the knowledge within a couple of post-war years.

Even now, new hedgerow birds are learning about the winter largesse of back gardens: woodpeckers, siskins, above all the glorious goldfinches – a dozen of them now at our feeders in the oak trees, battling it out with the sparrows. There are still e-mails asking, 'What is this wonderful bird?' from readers at a first rapt encounter, and a visit by 40 of them at a garden in Waterford must have seemed magical, indeed. A reader in Wicklow last month reported the success of a small feeder filled with nyjer, the tiny, black oilseeds from Africa: within days, up to 18 goldfinches were clinging there. 'How,' wondered Robert Myerscough, 'did they recognise it in the first place, and how did they get the word out to their mates?'

As the temperature plummeted this week, one's ecological concerns were softened by ordinary, irrational sympathies. In the battles over oat flakes on our kitchen window sill, we welcomed a pair of song thrushes, each with its own rich livery of speckles, and booed the anonymous blackbirds that drove them away. I have been out at first light to refill the box, hoping to give the thrushes a better chance.

Blackbirds are every bit the bullies they're painted, habitually robbing smaller birds of their food. David Snow, in a classic study of the species, thought them even more ruthless than mistle thrushes or fieldfares, both notoriously domineering. But at feeders it's the blackcap that seems most aggressive – a mere warbler that often seems able to chase everything else away.

As I write, a near-total absence of both fieldfares and redwings at this corner of the Connacht coast presents a disquieting mystery. These Scandinavian thrushes are regular migrants to Ireland in late autumn and fly west for refuge ahead of extreme winter weather.

In one day last January, the bird painter Michael O'Clery reported 20,000 redwings and 5,000–6,000 fieldfares arriving from the sea at Ballinskelligs, Co. Kerry. A few days later, the clifftops at Courtmacsherry, Co. Cork, were covered with hundreds of the birds 'so tired,' as Peter Wolstenholme wrote, 'that we were able to pick up the featherweight waifs, which almost expired in our hands.'

Thousands, indeed, did die, especially among the redwings, from Cork up to Mayo and beyond – among them, probably, the dozen I flushed unintentionally one morning from their roost at the heart of an escallonia bush.

Actor Brendan Gleeson, on whom an honorary degree of Doctor of Arts was conferred at a ceremony in the National University of Ireland in Dublin. Photograph: Eric Luke.

Surviving bitter nights is the big challenge for songbirds, which makes their different habits all the more intriguing. Blue tits and great tits, for example, seek individual shelter in crevices and tree holes, tucking beaks and legs into their feathers. (When blue tits have paired early, the male sees his mate to bed, then goes to roost nearby.) The slightly smaller long-tailed tits, on the other hand, flying in little flocks by day, clump together in a ball at night, tails sticking out, at the heart of a hawthorn bush.

Wrens may hold the record for snuggling down together: 50 in one nest box seems to be the current record. Last February, a reader in Co. Antrim e-mailed a photograph of wrens packed into a swallow's nest in a corner of her porch. Once they're all in, no one uses the front door.

Insect-feeders such as wrens are not drawn to peanuts, but will occasionally take crumbs or suet from the ground, and a Greystones reader last winter reported a treecreeper eating peanut crumbs beneath his feeders. Starlings, too, were coming to feeders for the first time in Co. Tipperary, and rooks in Co. Wicklow waiting patiently beneath them, for nut crumbs.

A pied wagtail joining our window-sill thrushes is different, but scarcely rare and certainly no match for the snipe in people's gardens last February, jabbing desperately into rose beds in the search for soil invertebrates.

WEDNESDAY, 8 DECEMBER 2010

Shattering the Myth of a World-class Education System

Seán Flynn

In the dark days – and there have been a good number of late – we could at least find comfort in the quality of our education system.

For years, ministers for education and the teacher unions told us we could take pride in our 'world-class' education system. It was the magnet that helped to draw inward investment to our shores – and it was something that differentiated us from troubled education systems in Britain and elsewhere. When it came to education, the land of saints and scholars could mix it with the folks at the top table.

It's not an exaggeration to say this portrayal of the Irish education system was almost entirely based on one authoritative study. In 2000, the OECD/PISA★ survey of 15-year-olds ranked Ireland fifth in literacy, well above the OECD average.

This glowing report helped to stifle much-needed debate about the quality of the Irish education system. Naysayers could be rebuked and brought to heel by reference back to that OECD survey. Over the years, the mantra from the Department of Education and the teacher unions became familiar: 'We can't be doing much wrong if we are in the top five in literacy.'

The truth, of course, was more complicated.

Ireland performed well in the 2000 literacy survey because it had an inherent advantage, a homogenous school-going population with few migrants. In simple terms, the task of imparting literacy in Irish classrooms was less challenging than that facing teachers in inner-city Paris or in central London.

But all has changed since 2000. By 2009, more than 8 per cent of the Irish school-going population are migrants and that has made all the difference. Ireland is on a level playing field with other OECD states.

The result? On literacy, Ireland has fallen from 5th place to 17th, the most dramatic drop of any OECD state.

Yesterday, the teacher unions and others were urging caution about the latest literacy figures. Potential problems with the methodology and the sample were cited. But it had the feeling of the players attacking the referee after losing the match. No such quibbles were raised when Ireland performed so well in 2000.

The steady focus on that 2000 literacy result had one other negative effect. Until recently, it crowded out debate on Ireland's performance in maths and science.

By any measure, this has also been disappointing for a country which sees a smart economy as key to its economic future. Ireland remains some distance from the premier league, ranked 26th in maths and at average levels in science in 2009.

Cumulatively, this year's OECD findings on literacy, maths and science represent a body blow to Irish education, shattering all those myths about a 'world-class' system.

And yet, it's fair to say the findings will not surprise those who have been sounding the alarm for years.

Frustrated primary teachers in working-class suburbs in Dublin will tell you about the appalling, persistently low levels of literacy in their classes. University presidents and the Higher Education Authority say thousands of students – weaned on rote learning in the Leaving Cert – cannot cope with university. Earlier this year, several of the main US multinationals expressed concern about the quality of Irish graduates.

So why was the decline in standards – now confirmed by the OECD – not picked up by the Department of Education?

Perhaps the answer is obvious: it was not asking the right questions.

At its core, there is what we might call an 'evaluation deficit' in Irish education. The focus is largely on resources, not surprising given the chronic under-investment in the sector.

Within the Department of Education, there has – until very recently – been no tradition of assessing the outputs from schools.

We have no idea, for example, how our 12-year-olds leaving primary school compare with children in England or France. For years, the Department of Education refused to participate in international reviews of primary education.

At second level, the department does not publish an annual report on the performance of schools. Every year, it congratulates Leaving Cert students and comforts us that standards are 'broadly in line' with previous years. There is little analysis of how this year's trends compare with 5 or 10 years ago.

The department – often dubbed the 'Department of Schools and Teachers' – has not traditionally cast a critical eye on the system it controls. It has opposed the release of information on school performance in the courts.

Mindful of its close relationship with the teacher unions, it has also been slow to mutter even the mildest criticism of teaching standards or teacher quality.

The good news is that a revolution of sorts may be sweeping through Marlborough Street. The new Chief Inspector of the department, Dr Harold Hislop, and Secretary General Brigid McManus are raising awkward questions about quality standards.

Last month, Hislop published a report of school inspections in primary schools. The results were devastating. Shortcomings in almost 15 per cent of English and maths classes were discovered when inspectors arrived unannounced in more than 450 primary schools in the past year.

At second level, inspection reports on schools – notoriously bland in tone – have become more robust and critical.

There are other encouraging signs. A new maths curriculum – with a fresh emphasis on problem-solving – is being rolled out in schools.

The initiative is largely in response to a succession of OECD reports highlighting our deficiencies in this key area.

The hope must be that the latest disappointing findings on literacy will have a similarly transformative effect. At the very least, it should remove the complacency and the denial about falling literacy standards.

In all of this, there may also be a need for some wider perspective. Yes, the Irish education system has been too self-regarding for too long. But, for all its faults, it has many positives – not least the strong, personal commitment of many teachers and school leaders.

The Irish education system may not be perfect – but it remains among our best-performing public services.

*The OECD is the 33-country-strong Organisation for Economic Co-operation and Development, members and associates of which are all committed to democracy and the market economy. PISA, the Programme for International Student Assessment, is an internationally standardised assessment that was jointly developed by participating economies and administered to 15-year-olds in schools.

FRIDAY, 10 DECEMBER 2010

Enda Kenny Could be Best Taoiseach for Decades

John Waters

It is clear that in the coming election campaign no radical proposals will be on the table. There is no stomach in the Irish political system for standing up to bankers, loan sharks or Eurobullies.

If there exists a plucky little nation that will tell the emperor he is naked, it won't be this one. We no longer do bottle, vision or core thinking.

Our best hope is either that the entire international debt pyramid collapses and we can roll clear or, conversely, that the whole thing is rebalanced to enable it to limp along for another few years, during which time we might be able to do some core thinking about ourselves.

Our political system offers no alternatives except at the rhetorical level. The best hope, bleak as it is, is for a government that will hold the line that has now been established and enable new

energies to emerge from a largely moribund and hollowed-out society.

Strange to say, but the most profound crisis we face as a society is not an economic one, but the fact that our political system has gradually become atrophied, having ceased to absorb new talent and energies from the younger generations, which skulk behind keypads lobbing witticisms at politicians but refusing to become involved.

This has more to do with the hogging of power by the older generations than with any innate 'apathy' among the young – a kind of constructive alienation that has suited the elder lemons until now.

It is obvious that Fianna Fáil will not have a sniff of government for an aeon. Yet, there is little confidence in any of the alternatives, which means that, more than likely, the next government will emerge more by default than for any reasons to do with inspiration or hope. The best chance, long term, is if we can find a way of fast-tracking the handover of power so as to replace the dead wood in the shortest possible time.

Rather bizarrely in some respects, Fine Gael is now the closest party in the Dáil to offering a representation of the overall national demographic. Whereas the Labour Party still offers essentially the same left-wing personnel as 20 years ago, Fine Gael has a number of interesting and smart young TDs.

In this the party is, theoretically at least, better placed than the others to lead a country in which more than 40 per cent of the population is under 30. Of the notional alternatives, a cabinet containing Leo Varadkar, Lucinda Creighton, Simon Coveney and Brian Hayes has the best hope of inspiring the nation with the idea of the torch at last being handed to a new generation.

Enda Kenny can claim a fair deal of the credit for the election of an eclectic and promising bunch of TDs in 2007. Unfortunately, right now, the defensiveness and paranoia that have built up around his leadership risk destroying this potential.

As leader, he must take the blame for the fact

Cartoon by Martyn Turner.

that, having brought these people in, he has failed to deploy them properly.

Fine Gael, therefore, also offers a reasonably accurate microcosm of the country in that the energies of its younger generation are being rendered frustrated by the reluctance of the elder lemons to move over in the bed. Olwyn Enright, once mentioned as a future leader, has ruled out contesting the coming election.

Varadkar, who has the potential to be a truly great politician, is in danger of running to seed, shooting his mouth off for cheap headlines.

Creighton, who on her election to the Dáil in 2007 displayed an ability and maturity far beyond her years, has recently been spending much of her energy gazing at her own political belly button and muttering about quitting politics altogether.

This is disastrous for Fine Gael but it presents Kenny with a challenge and an opportunity. He could do worse than reflect on the title of Brian Farrell's book about the role of the Taoiseach in Irish government: Chairman or Chief?

Kenny cannot be a credible chief. His focus should, therefore, be on managing the not inconsiderable talent available to him. Whatever personality shortcomings he may have, these can be more than overcome if he approaches correctly the task of ensuring that there occurs an effective and harmonious devolution of power over the lifetime of the next government – that at the end a new generation will have emerged in Fine Gael, leaving the other parties panting to catch up.

Kenny could obliterate most of his present image problems by simply declaring that his role as chairman in the next government would be to ensure that, at the end of it, a new generation of leaders will have emerged with the experience and moral authority to make decisions, radical or otherwise, in accordance with the true desires of those who will constitute Irish society. If he can dissolve the paranoia and defensiveness he has allowed to develop around himself, Enda Kenny might well become the greatest Taoiseach for decades.

FRIDAY, 10 DECEMBER 2010

In My Dreams, the Heat of Revenge will be White Hot

Michael Harding

One evening during the snow, the news on the television carried a story about the difficulty a bride was having getting to the altar for her wedding. When I went to bed that night I fell into a disturbing dream about a woman in a white gown walking towards me through the snow and then putting her fingers on my lips until I was burning up like a fire.

I woke up sweating and full of anxiety, but then I realised that I had left my new electric blanket on. So I presume that is what caused the dream. At least that's what I told myself the following morning as I opened the shutters and looked out on the white fields and the frozen trees enveloped in fog.

The phone rang in the hallway downstairs. It was a friend calling to say his mother had been taken into hospital and, since he lived too far away, he was wondering if I would go over to Cavan and turn on the heating in her house. He feared she might have turned it off when she was leaving.

I drove through Edgeworthstown and Granard, and arrived at the semi-detached house on the outskirts of Cavan without any bother. I opened the back door, as directed, with a key that is always left under the mat.

I entered and switched on a Dimplex heater in the kitchen. I turned the thermostat gauges in the two front rooms to max.

A swimmer takes the plunge at Sandycove Beach in Dublin before the expected return of the cold spell.
Photograph: Cyril Byrne.

The house was cluttered with things that conjured up the absent woman: a radio, a Sunday newspaper, a purse with old pound coins in it, a set of rosary beads, a half-empty box of Celebration chocolates, Lemsips, a packet of Panadol, her coat, draped on a chair, and a scarf of purple mohair on the floor.

In the dining room there was a sideboard of silverware, an armchair and an old-fashioned television set where the lady may have spent many hours, because the cushions retained the imprint of her body.

I, too, use the television as a refuge from pain. It numbs me with a noise that is not my own. I am released from the zone of my own anxiety by absorbing daily doses of soap opera and the deadening narrative of American movies.

As I stared at the empty chair, I imagined the old lady as a white ghost sitting there gazing at her television, her eyes moving occasionally from the television screen to me. It was her whiteness that unnerved me.

I drove home through the fog past fields of snow as white as the whale that Captain Ahab pursued with such diligence.

Whiteness, the author of *Moby Dick* tells us, wipes all colour from the earth. It takes the life and vitality that the world has and freezes it over. In whiteness there is always a hint of death. The new bride's gown and the infant's christening shawl are white because an old self has been abandoned. Whiteness erases all previous marks. It makes a space empty again and ready for new beginnings.

That night I made the same mistake again: I forgot to turn the electric blanket off. This time I dreamt I was in the visitors' gallery at Dáil Éireann sitting beside a newsreader in a wedding gown.

When I looked into the chamber, all the deputies were in long, white robes with white hoods covering their heads so that their faces could not be seen behind the gleaming cloth.

'Why are they covered?' I wondered.

The bride from RTÉ said, 'It's payback time, baby. You should never have put a motorway through the Tara valley.'

Then I saw a minister rising, resplendent in his white robes, like some imperial wizard, as he stood before the throne of the Ceann Comhairle. 'Behold,' he mumbled, 'I stand before you as the most innocent, among a legion of white-robed innocents. Yet it must be accepted that the axe is already at the root of the tree. The White Whale has triumphed. The White Hag has returned to the white bush.

'Cathleen has sprung once more from the ashes of the GPO and, through me, she now summons her children to attention and strikes them without mercy in retribution for the sacrilege at Tara.'

'Jesus protect us,' I shouted, as I woke up, sizzling like a rasher on a frying pan and disturbed by a sense of foreboding, though I consoled myself that it was only a dream.

Cathleen has sprung from the ashes of the GPO and, through me, she now summons her children to attention and strikes them without mercy in retribution for the sacrilege at Tara.

SATURDAY, 11 DECEMBER 2010

A Lesson from Iceland: Say you're Mad as Hell and are Not Going to Take it Any More

Elaine Byrne

The president of Iceland, Ólafur Ragnar Grímsson, expressed his deep annoyance at the start of the year at a joke about his country: 'What's the difference between Iceland and Ireland? One letter and six months.' The gag, first heard on the BBC's daily current-affairs programme *Europe Today* a year earlier, implied that Ireland was facing an

Icelandic demonstrator shouts slogans as hundreds of people protest outside the parliament in the capital, Reykjavík,
against evictions resulting from the financial crisis. Photograph: Halldor Kolbeins/AFP.

economic collapse as severe as Iceland's. In nationalistic vein, Grímsson said the joke was 'just a recent example' of the 'arrogance of the British'. A year later and the shoe is on the other foot. Ireland has embraced British generosity and Iceland has officially emerged from recession.

The British chancellor of the exchequer, George Osborne, published legislation on Thursday granting a €3.87 billion bilateral loan facility to Ireland. Two years after Iceland's €7.5 billion IMF bailout, the North Atlantic island has returned to growth for the first time, recording 1.2 per cent growth in the last quarter. Inflation is at its lowest level since 2004, at 2.6 per cent, and the official interest rate has dropped from 18 per cent at the height of the crisis to a more manageable 4.5 per cent.

The Nobel laureate Paul Krugman notes in his *New York Times* blog that although Iceland had by

far the biggest excesses, 'through the magic of default and devaluation, it's actually doing better than Ireland'. Patrick Honohan, the Central Bank governor, assessed this point in his report for the Banking Inquiry this year, noting that Iceland's losses were 'almost 10 times those of Ireland when measured relative to each country's GDP'.

So what can Ireland learn from Iceland? In a blunt comparison between the two, a senior Icelandic government source privy to his country's IMF negotiations said: 'I think the blanket guarantee given by the Irish Government on all bank obligations was a big mistake which now needs to be paid for . . . We were not going to have the Republic of Iceland go into a default situation. Which is why we did not guarantee the banking system in its totality.'

In a referendum in March to decide what to do about more than €5 billion lost by Dutch and

Lorraine Tran from Cherrywood in Co. Dublin with her 13-month-old son Jake, enjoying the Brown Thomas window at Christmas on Grafton Street in Dublin. Photograph: Bryan O'Brien.

British savers who had online Icesave accounts with Landsbanki, which went into receivership in October 2008, more than 90 per cent of Icelanders rejected a proposition to fully reimburse the money.

Despite impressions to the contrary, the Icelandic Government never defaulted on its sovereign debt. The commercial banks, however, did default on their obligations, burning foreign creditors, including senior bondholders. The country's three largest banks – Kaupthing and Glitnir held the top spots alongside Landsbanki – were nationalised immediately. The government did not pour good money after bad in a pointless effort to rescue its zombie banks. It cleanly pulled the plug on financial institutions that had no means of saving themselves.

There are other lessons too.

As a direct response to the country's economic cataclysm, Icelandic citizens adopted the mantle of Howard Beale, the frustrated anchorman from the Sidney Lumet film *Network*, and protested *en masse* – a virtually unknown phenomenon in Iceland's history. The 'kitchenware revolution' of January last year saw thousands gather outside the Althing, the national parliament, adopting Beale's slogan to proclaim: 'We're mad as hell, and we're not going to take this any more.'

This cathartic uprising brought down the centre-right government that had been in the ascendancy in Icelandic politics for decades. The subsequent April elections saw the centre-left win a parliamentary majority for the first time and the election of Jóhanna Sigurðardóttir, the first woman to hold the office of prime minister.

As part of her programme of democratic

Mark Kavanagh, aged six, from Celbridge, Co. Kildare, watched over by former presidents at Áras an Uachtaráin, where President Mary McAleese, her husband Dr Martin McAleese and 130 children switched on the Christmas tree lights. Photograph: Alan Betson.

renewal, the Icelandic parliament voted last June to establish a directly elected constitutional assembly 'for the purpose of reviewing the Constitution of the Republic'. This 25-seat body will essentially rewrite the constitution and prepare a Bill that, if passed in parliament, will be put to a referendum in 2012.

There is scepticism in Iceland about this unique constitutional experiment. Elections to the assembly last week recorded the lowest electoral turnout in the country's history, with only 35.9 per cent of voters going to the polls. Of the 523 candidates who put themselves forward, the successful ones tended to be celebrities. This low expression of support for Sigurðardóttir's constitutional initiative suggests Icelanders believe their government is trying to change too much too fast.

As the shock of the economic collapse has subsided, the popularity of the new government and its authority to implement political reform have taken a hit. The constitutional assembly may yet become the stick that a resurgent centre-right will use to regain popular support. Lessons, perhaps, for an incoming Fine Gael-Labour government: the dynamics of politics changed quickly in Iceland as the immediate memory of the collapse waned.

Ordinary Icelanders have mixed views about their future. When the property boom collapsed, two friends of mine, Brynhildur and Hinrik, lost their jobs in architecture and property conveyance. When I visited earlier this year, they were living in a tiny two-room basement of their house, having divided the rest of their home into rental apartments. Trapped in a cycle of negative equity,

Hinrik has no option but to work as a fisherman in the Arctic Circle two-thirds of the year. 'A dramatic shift in the mentality of the people has occurred,' says Brynhildur. 'We are re-evaluating every priority in our lives.'

Even more tax increases, spending cuts and salary cuts are promised for 2011. The Icelandic minister for finance cancelled a trip to Trinity College Dublin two weeks ago after the failure of attempts to legislate for a bailout for mortgage holders. In a country of only 320,000 inhabitants, up to 40,000 of them may now lose their homes.

Things will get much worse in the next year before they get better. A taste of the future?

WEDNESDAY, 15 DECEMBER 2010

Every Little Helps: Mary Comes Home to Hero's Welcome

Ronan McGreevy

A working-class hero is something to be celebrated in these straitened times when there is nothing but doom and gloom about.

X Factor semi-finalist Mary Byrne (51) left Ballyfermot with a dream and arrived back with a Garda escort to a huge crowd and a make-shift platform in front of the Tesco where she worked for 11 years.

The crowd were kept waiting for nearly an hour because Byrne's flight was delayed getting in from London where she had been at the *X Factor* wrap party on Monday night.

Despite the chill of a mid-December afternoon, the warm reception she received moved the singer to tears, though she freely admitted that the rollercoaster ride of her time on *X Factor* brought her to tears on many occasions.

Schoolchildren from St Gabriel's Primary School and St Raphael's Primary School,

Ballyfermot, carried placards and shouted 'Mary, Mary, Mary' as the singer was momentarily lost for words as she took in the sea of faces in front of her, most of whom she knew personally.

'I always thought Ballyfermot people were supportive, but that was beyond the call of duty,' she said.

Flanked by her daughter Debbie and brother Tommy, who is a singer himself, Byrne raised the biggest cheer when she revealed that she would be making an album.

Then her speech was drowned out by cries of 'sing, sing, sing'.

Byrne obliged with her version of James Brown's 'It's a Man's Man's Man's World', a song she sang on two occasions during *X Factor* – this time with a slight croak in her throat as a result of a throat infection.

'Go on, you good thing,' shouted one enthusiastic fan.

Afterwards, she entered her long-time workplace Tesco, trailed by staff and media and passed a phalanx of security officers who had to keep the enthusiastic crowd at bay.

Byrne posed at till No. 40, now surely the most famous supermarket till in the world.

Not since she entered the bear pit of the live finals on the *X Factor* has she been back to the supermarket.

Holding court in the training room of Tesco Ballyfermot, where she spent many hours in a previous life, Byrne was remarkably sanguine about the revelations that she polled more votes than teenager Cher Lloyd, though the judges opted to send Byrne home at the semi-final stage.

'It's in the past. First of all, I was given the opportunity and not many Irish people are given that opportunity in the UK and that was fantastic. It was what it is, and there are no hard feelings whatsoever,' she said.

She admitted though that she 'felt like slapping' the emotional Lloyd on several occasions 'and I've told her that to her face' and she

X Factor *contestant Mary Byrne at her former checkout till in Tesco, Ballyfermot, Dublin, meeting fans and former colleagues. Photograph: Alan Betson.*

counselled teenagers against taking part in the competition.

'It's emotionally draining, the politics are frightening. I felt sorry for the young kids at times. I really would say, wait until you are older. You have loads of years to be a pop star.'

She dreams of singing with big orchestras doing the big show songs that were her métier during the *X Factor*, but won't leave Ireland to live elsewhere in any circumstances.

'I'd never leave my country, I love it too much,' she said.

She plans to do the *X Factor* tour, make an album of covers followed by an album of original material, but her immediate priority will be *The Late Late Show* on Friday night.

'I have to look after it now, it's my job,' she said pointing to her throat.

WEDNESDAY, 22 DECEMBER 2010

Hairshirt Solstice Reflects National Mood but Darkness will not Prevail at Newgrange

Eileen Battersby

After weeks of white fields, vicious frosts, relentless ice and sharp, brilliant winter light, the chances of a glorious sequence of solstice sunrises had seemed likely.

No one was expecting rain or clouds, the sun would burst forth into a sky of blue, thus ending the longest night. But it did not go quite to plan.

The view across the famous valley stretching out from the great Neolithic monument of Newgrange, Co. Meath, was suspended in shades of silver and grey, broken by dark shadowy trees and ridges concealing hedgerows.

The faithful and curious had gathered yet again to celebrate the beginning of the end of winter, but the fragments of conversations were more dominated by tales of crashed cars, broken bones and hungry animals than by wonder at the genius of the late Stone Age farmers who watched the sun and honoured their dead.

The newly assertive winter appeared intent on continuing a masterclass in global warming. There were no hopeful gazes towards the horizon, no warm rays of sun, only cloud.

The setting was beautiful, the waters of the Boyne still and had anyone dared to sing 'I'm Dreaming of a White Christmas' they probably would have been accused of anti-social behaviour.

The gathered gardaí looked cold but philosophical, while the photographers decided that in the absence of a dramatic sunrise, humans would have to provide the pictures. Two musicians bravely played tin whistles with cold fingers.

A robin landed briefly on one of the tall standing stones, surveyed the scene and flew off, as if aware there would be no morning picnics this time.

The day had begun earlier than usual. At 4 a.m. the moon had been as bright as day in a cold, clear sky.

The frozen ground crunched with the sound of compacted European snow. It is unlikely that ballads will be written honouring the road-clearing efforts of Meath County Council and the surest route down the hard, white road leading to Newgrange was a quad and we raced along,

Queuing in the snow to enter the passage tomb at Newgrange, Co. Meath. Photograph: Dara Mac Dónaill.

The lunar eclipse, as seen from Newgrange, Co. Meath, where people gathered to witness the winter solstice.
Photograph: Alan Betson.

creating an icy spray, glancing up at the large white moon.

However, before the eclipse began to slide over the surface, eventually creating the impression of a slightly opened doorway just before it was abruptly closed, an irritating succession of clouds hurried across the face of the moon.

Eclipse watchers dutifully compared notes before moving on to the monument.

There was none of the usual anticipation that happens when there is a chance the sun could appear. Most of those present wore the contented expression of having achieved something slightly heroic, standing in freezing temperatures.

There were archaeologists lamenting the serious cuts to heritage funding and to research. The irony of placing heritage tourism, a valuable earner, at risk, was not lost on recession-hit citizens engaged in entertainingly explicit government bashing.

Minister of State Martin Mansergh arrived wearing his habitual expression of polite despair.

Inside the chamber there were no false promises. This would be a hairshirt solstice, in keeping with the condition of the country.

We could expect only the palest of grey light along the passage. Mary Hanafin, noticeable for her lack of ski wear, was interested and asked questions. It was her second time inside the chamber at the solstice, having been present in 2003 'when the sun did appear'.

The chosen few and sundry interlopers stood in the darkness, a stomach rumbled, and a watery brightness did gather momentum. Scottish astronomer royal Prof. John Brown, who twice called for a moment's silence, spoke about the archaeology of the Orkney Islands, while Prof. George Eogan, who has spent his career researching the Brú na Bóinne complex, placed the solstice architecture within a wide European context.

Whether in the shadows or bathed in golden rays, the ritual of being at Newgrange offers its own comfort; it is the beginning of the slow return of daylight.

One by one we left the chamber. Above our heads the corbelled ceiling was dry, except for two thin bands of ice that had formed between two of the carefully layered stones.

Outside it was snowing. Instead of walking into rich sunlight, we emerged into a soft flurry of snow, which had already frosted the woollen hats and bare heads of those waiting outside. How would our ancient ancestors have dealt with the cold weather?

Probably better than modern man. The sun might well break through the clouds this morning or tomorrow, but the most important battle has been won. However unlikely it may seem in the current weather conditions, the darkness will begin to yield and the light will return.

THURSDAY, 30 DECEMBER 2010

Russia's Great Defender of History and Protector of Cultural Wealth

Daniel McLaughlin

At the heart of one of the world's great cities, through the halls of one of the world's great buildings, moves the man who runs one of the world's great museums.

Mikhail Piotrovsky is the director of the Hermitage, whose Winter Palace was home to the Romanov tsars for two centuries, before the 1917 revolutions swept the Bolsheviks into power and saw Moscow replace St Petersburg as Russia's capital.

Piotrovsky presides, as did his father, over a collection of almost three million pieces that is not only a world-class treasure trove of art and historical artefacts, but a key element of Russia's claim to be a global cultural force.

His stewardship of St Petersburg's main artistic powerhouse makes him also a reluctant political figure in Russia's second city, as it regains strength and influence under two native sons who made their names in Moscow: President Dmitry Medvedev and Prime Minister Vladimir Putin.

'We think of ourselves as the centre of the city, and as the city orientates in the world and as a cultural capital it must ask us, orientate through us, and we provide an example of good taste and other things,' Piotrovsky told *The Irish Times*.

'In culture, as in sport, you have to prove every year that you are the best. And in culture you have to do it over hundreds of years. We have to keep the museum in good shape, we are always restoring and repairing, but it is our traditions that keep us great. Our role as a universal museum that presents different cultures and puts them in dialogue – that is the main purpose of our existence.'

As Piotrovsky (66) suggests, the scope of the Hermitage's collection is extraordinary. From ancient Egyptian, Greek and Roman artefacts, through Russian icons and imperial treasures, to an array of western European art encompassing da Vinci, Michelangelo, Rembrandt, Rubens, Monet, Matisse, Van Gogh, Picasso and most of their most famous contemporaries, a walk through the Hermitage's 365 halls can be overwhelming.

Not only do many of these masters have entire rooms to themselves, the walls covered with paintings familiar from posters and art books, but they are set among the splendour of palaces that were built and decorated to convey the wealth and power of the Russian Empire to awed visitors.

The vast scale of the Winter Palace – and the five smaller buildings that comprise the Hermitage – is also daunting, and means that even a museum that is toured by 2.5 million people each year still has plenty of echoing corridors and rooms in which the visitor finds himself alone with Scythian mummies, Babylonian bas-reliefs and ancient gold from the Caucasus.

Many of these items survived one of the great upheavals that periodically strike Russia and St Petersburg, when they were evacuated as Hitler's forces approached in 1941. About one million items were kept safe in the Urals city of Sverdlovsk – now known again as Yekaterinburg – where Tsar Nicholas II and his family had been executed in 1918.

Having been at the epicentre of the October 1917 revolution, the Winter Palace was bombed many times during the Second World War, and its basement provided shelter for thousands of people as the city withstood a 900-day siege in which

more than a million soldiers and civilians were killed.

It is this history, as well as the Hermitage's cultural wealth, that Piotrovsky is defending in his battles with big business and St Petersburg's political bosses.

He regularly rejects requests from major music acts to perform on the massive Palace Square, and only allowed the likes of The Rolling Stones and Madonna to play there after they promised to keep the volume down, and he also quashed a city plan to turn it into an ice rink.

More recently, Piotrovsky opposed state-run energy giant Gazprom's bid to build a new 400-metre tall skyscraper overlooking Smolny Cathedral, a baroque St Petersburg landmark created by Francesco Bartolomeo Rastrelli, the Italian who

Debbie Black, Róisín Lyons, Gráinne Lyons, Brian Kelleher and Shane McDonnell from Dublin get ready to enjoy the racing at Leopardstown after the weather forced the cancellation of the first two days of the festival. Photograph: Alan Betson.

also designed the Winter Palace. It was decided this month that the tower would be built elsewhere.

'It's a permanent fight . . . but it's about a philosophy as well as a question of how to protect monuments,' said Piotrovsky.

'People say St Petersburg is a museum and one can't live in a museum. I say that yes, you can. A modern museum is a big enterprise with culture, politics, economics, and it can educate people and help them work and live. And all the better if it doesn't do it in the usual Russian way – by demanding 400 per cent profit.'

Not that Piotrovsky is an enemy of power or big business. He says he sees Putin and Medvedev as allies, and several of Russia's billionaire 'oligarchs' have done their dubious reputations no harm by becoming some of the Hermitage's biggest benefactors.

When Armenian-born Piotrovsky took over the running of the Hermitage in 1992 it, and Russia, were mired in the poverty and chaos that followed the Soviet Union's collapse.

The Arab expert has since rebuilt the museum's annual budget from $1 million to $40 million, and put it on a sound footing for the future. Or at least as sound as it can have in St Petersburg, a city standing on the bones of those who built it in a Baltic bog, a 'window on the West' for Peter the Great and a window into Russia's turbulent past for today's visitors.

FRIDAY, 31 DECEMBER 2010

'It's Only Words, but Words are All We Have to Take Your Heart Away'

Brian Boyd

It's a truth not universally acknowledged. Most people will tell you, quoting some spurious study, that by far and away the most searched-for term on the internet is 'sex', followed by all the endless variations and permutations thereof. But what all these end-of-year 'most searched for' polls (aggregated from a number of popular search engines) actually show is that – and it's a big surprise – 'lyrics' is the most popular search.

You'd think only anoraks and demented teenage fanboys would be searching for the exact words to any given song, but apparently everyone is at it, in massive numbers. No one can quite understand why, but there are possible reasons aplenty.

The dominance of the MP3 file (which, unlike vinyl and CDs, doesn't contain the lyrics) means that, even with Auto-Tune smoothing the vocals out, a whole new generation is clueless about what is actually being sung.

There's the fact that newer artists such as Justin Bieber and Lady Gaga have obsessive 'I need to know every single thing about this person' fan bases. There is the 'I want to sing along and upload a funny video of me doing so on YouTube' brigade. There's also simply more music everywhere, from video games to advertisements to social networking sites to mobile phone apps.

Perhaps most importantly is the rise of shows such as *X Factor*, *Glee* and *American Idol*, which have introduced millions of new fans to the power of songs.

It's not your whey-faced indie types poring over Belle and Sebastian lyrics. Of the 300 million visitors a month to internet lyric sites, most are clustering around a small group of contemporary artists: Bieber, Gaga, Eminem, Taylor Swift, Shakira. It's no coincidence that fans of these artists commonly display an empathy and connection with the music over and above what you normally see in the rock music world.

There's a salutary lesson (somewhere) in the fact that, of all the social, political, economic and spiritual information now at our immediate disposal, one of the most searched-for items of 2010 was the lyrics to Bieber's 'Baby'.

Isabella Gerbola, who was born in her parents' jeep near Clonee at 3.13 a.m. on Saturday, 1 January 2011, with her mother Tara McFadden, a tour manager and former trapeze artist with Circus Gerbola in Navan, Co. Meath. Photograph: Matt Kavanagh.

And quite a revelation it is too: 'I was like, baby, baby, baby, oh/Like baby, baby, baby, no/Like baby, baby, baby, oh/I thought you'd always be mine, mine.' (It's the dramatic and unexpected repetition of 'mine' at the end that does it for me.) Not that far off was the search for the lyrics to Gaga's 'Alejandro': 'Alejandro/Alejandro/Ale-Ale-Jandro/Ale-Ale-Jandro (x2).'

There was at least something of substance in another huge search: the words to Swift's 'Dear John'. The song was not a massive hit, but millions were presumably drawn to find out the lyrics because it was about Swift's ex-boyfriend, the musician John Mayer: 'Dear John, I see it all now that you're gone/Don't you think I was too young to be messed with/The girl in the dress cried the whole way home/I should've known.' Which

reads like Jane Austen compared to the other two above.

Leaving aside individual songs, perhaps the most searched-for artist (lyrics-wise) was Eminem, as indeed he has been for the past number of years.

Because of a new album and his breakout hit with Rihanna ('Love the Way You Lie'), Eminem searches have exploded in the past three months. And despite all the front and the controversy, he remains one of the best lyricists at work today. It wasn't for nothing that Seamus Heaney once lauded Eminem's 'subversive attitude and verbal energy' and noted that 'he has sent a voltage around a generation'.

Still, Marshall Mathers notwithstanding, there's a terrible irony in the fact that 'lyrics' has become the most searched-for term at a time when the craft of song-writing is at an all-time low. It seems like the whole R'n'B genre is incapable of coming up with a memorable lyric, while hip-hop can veer from sublime (rare) to pathetic and ridiculous (common).

Is there anything at all from the past five years – even from the rock-indie spectrum – that has the impact and staying power of an 'Eton Rifles' or 'Up the Junction'? I'm thinking, like, baby-baby-oh, baby-baby-no there isn't.

SATURDAY, 8 JANUARY 2011

The Bull in Winter

Sara Keating

Brian Dennehy is sitting in a strange, half-supine position when I arrive to meet him, as if in meditation. In repose, he looks like a character in a Eugene O'Neill play; Con Melody, perhaps, the deluded Irish-American soldier from *A Touch of the Poet* whom O'Neill defined by the 'map of Ireland written on his face'. With his wide brow, large features and pale blue eyes, there is indeed something particularly Irish about his bearing.

O'Neill seems like a third member of our party as our conversation starts. Dennehy has performed in several O'Neill plays over the years: as the complex actor patriarch of the Tyrone family in *Long Day's Journey into Night*; the parsimonious farmer Ephraim Cabot in *Desire Under the Elms*; the small-time hustler Erie Smith in O'Neill's monologue play, *Hughie*; and the tragically evangelical Hickey in *The Iceman Cometh*, at the Abbey Theatre in 1992.

Dennehy was even awarded the prestigious Eugene O'Neill Lifetime Achievement Award earlier this year, although he is too polite to mention it during our meeting. Indeed, he is happier talking abstractly about his love of the Irish-American O'Neill and his passion for Irish literature – Samuel

Beckett, Sebastian Barry, John B. Keane – than he is about himself, his achievements or the longevity of his career in film, television and stage.

The life of O'Neill gradually opens into a discussion of Dennehy's own background and the complexity of his Irish-American heritage. 'O'Neill was Irish-American, remember, not Irish,' he says, as if qualifying his own connection to the island. 'And that's a whole lot different.'

Dennehy's parents were children of Irish parents who emigrated around the same time in the late 1890s and settled in Connecticut. Their relationship with their homeland was very different from Dennehy's parents' understanding of their heritage. 'My grandfather had a really bitter childhood,' he says. 'He went to America to lose himself. He hated being reminded of Ireland and hated everything Irish: Irish music, everything. And maybe that wasn't an unusual reaction for the first generation – all they remembered was poverty and oppression.

'But my own father, he became a typical Irish-American, a typical sentimentalist. Me, third generation, I fell in love with Ireland when I first visited, but I am no idealist; I know the good and the bad points – the joy and the craziness – but at the same time it all works for me.'

In the same way O'Neill's father, James O'Neill, defied convention by becoming an actor, so Dennehy shocked his parents by deciding to take to the stage. He had flirted with the military ('service was compulsory in those days'), driving a cab and going to law school (he got a scholarship to Columbia University), so when he eventually settled on acting his parents were confused.

'"Why do you want to be an actor?" my father asked me. "Because it might make me happy," was what I said. "What's that got to do with it?" my father wanted to know – and he was right. It was a whole generational thing, and we got carried away with it – the pursuit of happiness – and I think it is what left us with the whole mess we are in right now, in Ireland, in America, and that is something my children and your generation will have to live with.'

Dennehy first visited Ireland almost 40 years ago on a brief sojourn from a film shoot in the UK. After working at the Abbey Theatre in 1992 he bought a cottage on the Beara Peninsula, to which he made an annual pilgrimage with his family until a few years ago. He visited J.B. Keane in nearby Listowel one year, just before the writer died, and is thrilled now to have the chance to perform in *The Field*, 'a great melodrama that is also unbelievably profound'.

'When you read it and remember that it was written in 1965, it is just astonishing in the way it's so anti-authoritarian, so anti-Church. It was written right at the cusp of a whole new mood . . . and it was based on a real-life local incident. It was a really brave play.'

Dennehy is taking on the role of the fearsome Bull McCabe, a complex, particularly Irish figure whose tragedy is his stubborn determination to uphold his principles, despite the consequences. He may not be a sympathetic character, but Dennehy sees 'a grace note there'.

'Aside from committing a murder – and that was an accident; I don't believe he intended to murder this guy – and aside from being a bit of a pig when it comes to gender, there is a real integrity to his character. He embodies this struggle against primitive capitalism. He is closely related to nature.

'He resents modernisation. It will result in a field being turned into a concrete factory, nature being sacrificed on the altar of commerce. He might not be a sympathetic character – but he might be right.' In light of the crazy overdevelopment of the Irish landscape since the mid-1990s it seems prescient, too, but Dennehy is careful not to shoehorn *The Field* into a reductive argument about political relevance.

'It is not contemporary, because the Bull's solution is so fascist. Perhaps the more modern part of it would be the total condemnation of what he

Actor Brian Dennehy: 'I don't want a new jacket. I'm 72. I have enough jackets for the time I have left.'
Photograph: Bryan O'Brien.

calls "the gang" – the priests, the doctors, the law-men, the schoolmaster – who have the world wrapped up between them. And how people like the Bull are constantly thwarted by their desires.'

Having just done the first read-through with the full cast, Dennehy is excited to get into the rehearsal room to work the play out, but rehearsals, he says, are merely the beginning of his journey with both character and play.

'It is not until you are out on the stage with the audience that you really begin to know what you are doing,' he says. 'That is when you learn. The more you do it, the more you understand it, but I don't know if you can ever really put your finger on it.' He played Willy Loman in Arthur Miller's *Death of a Salesman* more than 700 times, he says, 'and maybe three weeks after I finished it – and I spent 10 years with that play – I was driving home when something came to me. I had to pull into a rest area on the highway, and I sat there for 20 minutes going through it in my head, a whole new way of doing a scene, even though I knew I was never going to do it again.

'Sixty performances for a straight run?' he continues. 'That's nothing. I don't know that, after such a short time, you can really figure it out, but you're trying. When you're shooting a movie you might do a take 50 times; you're trying to achieve a certain thing. But in the theatre you're chasing something different every time. A door you didn't realise existed might open up suddenly, and you might want to follow, and it might bring you somewhere entirely new, and that's much more exciting than some jerk-off TV series.

'The thing you're really looking for is the thing you have no control over. Because what you want is not applause but silence, where nobody moves or opens their programme or shifts in their seat. That's when you know you have them. There's this thing actors and directors say: "Can we make them lean forward in their seats?" That's what you want: 850 people leaning forward to try to catch the next sound.'

Dennehy is 72 now – 'and I feel it. I feel really old' – but his enthusiasm for performing hasn't waned. If anything, he has done more and more theatre over the past 10 years.

'Why would I not?' he asks. 'I mean, you get the opportunity to spend two hours a day exploring, making an effort in the thing you love and enjoy the most and they want to pay you. That is not a chore. That makes me a very, very lucky person. Some people might say, "Oh the repetition," but that's bulls★★t.

'I suppose the thing about getting old is that certain things become more important to you. I went shopping with my wife one day and she said, "Why don't you get a new jacket?" and I thought, I don't want a new jacket. I'm 72. New socks, underwear, fine – but I have enough jackets for the time I have left. And that's what it's like professionally. I only want to do things I really care about, and I'm happy to do that until I collapse.

'An actor friend of mine . . . His name was Davy Byrnes – a wonderful actor but no one heard of him – he died on stage in Chicago one night. And Tommy Cooper collapsed one night after a show, his feet sticking out from underneath the curtain, and the audience thought it was a joke, part of the show. That's how I want to go – feet sticking out from underneath the curtain.'

SATURDAY, 8 JANUARY 2011

Perhaps Political Reform, Like Sex, is Best Left to the Young

Elaine Byrne

Alfred Kinsey's pioneering research on human sexuality has profoundly influenced the study of sex since the 1940s. Although some of his findings have since been contested, his conclusions about sexual activity have become mainstream assumptions.

Cartoon by Martyn Turner.

Kinsey asserted that the male sexual drive hits its peak between 20 and 30 years of age because physicality at that point in a man's life ensures high libido and greater staying power. Women, on the other hand, achieve their peak in their 30s because they are, apparently, more self-confident and comfortable with their bodies and know how to communicate their needs more assertively.

Kinsey also believed that age determined the nature of sexual activity. When people are young, they are more inclined to be strong-willed, passionate, have greater stamina, are more adventurous and open to alternative ideas. For example, scientific research suggests that heightened sexual activity is responsible for higher levels of creativity in an individual because it releases greater levels of dopamine. This neurochemical generates arousal and limits latent inhibition that thereby increases energy and drives ideas within the brain.

W.B. Yeats certainly believed in these positive effects of sexual activity and associated his loss of inspiration with an inability to have erections. He held that there was a direct relationship between sexual desire and originality in his poetry. In a book published last year, *W.B. Yeats and the Muses*, Joseph M. Hassett outlined how the poet underwent a 'rejuvenation operation' in the mid-1930s to address this personal inadequacy. After the surgical procedure, Yeats described a 'strange second puberty the operation has given me, the ferment that has come upon my imagination'.

Ostensibly, frequent sex for those in their 20s and 30s has the unintended consequence of promoting less conservative behaviour. On the other hand, Kinsey found that older generations tend to revert to familiar and traditional sexual practices. In time, experience begets a reluctance to do anything remarkably different. The option often chosen, though not in Yeats's case, is to put up with discontent. It becomes easier to live within the parameters of disappointment when expectations have been blunted over time.

Are there lessons within Kinsey's research on sex for politics? Does the political development of the Irish State share a similar disposition to the different characteristics of sex among the young and old?

Since the foundation of the State, just three generations of political leaders have held office.

The first stage of Irish political development was defined by men primarily in their 30s. W.T. Cosgrave was regarded as the elder statesman in the 1920s Free State government, at only 42 years of age. Despite having no political experience, they established the legislative framework and institutions of the state.

The second phase of change in Irish public life came in the 1960s when dominant first-generation political figures permanently departed the political stage with the deaths of W.T. Cosgrave in 1965, Seán Lemass in 1971 and Éamon de Valera in 1975. The revolutionary elite of the old guard was gradually replaced by career-orientated politicians who challenged economic orthodoxy and opened Ireland to external investment with the Whitaker reforms.

The 1960s saw a new generation of young, urban, educated, middle-class voters who were more concerned with social and economic matters than the Treaty.

In Fine Gael, this manifested itself into internal policy struggles on Declan Costello's 'Just Society' document that challenged the party to orientate itself left of centre.

This produced a more robust, articulate and energetic opposition with the election of John Bruton, Garret FitzGerald and others. It became no longer acceptable for the Fine Gael front bench to operate on a part-time basis because of outside career commitments.

The stagnant electoral market of previous decades became more competitive with the emergence of younger politicians within Fianna Fáil, such as Donogh O'Malley, Charles Haughey, Brian Lenihan, Des O'Malley and Bobby Molloy.

A new sense of optimism within the Irish Labour Party was prompted by consecutive victories by the British Labour Party in 1964 and 1966. This motivated the party to fundamentally reorganise its structures. The appointment of 31-year-old Brendan Halligan as general secretary at the party's Gardiner Place headquarters in 1967 created a new dynamism in Irish public life.

A third phase of renewal in political representation occurred in the late 1970s and early 1980s with the entry to political life of dominant personalities such as Bertie Ahern, Jim O'Keeffe, Michael Woods and Michael D. Higgins – all of whom have announced their retirement in recent weeks.

Are we about to see a fourth generational shift in Irish politics?

With less than three months to go to an election, 25 TDs have already said they will not stand again. This is up on 2007 levels with others yet to confirm their intentions. The average age of TDs is considerably higher than that of the general population. More than 70 per cent of deputies are over 50 and the selection processes within Fine Gael and Labour indicate that this is not about to change.

According to a Red C poll by Paddy Power this week, 61 per cent say that a new political party is needed. Support for the proposition is strongest among the young.

Kinsey's research loosely suggests that the act of sex is best appreciated or most enjoyed among younger people. Maybe politics is too.

FRIDAY, 14 JANUARY 2011

Voice of Experience

Tony Clayton-Lea

We are 20 minutes into a right old natter, and Tottenham's Aretha Franklin is wrinkling up her nose. 'I'm so sorry, but the dog has farted.'

Louis Armstrong, Adele Adkins's petite, tubular dachshund (aka Sausage), is soiling the atmosphere of XL Records' headquarters in London's Ladbroke Grove, but the apology is shot through with a bit of a cackle and a carry-on-regardless demeanour. Spend any length of time in the company of Adele and you'll come to learn pretty damn quick that the classiest singer of her generation has little time for airs and graces.

Truth is, Adele is as rooted as they come, a 22-year-old woman with strong Irish connections and what appears to be a direct line to a heaven-sent range of musical influences that themselves are underpinned by straight-as-they-come emotions. Three years ago, Adele's debut album, *19*, ushered in a singer and a voice that knocked her contemporaries and main competitors (Duffy, Lily Allen, Kate Nash) out cold. Now, with Duffy and Nash clearly showing their shortcomings on follow-up albums, and with Allen currently hiding in the long grass, Adele's new album, *21*, is geared up to be this year's model.

But *21* is more than just a Mexican stand-off with her music chart mates. It's unlikely that an album released this year will match its often profound depths or its peaks of euphoria, all of which are enveloped by a stirring mixture of stripped-down, subtle soul, blues, country, gospel and pop.

'It was always music for me, as I'm not, and never have been, very academic.' Dressed top to toe in black, with a beehive hair-do out to there and curved eyelashes out to here, the dog on her lap, Adele is a charmer. She's the anti tits-and-teeth, barely-there female pop star, falling over herself, almost, to make me a cup of tea before she gets down to chatting.

'I get bored very quickly – I have the attention span of a fly. So music, yes, but it was never something I purposely pursued.

'In other words, I never had the aim of being a professional recording artist. Like my friends at the time, we all had a dream and none of theirs was

coming true, so I reckoned why the hell would mine? The only reason I ended up studying music at Croydon's Brit School was because I knew I was going to fail all my GCSEs, so I panicked. Whereas I knew I'd pass all the music and performance stuff, and because of that I thought I'd get work somewhere in the music industry.'

Adele had been writing songs since she was 16, and while at Croydon had set up her MySpace page where songs such as 'Hometown Glory' were being listened to.

With her Brit School qualification in her bag and a job at Gap keeping her in pocket money, Adele eventually rolled up at the offices of XL (home to The Prodigy, Badly Drawn Boy, M.I.A., White Stripes, Sigur Rós, Peaches, Vampire Weekend, Dizzee Rascal, The xx), where she had hoped she'd land a position as a talent scout.

'They offered me a record deal instead – but getting signed was never an ambition. I knew I'd be involved in music somewhere, but I never – ever – thought I'd be a recording artist. It just seemed pretty unlikely. I clearly remember the day I came to them, as it's one of the pivotal days of my life. They asked me if I had a manager, and I said, "Well, I have one at Gap!"'

And so Adele's story began. Debut album *19* followed, its success quickly setting her up as an authentic voice of the emotionally bruised teenager. But how does anyone follow up such a stirring debut? The answer, in Adele's case, with relative ease, and with, apparently, none of the shortcomings that usually undermine highly anticipated second albums: lack of material, insight, guidance and a surfeit of ego.

'When I was 16,' recalls Adele, 'I wrote my first song, "Hometown Glory", which is the song I got signed on the back of. Then, of course, the rest of the songs for *19* came after that. But I remember when I was promoting *19*, I started to think, "What the fuck am I going to write about for the next album?" It's not life, is it, when you're spending your time in hotel rooms and airport

Adele. Photograph: Mari Sarai.

lounges? What if I turn into one of those people I hate? What if I had ended up writing a really egotistical record, about being lonely while you're raiding the minibar? People aren't sympathetic to that, and I'm not, either.'

Life, as is so often the case, had other plans for Adele. She hooked up with what she calls 'the complete love of my life, and the most amazing immense relationship so far in my life. It didn't last, unfortunately – it ended because it stopped being fun, and thankfully the ending wasn't bitter – but the whole thing changed me. It made me really passionate about love, life, myself, pretty much everything. I had so much to write about. It was like a tap that was difficult to turn off. The relationship just consumed me, which is where the songs came from.'

As on *19*, the songs on *21* ring true. With such a resonant source from which to mine authentic heartbreak, Adele has achieved that rare thing: you believe utterly in what you're listening to.

'It's important to me that people believe the songs are honest because they totally are. I would hate if someone thought that, "yeah, whatever, she's made them all up".

'My primary inspirations for this record were the likes of Etta James, Carole King, Roberta Flack – people behind completely convincing love songs that I fully believed when I first heard them. I remember hearing *The Miseducation of Lauryn Hill* when I was 10. I was waiting for the bus outside Woolworths in Brixton, and my dad bought that record for my mum and a video of *Flubber* – fucking *Flubber*! – for me.

'But I nicked the album and listened to it every day after school in my bedroom, sitting on my little sofa-bed, reading the lyrics, and hoping to God that one day I'd be a singer. So that conviction, the breathtaking delivery of songs – the believability – is almost part of my DNA. I'm not happy unless I feel I'm offering that – even if it's just a little bit.'

A little bit? Adele is underselling herself here, as *21* is the work of someone whose heart was shattered but whose dreams have come true, a songwriter adept at mining gold from despair. It must make certain people livid to realise she had no career strategy whatsoever.

'Maybe it was just having a kind of self-belief, and also having to bear the brunt of attitudes from authority figures such as teachers who were saying that, for me, success was unrealistic. So I chose to survive rather than live in a fantasy world. I suppose I could have been more determined, but, well, here we are anyway.'

The fallout from Louis Armstrong has drifted away, and Adele has more things to do, more people to charm, more cups of tea to make in order to put them at ease.

'It still feels odd, though, if you know what I mean,' she concludes, eager to explain, if not quantify, the huge changes in her life from then to now. 'In many ways I'm still a ratty-haired blonde girl from Tottenham. So far, my music has passed all expectations, and occasionally reactions from fans take my breath away.

'Sometimes it's difficult to let things sink in, and that can come across as me being a bit icy or unappreciative, particularly on television. But I often feel that if I let it sink in I'll just melt into a puddle.'

MONDAY, 17 JANUARY 2011

Munster Bid *Au Revoir* to an Era

Gerry Thornley

All good things come to an end. This felt like the end of something alright, and because it was something special that made the ending more profound. Munster have given us many unforgettable days along the way, but after their unbroken dozen years in the knock-out stages (a record liable never to be equalled), yesterday here in the throbbing Stade

The cortége carrying the remains of Michaela Harte is escorted by members of the Tyrone senior Gaelic football team and local club Aireagal Chiaráin to St Malachy's Church for the funeral Mass in Ballymacilroy, Co. Tyrone. Photograph: Matt Kavanagh.

Félix Mayol it was time to say *merci* and *au revoir*.

In truth, they comfortably came off second best to Toulon in front of a baying 14,800 crowd, beaten in most facets of the game on the way to a 32–16 defeat, which, in terms of the Cup, makes next week's game at home to London Irish their first dead rubber in over 12 years.

'We're absolutely shattered to be out of the Heineken Cup campaign, especially after such a disappointing performance,' admitted coach Tony McGahan.

The highly voluble and visible Toulon club president Mourad Boudjellal had built this game up as the biggest in their recent history, and, given the context, that made the performance their best in recent times.

This is a proper rugby town in the south of France where even the buses welcomed the Munster supporters, about 2,000 of whom mixed in good humour with the locals en route to the ground in the heart of the town as the sun bounced off the sea in the marina.

You didn't have to speak French to understand the word on most lips as the crowd made their way to the ground: Wilkinson.

In temperatures of 15 degrees, the home support even applauded a pre-match rendition of 'Stand Up and Fight'.

But all hospitality temporarily and predictably ceased with a vengeance for 80 minutes of often feisty, edgy rugby.

Fired by the memory of their 45–18 defeat in Thomond Park last October, Toulon more than matched Munster in the physical collisions and, with Jonny Wilkinson especially pulling the strings, also played the smarter cup rugby.

By contrast, Munster played too much rugby too deep, and much of it laterally, and – cracking a little under the pressure Toulon put them under – were error-prone.

The cup-final-like occasion and febrile atmosphere also demanded cool heads. But while Munster could argue about some of the decisions by referee Dave Pearson – especially the yellow card handed out to Ronan O'Gara – the sinbinning of Donncha O'Callaghan in the 33rd minute for taking out Rudi Wulf with a high arm off the ball was indicative of the way they did not keep their emotions in check sufficiently.

In the lock's absence, Toulon turned the screw, building an already ominous 16–6 advantage into a relatively unassailable 29–9 lead. Wilkinson was tormentor-in-chief, profiting from Munster's ill-discipline and troubled scrum to land 8 kicks out of 10 for a 22-point haul.

'The first thing was our discipline,' said McGahan. 'Thirteen points with two men off the field and a couple of penalties off scrums certainly added to the scoreline.

'I think most of all the lack of accuracy in trying to put anything together. I thought we were very frantic at times, especially in the first half. Our ball dried up a bit from the set-piece, so we really needed to make sure we controlled the ball and play it in the right areas of the field, but unfortunately we weren't able to do that.

'We needed to tighten things up at times and we didn't give ourselves an opportunity to do that. We needed to show some patience with regard to getting ourselves into the game away from home and being able to outwork the opposition, which is one of our strong traits. But when you are playing from side to side, a little bit frantic, trying to get something to happen, it's difficult.'

McGahan spoke of fronting up next week and then using the Six Nations break, adding: 'There is the Magners League, but certainly to be competing for just one trophy is an unusual situation for everyone concerned.'

John McAreavey and wife Michaela Harte on their wedding day at St Malachy's Church, Ballymacilroy, Co. Tyrone on 30 December 2010. Photograph: **The Irish News.**

Inevitably, this will be seen as the end of an era, with Munster now obliged to rebuild more than any time in the last dozen years.

'That's certainly a very pertinent question and certainly a very realistic one. This group has gone through a lot of time together and we are certainly making changes to the playing group, and I think that has been well evident over the last two years. But, again, we need to deal with where we are at, and we need to make sure to get results for the rest of the year.'

Coupled with London Irish's surprising 24–12 win over the Ospreys (their first of any kind in 11 matches) in Reading yesterday, Toulon have

Referee Dave Pearson sends Ronan O'Gara to the sinbin during Munster's 32–16 defeat to Toulon in their Heineken Cup clash at Stade Félix Mayol in France. Photograph: Billy Stickland/Inpho.

advanced to the last eight in their debut Heineken Cup season. The Ospreys and Munster can both still advance to the Amlin Challenge Cup.

Indeed, Munster weren't the only team to have their fate sealed over the weekend.

Unusually for the cup, much across the six groups was resolved over the penultimate weekend, leaving little in the way of issues to be resolved or major head-to-heads. Following on from Northampton having won Pool One on Friday night, and Leinster joining them on Saturday from Pool Two, a 76th-minute drop goal by Ruaidhri Jackson completed a shock 20–10 win for Glasgow over Wasps in Pool Six yesterday, which knocked out the two-time English winners of the

tournament and ensured Toulouse progressed.

This also makes next Sunday afternoon's finale between Wasps and Toulouse something of a dead rubber, save for the final standings and deciding whether Toulouse earn a home quarter-final.

This also had significance for Ulster in Pool Four in one of only two pools, which will go down to the wire, for it means a win in Aironi next Saturday of any hue will guarantee them a place in the knock-out stages for the first time since they won the trophy in 1999 as one of the two best runners-up.

They trail Biarritz on the head-to-head record in their meetings after Saturday's 9–6 win in Ravenhill, although they could still top the pool if they can better Biarritz's match result at home to Bath next Saturday.

The other pool that will almost certainly provide one of the best runners-up is in Pool Five, in which Leicester and Perpignan are tied on 17 points with the Scarlets two points adrift. Perpignan host the Scarlets in what amounts to next weekend's only winner-takes-all, with Leicester best placed to qualify one way or the other when entertaining Treviso.

Although the world will still be spinning on its axis, Munster won't be there with them.

MONDAY, 17 JANUARY 2011

Cowen Unanimous with Himself on Issue of Confidence

Miriam Lord

Crisis management. Confidence. Clarity. It's comforting to know Ireland has a steady hand at the helm and competence in the wheelhouse at this most difficult time.

Doubtless the IMF and EU boys are penning glowing reports back to base. That's if they can steady their biros long enough between the laughter.

What must they be thinking? If it's anything like the rest of the country, their thoughts are far too distressing to dwell upon.

The only shred of certainty to emerge yesterday from the people who purport to run this country is that the panto season isn't over yet. And that's not funny anymore. (Unless you happen to be a member of the Opposition. They're riveted to the cheap seats, laughing like drains.) The Taoiseach has tabled a motion of confidence in himself. And he is unanimous with himself in that.

His Minister for Foreign Affairs has resigned. And yet, he hasn't.

Why? Because the man he has no confidence in asked him to stay, and when somebody you think isn't up to the job asks you to do something, well, you jump to it.

Don't try to figure it out. Nothing makes sense.

Except the ship of state continues sailing into the maelstrom with passengers who are sick with worry while the crew members fight among themselves.

It's frightening.

Such a huge palaver over the Fianna Fáil leadership crisis for the last week. It was supposed to come to a head yesterday. The Taoiseach – he was the uncomfortable looking man in the grey suit who presided over the first of the day's two press conferences, for those who have forgotten what he looks like – went out to assume command.

He hasn't done that much since taking over the top job, but seldom is wonderful and there's nothing more commanding than a Biffo with his back to the wall when his future and the future of his party are at stake.

What's that? Economic crisis? Citizens crying out for direction? Normal business suspended? National paralysis? Never mind all that. There's a man's posterity at stake – which has nothing to do with protecting a person's, or a party's, posterior. How dare anyone imply otherwise.

Oh, and there the interest of the people has to be taken into account also. So when Brian Cowen arrived in the Alexander Hotel yesterday afternoon – the hotel where he celebrated with his supporters on the day he became Taoiseach – he was fighting for Ireland.

You'd better believe it. He had Mary Coughlan and his Chief Whip, John Curran, by his side just in case you didn't.

Where was the rest of his Cabinet? The usual drill, when one of their number is in difficulty, no matter how embarrassing it might seem, is for them to muster in strength and show support.

Not yesterday.

Fine Gael TD for Roscommon–South Leitrim, Frank Feighan, wasting no time getting on the campaign trail on Kilronan Mountain, Ballyfarnon, Co. Roscommon, after the calling of the general election. Photograph: Brian Farrell.

The Taoiseach is staying put. He is remaining as leader of Fianna Fáil because, after two-and-a-half days of asking them if they still want him, he reckons they do. That's a great recommendation for the CV.

Brian Cowen went in for group counselling with his parliamentary party, it was 'cordial, mutually respectful and productive' and at the end of it all he 'was heartened' by their response. As a result, he thinks they will back him in a secret ballot.

A billet among a nest of vipers sounds more comfortable.

Biffo is a proud man. He doesn't want to be ousted. He came out fighting yesterday. 'We live in transformative times,' he explained. Times are difficult, so it's understandable that folk might be unhappy with him. But Cowen feels the majority of his colleagues are behind him.

'Excellent conversations' have been had over the last week. Sadly, for the citizenry, who would prefer a conversation with our crisis, they were with backbench members of Fianna Fáil.

It'll all be over by Tuesday, reckons Brian, by which time he can get back to running the country. That's obviously the confidence bit.

Such decisiveness from the Taoiseach. After his week of conversations, he tabled the motion of confidence in himself 'on my own initiative'. Where initiative is concerned, it's a bit late, granted, but it's a start.

The Taoiseach seemed up for the internal fight. When he spoke, he rose up and down on his toes, waving his hands, stressing that he is the man to bring Ireland through the crisis. Or through the passing of the Finance Bill, which could take a couple of months. And then he'll be gone anyway. Cowen is ready, he said, to fight the election.

Some people watching the press conference, which was televised live, might have been wondering why they had to wait another couple of months to have their say.

He turned the tables on his opponents for the party leadership, apparently. By tabling this motion of confidence in himself, he had taken the wind out of Micheál Martin's sails. Micheál having emerged as the most likely successor. Although as he hadn't been seen or heard for a week, 'emerged' might not be the right word.

It turned out yesterday that Minister Martin was waiting to hear what his boss had to say before outlining his side of the story.

What would he do? If he did nothing, his ambitions would come to nought and he would be consigned to history as the nearly-ran who hadn't the backbone for the fight.

Resignation, came the word.

In the aftermath of Brian Cowen's press conference, his people rang around city hotels to find a venue. Late in the evening, the Minister for Foreign Affairs arrived in the Burlington Hotel for his press conference.

This would be more like it. A bit of fire. Movement. Clarity. A man who can communicate. This would be good.

Merciful hour.

Micheál looked as traumatised as the Taoiseach. He delivered a speech and then he took questions.

Clarity? As clear as mud.

Cartoon by Martyn Turner.

Except that the Minister for Foreign Affairs (reluctant) was straight up in relaying that this whole farrago has been about Fianna Fáil and its future. He said the bit about the nation, and not being in it for 'the spoils', but he was clear that he wanted Brian Cowen out because he is killing the party.

Micheál listed the reasons: low morale, no preparation for the election, no readiness for it, the continuing slide in support, no sense of direction. The spate of resignations after Christmas only strengthened his resolve to make a move. When Cowen seemed to be appealing to a national audience when he auditioned to stay in the job, his Minister was bringing things down to brass tacks. 'The survival of the party was at stake now.' The Minister said backbenchers have been coming to him for months asking 'what are you guys going to do about it?'

He went to his Taoiseach and said he should step down as leader. He resigned. Cowen said he wouldn't accept it. What could Micheál do, when 'a Taoiseach puts it passionately: "I don't want you to go?"' One would have thought you tell him to stuff it, but apparently Brian was clinging to his leg as he left the Taoiseach's office, and what was he to do? Reporters at the press conference were perplexed. The Minister arrived in a ministerial car, and he left in one.

He is not canvassing for the leadership, but he, doubtless, will be available for conversations in the coming days.

The Minister pointed to one of his great achievements during his time in politics: the smoking ban. Sad to say, after the two performances yesterday, people who had to listen to them were contemplating going back on the fags. Marvellous.

Maybe Mary Hanafin will come out tomorrow and blow them both out of the water. Or Brian Lenihan might try short circuit matters.

The Greens seem a lost cause.

Model Nadia Forde in the Royal Hospital Kilmainham during a reception to announce details of Showcase Ireland at the RDS. Photograph: Brenda Fitzsimons.

The people gave up long ago.

Meanwhile, the ship of state drifts while hand-to-hand combat continues on the bridge.

The IMF/EU boys must be enjoying it though.

Marvellous.

SATURDAY, 29 JANUARY 2011

'It's Seán FitzPatrick's old BMW. I bought it for you online.'

Ross O'Carroll-Kelly

'Oh my God,' Honor goes, staring at the cover of *Heat*, 'is Jordan wearing that dress or is that dress wearing Jordan?' Me, I'm staring at the front of the *Mail*, cracking my hole laughing. 'Look at the state of Jackie Healy-Rae,' I go. 'He looks like he escaped from an old folks' home after stealing the clothes of the man who comes to give out the Eucharist.'

She's there, 'And, oh my God, when is Jennifer Aniston going to build a bridge? You lost Brad Pitt to someone way hotter. Er, deal, girl!' And of course I can't help but chuckle? This is me and my daughter, by the way, in Eason's in Dundrum Town Centre, enjoying an afternoon of unsupervised quality time. And I'm looking at her, wondering was I as clued-in at five years old as she obviously is? I'm forced to admit that I possibly wasn't, and I blame my old man for that. My earliest memory is of standing in our back gorden in Glenageary slash Sallynoggin, with him throwing that Gilbert ball at me. I think I'd racked up eight concussions by the time I was five. A lot of people would say that actually explains a lot.

I suddenly laugh out loud. 'Kerry Katona on Ice,' I go. 'Am I the only one who read that headline and thought she was back on the gear?' Honor laughs. She's like, 'That's lollers, Daddy,' which is

an amazing thing for any, I suppose, south Dublin father to hear. 'That is, like, so lollers!'

We wander back to the cor pork and I watch her, walking three steps ahead of me, like a Mini-Me version of her old dear, struggling with her Cath Kidston, D&G, House of Fraser, Fran & Jane and Sunglass Hut International bags. Sorcha reckons I spoil her. And, yeah, I possibly do. All I'm trying to do, though, is give her the happy childhood that I never had? I check out her happy little face in the rear-view mirror. Even though she's long outgrown her child seat she still insists on sitting in the back. She says she likes to feel like she's being chauffeured.

On the drive back to Sorcha's I have some of my famously deep thoughts about the whole, I suppose, parenthood thing? As in, if you had a really rubbish old man like I had, then you end up being an amazing one yourself. He forgot my birthday a few weeks back. Can you actually believe that? Oh, he knows the date of the general election, because he's been texting it to me all week, with comments like, 'Let the people have their revolution – see are they any happier.' But the birthday of his only son? No, that'd be too much to keep in his head.

We pull up outside Newtownpork Avenue. I turn around in my seat. 'Okay, Honor, let's get our stories straight. What did we have for lunch?'

'Sushi. Er, puke?'

'Very good. And what did we very definitely not have?'

'Eddie Rocket's.'

'Well done.' Sorcha opens the door, cops the shopping bags and gives me what would have to be described as a disapproving look. Honor just goes, 'Oh! My God! You should see the photograph of Cat Deeley in Heat. Dressed to kill? Er, dressed to spill, more like. It's like, whatevs!' and morches straight into the kitchen.

Sorcha just goes, 'Your dad is here.' I end up losing it a bit. I'm like, 'What does he want? It's not another rant about how Brian Cowen is the most wronged Irish politician since Michael Collins?'

'He's here to see you, Ross.'

'Who even is Michael Collins?'

'Ross, just hear him out.'

I just shrug, roysh, then follow her into the kitchen, where Honor is talking him through her various purchases, telling him that peplum dresses are going to be rocking the catwalks all over Europe this spring.

'Hello there, Kicker,' he tries to go. And I'm obviously there, 'What do you want?' Except he ends up, like, totally disorming me by waving a set of cor keys in front of my eyes and going, 'A belated – inverted commas – happy birthday!'

'Okay,' I go, happy to hear him out, 'this better be good.'

'Your birthday present, Ross, it's parked outside.'

'The only thing I saw porked outside was a shitty 92WW three-serious Beemer.' He just looks at me with a big stupid smile, then motions for me to follow him outside, which I do.

'This?' I go. 'You're telling me this is what you bought for me for my 31st?'

'Do you like it?'

'Like it? I was barely even born when it was built.'

'It's Seán FitzPatrick's old BMW,' he goes. 'I bought it for you – what's this they say – online?' I'm like, 'What?' genuinely meaning it. 'Oh, Sorcha helped me. Gave me a tutorial on how these internet auctions work. They were taking bids, you see, for the right to press the button to crush old Seánie's pride and joy. Well, I was, of course, appalled. I said it to Hennessy. That car is a bloody monument, I said, to the good times we enjoyed in this country and seem in far too much of a hurry to forget. It should be preserved. So I put in a bid to buy the bloody thing – €6,000, Ross!'

I open the driver's seat and climb in. It's still got that new-cor smell. 'Oh,' he goes, suddenly all misty-eyed, 'driving it out here today brought back a memory or two, I don't mind telling you. Seánie

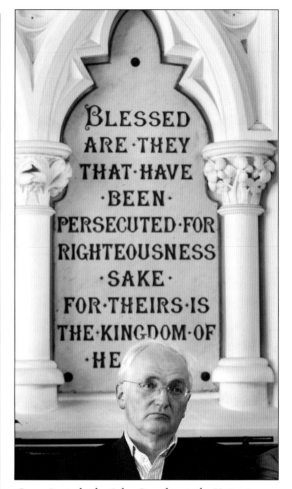

Green Party leader John Gormley at the Unitarian Church in Dublin, where he took part in a climate change debate. Photograph: Leon Farrell/Photocall Ireland.

and I, driving home from Delgany, having just played 18, tiring the bloody stars with our talk of everything, from the over-regulation of the banking sector to the good old days when a try was worth four points, a conversion three and kicking was considered an art, a bloody art.'

I pull the door shut, just to drown out his voice, then I run my hand along the polished leather interior and the walnut detailing. I'd actually forgotten what a classic cor the old three-serious was. Driving Seán FitzPatrick's old motor.

The idea is suddenly growing on me. And it's like Honor said to me, as she was wrapping her face around a Classic in Ed's: the beauty of vintage is that it never gets old.

So I'm sitting there, thinking, 'Six granding-tons, though? Why so cheap?' when I suddenly spot two dudes on the other side of Newtownpork Avenue, basically pointing at me? The next thing I know, one of them throws a full can of Coke at my windscreen and shouts, 'Wanker!'

And what can I do except wind down the window and tell my old man, 'It's perfect.'

TUESDAY, 8 FEBRUARY 2011

Fancy That – A Paragon of Radical Reform Languished in Cabinet for 14 Years

Miriam Lord

Why couldn't the poor man have sent us a sign? A scribbled note dropped from the window of his State car. A coded message to Charlie Bird. A hint of off-message behaviour.

But nothing. No indication of how he must have been suffering while serving as a senior cabinet minister in three successive governments. Micheál, forgive us. We never knew.

To think that this paragon of radical thought languished for 14 years under the oppressive leaderships of Bertie Ahern and Brian Cowen, forced to go out and defend the worst of Ahern's tribunal tales and forced to denounce the critics of Cowen as Ireland fell apart.

In his defence, we now know that Martin was drugged for most of the time. The truth came out at the Fianna Fáil minifesto launch.

He was high on 'the consensus', which, apparently, is even worse than the cigarettes. But Micheál is clean now and happy to face his demons. Militant humility is his stock in trade these days.

Everyone was at it back then, he argued. Even Fianna Fáil couldn't resist the temptation. He regrets this.

'We didn't stand up to the consensus – including myself,' he confessed.

He's free now. Thank God. But all the money is gone.

On the plus side, Martin, former strung-out stalwart of the boom years, is a man reborn.

Note to Mount Street: is it too late for a new election slogan? 'THEY made me do it.' Loads of billboard options there – lovely full-page colour photo of Micheál from page 2 of the minifesto teamed with a varied cast of baddies in the background. Ahern and Cowen, glowering malevolently at the back of his head; Enda and Eamon, grinning like half-wits; the general public, surrounded by designer handbags and SUVs.

Because according to the vaguely contrite former minister, we were all cheerleaders for the consensus. We share the blame.

Now that he is reconstituted, he wants to join the Reform Club. It's a very popular spot in Irish politics at the moment.

Things are different now, stresses Micheál in his application. Just because he used to be a leading light of the Bertie and Biffo years doesn't mean he can't change. He is anxious to forget the past and move on and he hopes the voters will do likewise.

Micheál Martin: accessory to the crime or architect of the recovery? The public will pass judgment shortly.

He's good at what he does, is the new leader. They must be kicking themselves in Fianna Fáil for not having the bottle to get rid of Brian Cowen earlier.

Given that he has few shots in his electoral locker, Martin handled the launch well, even if calling it a manifesto raises trade description issues – there's damn all in it. Micheál's minifesto is a slim volume.

Fianna Fáil leader, Micheál Martin, speaking at the launch of his party's general election manifesto in Dublin City Gallery, The Hugh Lane. Photograph: Dara Mac Dónaill.

But he was keeping it 'real'. The event was about showcasing his 'Real Plan'.

It reminded us of a popular brand of potato crisps which boasts on its packaging: 'made with real ingredients'. As opposed to what? The launch took place in the Hugh Lane Gallery of Modern Art on Dublin's Parnell Square. An exhibition of the work of Richard Tuttle is on at the moment. It's called 'Triumphs'. That's just teasing.

Tragedies, would be more like.

Tuttle is a leading 'post-minimalist artist', as opposed to Micheál, who will be a leading minimalist politician after the size of his parliamentary party is slashed.

Upstairs at 'Triumphs', visitors to the gallery would have seen an, er, 'polysemous multipart horizontal installation'. Downstairs, in the beautiful Sculpture Gallery, visitors would have seen a collection of mute figures known as 'the Fianna Fáil front bench'. One of them, Éamon Ó Cuív, slept for most of the launch. He woke once or twice, but couldn't keep his eyes open. He has since apologised, saying he only had a few hours of sleep before he had to travel from Galway for the morning kick-off.

At least he turned up. 'Where's Willie?' was the question of the day. Willie O'Dea, newly restored to the front bench, was missing.

Are they hiding him already? Micheál made a virtue of his Government's mistakes. Fianna Fáil will be making no new spending commitments, he pledged. There will be no gimmicks. No soundbites (he keeps saying that, then contradicting himself. Yesterday, he talked about 'the Punch and Judy show' that is the Dáil).

Why this no-spend minifesto? 'The reason for this is simple – the money is not there,' declared Deputy Martyr.

And whose fault is that, then? The atmosphere at the launch was flat, nothing like the razzmatazz of old to add a touch of excitement. That's understandable. What was very different is the air of irrelevance that is beginning to envelop Fianna Fáil. Journalists dutifully asked their questions, but there was less urgency about the exchanges.

Micheál's big talk about reform is easy for him now – he won't have to implement it. Everyone knew that.

RTÉ's Seán O'Rourke summed up the problem that faces the new Fianna Fáil leader – while he has great plans now, he can't divorce himself from his involvement with the last three governments, when these plans could have been implemented.

'You've the credibility of somebody who claims he was abducted in Kingsbridge about 15 years ago after getting off the Cork train.'

Everything Micheál says invites comparison. 'The government can't afford to travel on a wing and a prayer,' he remarked, referring to some of Eamon Gilmore's pious aspirations.

Ah, yes. Micheál was always a great fan of the government jet . . .

SATURDAY, 12 FEBRUARY 2011

Egypt Celebrates as Mubarak Finally Concedes and Leaves Office

Michael Jansen

A roar of joy rose up that could be heard around the world when the Egyptian people heard that their president, Hosni Mubarak, had resigned. In Cairo, Alexandria, Suez and Port Said, hundreds of thousands of democracy demonstrators chanted: 'The people ousted the regime'.

'Hurriyeh, hurriyeh, freedom, freedom,' they shouted, dancing, hugging one another, weeping, laughing. 'Goodbye, goodbye,' they called.

One moment the streets of the capital were almost empty, the next they were filled with honking cars flashing their lights in time with the hooting horns.

The ousting of Mr Mubarak (82) was announced at dusk on Egyptian national television by his grim-faced vice-president, Omar Suleiman, after an emissary from the supreme council of the armed forces delivered an ultimatum to the presidential palace, which had been besieged by thousands of democracy demonstrators.

Egypt's streets and squares had been taken over by them over the previous 18 days of non-stop protests against the autocratic regime.

Mr Suleiman said: 'In the grave circumstances that the country is passing through, President Hosni Mubarak has decided to leave his position as president of the republic. He has mandated the armed forces' supreme council to run the state. God is our protector and succour.'

The top man in the new regime is defence minister Mohammed Hussein Tantawi. The army command took action 18 hours after Mr Mubarak announced, for the second time, that he would remain president until his term was set to end in September and his successor elected.

Hundreds of thousands of pro-democracy demonstrators had converged on Tahrir (Liberation) Square on Thursday night expecting him to at long last declare he was stepping down in a scheduled television and radio appearance.

However, their expected night of triumph was not to be. After Mr Mubarak's announcement that he would not resign, Egyptians flooded in ever greater numbers into Tahrir Square and other prominent locations around the capital, calling for his immediate dismissal by the still powerful military.

The pro-democracy demonstrations, the largest people's power movement ever seen in the Arab world, were launched on 25 January by youth activists from different cities and provinces who were connected by the internet.

Yesterday at noon, on the 18th day of their protest, the military announced it would end the state of emergency, one of their chief demands, but only when the demonstrators had ended their protest and gone home.

Then at 6 p.m., beneath the Belle Époque domes of the building from which Mr Mubarak had ruled for so long, a cry went out that he was gone.

'For 18 days we have withstood tear gas, rubber bullets, live ammunition, Molotov cocktails, thugs on horseback, the scepticism and fear of our loved ones and the worst sort of ambivalence from an international community that claims to care about democracy,' said Karim Medhat

Ennarah, a protester with tears in his eyes. 'But we held our ground. We did it.

'My late father was part of a sit-in at the faculty of engineering in Cairo University in 1968 – the first protest seen in Egypt since Nasser took over in 1952,' he added. 'His generation tell me that they were not as brave as us, but they started something and played their part. Today, we finished the job for them.'

More than 300 people died and 5,000 were wounded during the 18 days. Yesterday one person was reported killed in the port city of Arish where protesters attempted to storm a police station.

Mr Mubarak, a former air force commander, took power in 1981 following the assassination by

Pro-democracy protesters celebrate in Tahrir Square in central Cairo after the announcement of Egyptian president Hosni Mubarak's resignation. Photograph: Dylan Martinez/Reuters.

Celebrating the fall of Egyptian president Hosni Mubarak. Photograph: Dylan Martinez/Reuters.

Muslim militants of his predecessor Anwar Sadat, who was condemned for signing a peace treaty with Israel.

During his three decades in power, he maintained his grip by repressing dissent, promoting the interests of wealthy supporters, projecting his regime as a bulwark against Muslim fundamentalists and courting the support of the US. He refused to countenance calls for political reform, an end to rampant corruption and reconstruction of the country's collapsing infrastructure.

Mr Mubarak rejected appeals to address unemployment, the deteriorating educational and healthcare systems, and the hunger of the 50 per cent of Egyptians who live on or below the poverty line.

His fall came 32 years after the shah's regime was toppled in Iran.

WEDNESDAY, 16 FEBRUARY 2011

Micheál Wants Evolution of Fianna Fáil Knuckle-Draggers – and He's the Missing Link

Miriam Lord

With things so awful for them at the moment, it is a blessing for Fianna Fáil to have a new leader who looks for the silver lining in every cloud.

Years of unbroken rule by his party has delivered a broken country. This may be a minor consideration for Micheál Martin, who refuses to look

Some of the 317 people who broke a world record in Dublin for the most number of heads shaved in one hour by a team of 10 barbers on Today FM's Ray D'Arcy Show, *raising over €300,000 for patient care services provided by the Irish Cancer Society. Photograph: Alan Betson.*

back, but it is proving a bit of a hindrance when it comes to mounting a credible election campaign.

Still, Micheál the optimist is facing the future, going forward. And the future is radical. 'I am not afraid of radical departures,' he said at the launch of his proposals for political reform. Just as well, because most of his TDs will have radically departed by the end of the month.

Since the election began, whenever Martin talks of innovative solutions he is slapped around the head with his record and asked why the hell he couldn't have implemented some of them when he had the chance? It happened again yesterday. It was a bit ironic, somebody suggested, for him to bang on passionately about Dáil reform now, when he had the previous 14 years to do something.

'The 14 years can be of benefit because one can draw on the experience that one has had . . .

to the benefit of the country,' said Micheál, extracting the silver lining. 'That's a plus that I'd like to bring to the table.'

Three governments, of which he was a part, ate the Irish economy alive – without the fava beans or a nice bottle of Chianti. Now Martin wants to help: a political Hannibal to our national Clarice. No wonder voters don't want to touch his party.

At least the morning briefing wasn't broadcast live. Hearing Micheál vow to make things better for the nation by sharing his experience of life from inside a State car might have upset some.

But there is an election to be fought and the party leader can't simply hoist the white flag. His best shot is to distance himself as much as possible from the past, while also distancing himself as much as possible from minglings with the great unwashed. Presumably, this is why he spent the early afternoon in a commercial vegetable plot, communing with green peppers.

The recent past must be erased. Micheál has a plan: it is the evolution of the Fianna Fáil knuckle-draggers – and he is the missing link.

Back in the prehistoric days when Bertosaurus and Bifflodocus roamed the plains of Leinster House, Martin ran with the dinosaur set. During those years, their approach to the issue of political reform and parliamentary co-operation was positively Neanderthal.

Micheál was never known as a reformer in his knuckle-dragging days. But then, as he confessed at his manifesto launch last week, he was addicted to 'the consensus'.

He returned to the pernicious influence of 'the consensus' yesterday. The prevailing view of society then was that everything was wonderful and nobody challenged how things were done. 'The consensus' made everyone lazy. He's able to think for himself, now that he has evolved and become party leader.

The laziness is gone.

It's been a very rapid evolutionary process for Martin. Last May, still in cahoots with his fellow knuckle-draggers, he categorically ruled out the appointment of people from outside politics to ministries. Now it is in his political reform document. What's that all about? 'What I said last May, or sorry, as I said last Monday, I always had issues around the list system and I had issues around whether we should appoint people from outside. But I evolved my thinking . . . and I think we have to learn lessons from the crisis.'

This big push for political reform isn't an election wheeze for Fianna Fáil because nobody

Fianna Fáil leader, Micheál Martin, during a visit to Keelings fruit and vegetable farm, St Margaret's, north Co. Dublin. Photograph: Dara Mac Dónaill.

will take them seriously when they talk about the economy and the health service. It's not been a sudden conversion because they're going into opposition and won't be irritated by the notion anymore. Here's new man Micheál: 'One is always evolving one's thinking, learning and reflecting on whether or not your political system is fit for purpose.'

Evolution or extinction. That's the choice facing Fianna Fáil. Micheál Martin, the missing link, knows this. The modern FFer is represented by people like Averil Power, who joined him on the platform yesterday. Despite not holding public office, Power, who is standing for the party in Dublin North East, was appointed to the front bench in November as spokeswoman on political reform.

Like her party leader, Averil is of the opinion that Fianna Fáil has taken the issue centre stage. All the other parties – who have produced policy documents – are only interested in 'gimmicks'. She concentrated her fire on Fine Gael, dismissing the party's proposals as the most conservative of all. 'I'm not surprised they're conservative, I guess, in that Enda Kenny has been in the Dáil since before I was born,' said Power (32).

This would be in contrast to Micheál Martin (51), who entered the Dáil 22 years ago and was wedded to the recent way of doing things until the game was up for the administration he served in as a senior minister for 14 years.

The woman who accused Pat Rabbitte of being sexist denied she was being ageist. Micheál kept out of the exchanges. He's involved in new politics now, unless he's attacking Gerry Adams.

Later in the day, the radically evolved Martin paid a visit to the Keelings fruit and vegetable farm in north Dublin. It's a multinational company that grows, sources and distributes fresh produce all over Europe. Micheál toured the peppers department. 'Salads Only' said the sign on the gate, which was apt for the health-conscious Corkman.

An Irishman's Diary

Frank McNally

Like eagle-eyed reader John O'Hagan, I at first welcomed the news – as reported in our Page 2 digest on Wednesday – that 'an English BMW dealer has banned foreign sales of used cars which will hit Irish buyers'.

The wonder of this, it seemed to me, was why BMW would produce cars that it was known would hit people, Irish or otherwise, in the first place. And why buyers, in particular? Not that any sane BMW driver would want the car to hit anybody else. But surely the act of buying it should confer some sort of privileges.

On the other hand, the reference was to 'used cars'. Which could imply that, somewhere in England and unknown to BMW, the vehicles were being modified to hit Irish buyers, perhaps as some kind of sick practical joke.

This immediately suggested the involvement of Jeremy Clarkson and his fellow middle-aged scamps on *Top Gear*, who are always trying to think up new motoring stunts to amuse viewers and who have been accused of using racist humour before.

But after allowing my confusion about the digest item to last long enough that I could get half a column out of it, I eventually turned to the actual story in the Motors section to read more about this car-dealing English philanthropist who had intervened to save us.

And imagine my disappointment when he turned out to be the villain of the piece. For, alas, it appeared that the report had lost something during the digestion process.

A meaning closer to what was intended might have been achieved by using a comma after 'cars', followed by the words 'a move that' instead of 'which'. This would have eliminated any implied physical threat to Irish car buyers, while allowing us to retain the word 'hit': which is a great

Cartoon by Martyn Turner.

favourite of journalists, especially the ones who write headlines.

You can see the verb's attraction. It's dynamic. It packs a punch, sometimes literally. And above all, it's short, fitting into even very confined spaces. Indeed, there are similar reasons behind the popularity of another three-letter word you regularly see in headlines: 'set'. As in: 'Election set for February' or 'Government set for defeat'.

'Set' is one of those terms that has become almost a badge of our profession, like an NUJ card. So much so that one now regularly sees and hears it in places where, defeating the whole purpose, it's superfluous. Many radio reporters seem to be addicted to writing headlines like 'Taoiseach set to resign', even though the S-word could be dropped there with no effect on meaning.

Back in January, I recall reading a headline somewhere that said: 'Ireland set to be hit by snow again'. The word was similarly redundant in that case – unless the reference was to a group of people known as the 'Ireland set'. And barring the possibility that these were tax exiles living in the Swiss Alps, it was hard to think of a scenario in which snow would affect them uniquely.

Of course, I speak as a member of another set – the Dublin cycling one – which was all too frequently hit by snow during the big freeze. It usually arrived in small, compressed lumps thrown by gurriers. But it could have been worse. So long as used English BMWs and other larger projectiles left me alone, I wasn't complaining.

Prone as it may be to misunderstanding, the word 'hit' is not (yet, at least) in the same category as 'inflammable', a term that had to be downgraded in the interests of public safety.

In fact, as one of my favourite reference books – Fritz Spiegl's *Contradictionary: an A–Z of* confusibles, lookalikes and soundalikes – suggests, this may be 'the only instance of an official change in meaning and usage demanded by a British government body'.

Inflammable means, and has always meant, 'easily set on fire'. But the problem, historically, was that many people thought (or were thought to think by officials paid to worry about them) that it meant the opposite. And it's true that, if you were to make the mistake of assuming English to be in any way logical, 'inflammable' would seem to bear the same relation to 'flammable' as 'insane' does to 'sane'.

Unfortunately there was no such word as 'flammable' until it was deemed necessary to invent it. Now you see it on everything from nightdresses to oil-tanks. And the usage has spread far beyond British English. Even that fusty old American language classic, Strunk & White's *The Elements of Style*, acknowledges the new word's role in 'saving lives', before sniffily advising that this is no excuse for writers to use it.

Their ruling on the matter concludes: 'For [safety reasons], trucks carrying gasoline or explosives are now marked FLAMMABLE. Unless you are operating such a truck and hence are concerned with the safety of children and illiterates, use inflammable.' I suppose the same advice applies in Ireland, for both trucks and literature, with one possible addendum. If it's a used truck, especially one imported from England, drivers and writers alike are urged to exercise maximum caution around it at all times.

TUESDAY, 22 FEBRUARY 2011

Voters Set to Endorse EU–IMF Deal in Election

Fintan O'Toole

Whatever sceptics may think, the election will make at least one huge difference.

Up until 25 February, there will have been no popular mandate for turning bank debt into public debt and imposing another four years of austerity. After Friday, unless all the polls are completely askew, there will be a popular mandate for the bank bailout, the EU–IMF deal and the cuts. Behind all the excitement of a historic changing of the guard, this is the real big event.

Come Saturday morning, like every morning after every election in the history of the State, right-of-centre establishment politics will be triumphant. Fine Gael and Fianna Fáil will have well over half the vote between them, 53 per cent according to yesterday's *Irish Times* poll. More strikingly, it is precisely the same as the 53 per cent that Fine Gael and Fianna Fáil between them got in the European elections in June 2009.

Everything that has happened since then – the revelation of the abysmal depths of the banking crisis, the loss of economic sovereignty in the EU–IMF deal – has resulted in little more than a shift in support between the two right-of-centre parties that have dominated Irish politics since the foundation of the State. Leave aside the 'vingince, by Jaysus!' factor in relation to Fianna Fáil and there is nothing to trouble the seismologist. To adapt the fictitious *Times* (of London) headline invented by Claud Cockburn: Small Earthquake in Ireland, Not Many Dead.

This outcome will be greeted with relief by the European Central Bank and the fiscal hawks within the EU.

It will mean that all the rage and disgust, all the cursing and fist-shaking, will have amounted to nothing very much. Internally, of course, Fianna Fáil's worst result to date (even the defeated and disarrayed republicans in 1923 got 27 per cent of the vote with many of their candidates in jail) will be a big deal. But externally, where the real power now lies, it will seem that nothing of great significance has happened.

The Irish will have a new government, surely more competent and energetic than the exhausted and demoralised one that rolled over when the IMF and the ECB came to town. The new boys will be rewarded with some promises of adjustments to interest rates that will allow them to claim victory. And they will get on with the job of nationalising private debt while attempting to bring the public deficit to below 3 per cent of GDP by 2014.

From the point of view of the ECB, the Irish will be even more onside than they are now. There was always a worry that Fianna Fáil and the Greens did not have public consent for the four-year plan they signed up to. These parties, after all, took just a quarter of the vote between them in 2009. That consent is now in the process of being secured. A few small concessions may be necessary but, after Friday, it will be essentially in the bag.

This is, surely, a remarkable state of affairs. Is there any other democracy where 55 per cent of the electorate would freely vote for a €15 billion austerity programme combined with a €100 billion transfer of wealth from citizens to banks? And let's be clear – this vote is free. For all the limitations to Irish democracy, and all the unhappiness that people may feel about the alternatives, there is nothing to stop people using their votes to send a very different kind of message. Most people will freely choose not to do so.

That's their right, but it is tough on those who don't have a choice at all, particularly the hidden people in this election – children. I've written before about the Irish capacity for 'unknown knowns', things we know to be the case but choose not to be aware of. One of those big unknown knowns is that children will pay a heavily disproportionate price for our collective consent to the current policy.

Cartoon by Martyn Turner.

Children in the poorest families are the most dependent on public services. The inevitable rise in poverty and the cutting of those services will hit them hard, at enormous long-term human and economic cost.

But that cost is tacitly written into the deal. It is not even up for discussion in any substantial way. Fianna Fáil's manifesto says nothing at all about poverty or children.

Fine Gael's has 860 words on the burning issue of defence policy and 360 words on children, all of them decent but most of them vague.

Labour has good intentions about eliminating poverty but the main specific proposal for breaking the cycle of child poverty is the rolling out of an area-based strategy in 'up to 10 of Ireland's most disadvantaged communities, at a cost of up to €15 million' – very nice, very fuzzy and very, very modest.

The three biggest parties clearly decided that, whatever we tell Joe Duffy, we are actually a timid people, willing to put up with what's happened to us and scared of any great change in the way our society works. The evidence is that they were right.

SATURDAY, 26 FEBRUARY 2011

Taking the Long View When it Comes to Elections

Garret FitzGerald

While we await the election results, there isn't much more that I can usefully say about this election, the outcome of which will emerge during this weekend.

So, while awaiting the outcome, I have been reflecting on my past experience of elections, which began in 1943, when my father, Desmond FitzGerald, was coming to the end of a 30-year political career. In that election 68 years ago, I addressed envelopes for Fine Gael at a temporary office at the end of Nassau Street, and also faithfully recorded the election results – a practice I continued thereafter, sometimes even including the time at which each count came through.

In the following year's general election, my father stood in Dublin County, which had been his constituency in the 1920s before he was sent by the party to Carlow–Kilkenny in 1932, and with my elder brother, Pierce, I went around the constituency to public meetings with him. And in the 1948 election my wife Joan and I canvassed for Fine Gael in Ballsbridge. However, as I was now a member of the staff of Aer Lingus, I decided that from then on I should opt out of any engagement in party politics.

But my interest in politics remained intense, and from that year onwards, Joan and I always invited our friends around to listen to – and later, when television began, to view – the results of all Irish and British elections.

In 1965, RTÉ faced the challenge of presenting the election results on TV for the first time, and they asked me to join the panel of commentators. I agreed, but I didn't think that they realised how much more of a problem the presentation of the results on TV would pose by comparison with radio. So I proposed that I would prepare a simulation of the first 70 counts likely to come through, with a possible time for each of them. Our election results have tended to peak between 6.30 p.m. and 7.30 p.m. on the day following the election and I knew that acute problems of TV presentation of counts would arise around that time.

When on the morning of the election count our panel met at 10.30 to test the system using my simulated results, we had to wait almost two hours for the first such result to emerge from what must have been a very early computer. As soon as we started to comment on that result a whistle blew, and everybody started running for the exits.

'Fire?' I queried, anxiously.

'No, lunch,' I was told.

Labour's Eamon Gilmore; the Green Party's John Gormley; moderator Pat Kenny; Fianna Fáil's Micheál Martin; Sinn Féin's Gerry Adams; and Fine Gael's Enda Kenny prior to the leaders' debate on RTÉ One's **The Frontline**. *Photograph: Julian Behal/PA.*

But the bugs had been got out of the system, and for the first two hours of the results programme all went smoothly. However, as we approached 6.30 p.m. our commentary began to be inhibited by the presentation of a rapidly rising flow of election count figures.

Believing that the fairly newly established RTÉ had not yet worked out what to do if a member of a panel absented himself, I had decided that at that point I would return to my nearby home to join our domestic election party for an hour or more. As I had calculated, in my absence from RTÉ the panel was suspended, thus enabling all the peak-time results to be presented!

I am not sure that this has ever happened since – to the distress of many serious psephologist viewers!

There was an unexpected, and unintended, consequence of my presence on TV for the bulk of this 10-hour programme. Shortly before that 1965 election I had decided not to stand for election to the Dáil, but in its aftermath I was persuaded to stand for the Senate in the Fine Gael interest – something I had never thought of doing.

As I sought the votes of county councillors around the country, it became clear that a number of them – I guessed about a dozen of the 64 whose votes put me into that House – did so because of that TV programme.

On my election to the Senate, Liam Cosgrave appointed me to the Fine Gael front bench – but, curiously, nobody thought to ask me to join the party! So, when Tom O'Higgins stood for the presidency in early 1966, I went to my local TD, John A. Costello, to find out how I could join Fine Gael so as to play a part in this presidential election.

His response was disconcerting.

'Forty years in politics; twice taoiseach. Never joined Fine Gael!' he said.

Nevertheless, I persuaded him to tell me where to join the party at local level. I then had to address meetings in Co. Wicklow, at the first of which in Bray, beside the courthouse where half a century earlier my father had received a six-month sentence for seditious speech, I made my first political address.

My acute nervousness was intensified by the fact that friends of mine, Michael McDowell's parents, had chosen to have dinner at a window of the Royal Hotel, right beside the platform. I also had to speak at a final rally (the last of its kind in Dublin – at the GPO), all of which I found quite terrifying!

The 1977 election gave Fianna Fáil the last overall majority ever secured in Irish politics. When, after the declaration of my own constituency result, I arrived at RTÉ, Liam Cosgrave was in the process of conceding defeat. So, when I joined the panel of commentators I did not have to pretend that things were better than they actually were for Fine Gael.

In those days, the media had no belief in polls, and none was published showing likely party voting strengths. But in Fine Gael we had the benefit of two post-dissolution polls, the first of which gave Fianna Fáil 59 per cent. However, after a vigorous campaign a second poll showed that we had pulled Fianna Fáil back to 51 per cent – which, of course, still gave them a clear majority. But the media knew nothing of this and continued to delude themselves into believing that the coalition of Fine Gael and Labour were on course to win. Listening to broadcasts during the day of the count I had formed the impression that because of this delusion, media commentators had been unable to take in the scale of the swing to Fianna Fáil that was emerging.

So, when I joined the RTÉ panel I inquired about their forecast for Fianna Fáil. 'Seventy-eight seats,' I was told. I challenged this, saying that nine hours earlier on the basis of lunchtime tally figures, Jim Dooge and I had calculated that they would win between 80 and 84 seats – and that now the outcome clearly lay between 82 and 84 – the latter figure proving to be the actual result.

I could see that Séamus Brennan, Fianna Fáil's spokesman on the panel, foreseeing the destabilising impact of such a large majority upon Jack Lynch's capacity to survive an onslaught by Charles Haughey's supporters, was clearly horrified at the prospect of 84 seats for his party.

Those were among my experiences during the first half of my 68 years of involvement in general elections.

MONDAY, 28 FEBRUARY 2011

Angry Electorate Coldly Voted to Liquidate Fianna Fáil

Miriam Lord

Finally, the tall grass parted. By God, but this was no rush job. It was a long time coming. When the verdict came, it was crushing. Moreover, it was thoroughly considered.

For this is the new politics; history, tradition, old allegiances and overweening presumption hold no sway anymore.

The Irish people looked back in anger this weekend and then they coldly voted to liquidate the party that plunged their country into liquidation. After decades of Fianna Fáil dominance, they turned and taught Fianna Fáil a devastating lesson: You call yourselves a national movement? Now, let us show you the real meaning of a national movement . . .

And with that, they emerged from the long grass and gutted the Soldiers of Destiny. Extraordinary.

Unthinkable, once.

The general election of 2011 will be remembered as the one that shattered another of the three great pillars of old Ireland. It was always a proud boast of the faithful multitude that they belonged to the Untouchable Trinity of the Catholic Church, Fianna Fáil and the Gaelic Athletic Association.

No more. Only the GAA remains, standing proud and rightly cherished.

FF big beast after big beast falling, as the ticker-tape pulsing across the bottom of television screens announced the end of political dynasties and shell-shocked household names watched stronghold constituencies desert them. It made for compulsive viewing.

The winners were almost overlooked as the compelling story of Fianna Fáil's momentous meltdown unfolded.

But not in Co. Mayo, where Enda Kenny led from the front, bringing home an unprecedented three running mates.

Fine Gael fought a brilliant election. Kenny, the underestimated man from Mayo, is now taoiseach-designate. He stepped into his new role on Saturday night with a refreshing humility and a pledge to restore public trust in the debased currency of Irish politics.

You could see how much he wanted the job. His energy and passion undeniable; his determination to make a difference an encouraging contrast to the jaded nature of what went before.

Willie O'Dea watches as members of his election team knock on doors while out canvassing in Limerick. Photograph: David Sleator.

Given the level of public expectation surrounding him and the scale of the task facing his new government, it's hard to know whether to feel happy or sorry for the man.

The Labour Party put in its best electoral performance ever, exceeding the seats won in the Spring Tide of the early 1990s. When Eamon Gilmore ties the knot with Kenny – don't expect a long engagement – their union will produce a government of well over 100 TDs.

Labour's campaign was a rollercoaster ride, from the high expectations of the 'Gilmore for Taoiseach' days to a worrying slide in the opinion polls and a final-week rally that pulled them back to respectable territory.

Sinn Féin's Gerry Adams romped home in Louth as his party returned a record number of TDs and post-election Tricolours. They will be a major Opposition force, within touching distance of Fianna Fáil. How the two parties will rub along together on the very much depleted Opposition side of the Dáil will be a fascinating feature of the 31st Dáil. Drawing up the seating arrangements should be an entertainment in itself.

The Green Party won't figure in those plans, as none of their TDs made it back.

Adding their considerable bulk to the fascinatingly diverse make-up of the Opposition will be a large assortment of Independent deputies from the right, the left and the whatever you're having yourself wing of Irish politics. The stuffy and prissy powers that be in Leinster House must be having palpitations over the imminent arrival of the flamboyant likes of Luke 'Ming' Flanagan and Mick Wallace.

Whatever else happens in the coming months or years, it won't be boring in Dáil Éireann.

If it won't be easy for Kenny and his incoming administration, heaven only knows what it will be like for Micheál Martin and his traumatised little band of Fianna Fáil survivors. No women in their ranks, the much vaunted Ógra generation almost wiped out, the party in a shambles at local level.

Dara Calleary, the only outgoing junior minister to retain a seat, began the fightback on Saturday night in Mayo.

'This is our darkest hour, but we will rebuild and I will roll up my sleeves and work for our party.' Fianna Fáil will regroup, but things will never be the same.

The shape of Irish politics is changed forever. And it was the people, no longer passive in the tall grass, who did it.

MONDAY, 28 FEBRUARY 2011

FF Will Never Recover Former Position

Stephen Collins

Irish politics will never be the same again. The era of Fianna Fáil dominance, which lasted for three-quarters of a century, came to an abrupt end at the weekend as the voters expressed their fury in the ballot at the way the party has run the country for the past decade and more.

While opinion polls had given plenty of warning that big changes were on the way, it was only when the ballot papers came tumbling out of the boxes on Saturday morning that the breathtaking scale of the Fianna Fáil rout became clear.

Nothing like it has happened since the Irish Party was swept into the dustbin of history in 1918. In fact, the Irish Party performed better on that occasion than Fianna Fáil has in 2011 but was undone by the first-past-the-post electoral system.

Proportional representation saved Fianna Fáil from total obliteration, but whether the party can survive as a serious political force is open to question. One thing is certain; it will never recover its place as the dominant party of power.

The electorate had clearly determined some time back to wreak vengeance on Fianna Fáil for all that has gone wrong and the EU–International Monetary Fund bailout was the final straw. The

Cartoon by Martyn Turner.

anger was probably fuelled by a sense of guilt among those who voted for it in 2007.

The implosion of the party in Dublin Central where Bertie Ahern and his Drumcondra mafia had ruled the roost for so long was one indication of that mood of guilt turning itself into anger.

The election has transformed the political landscape in one fell swoop, reflecting an obvious thirst in the country for a different kind of politics.

While people clearly don't want a radical shift to the left or right, they want a government that will be honest, open and courageous as it tackles the enormous challenges facing the country.

For Fine Gael, which has spent so much of its history in the wilderness of opposition, the extent of its election victory was beyond the wildest dreams of generations of party supporters. The astonishing thing is that not only is it the biggest party in the Dáil for the first time in its history, it is so much bigger than any other party.

'We have managed to see off the PDs and the Greens but I never thought we'd see off Fianna Fáil as well,' remarked one Fine Gael TD over the weekend.

The professionalism of Fine Gael's vote management was stunning. On a purely proportional basis, the party was entitled to 60 seats but it won 16 more than that.

When Enda Kenny arrived in the Burlington Hotel for a restrained victory celebration on Saturday night, there were a few tears shed when he told an emotional gathering of party supporters that he had received a congratulatory phone call from the 91-year-old former taoiseach Liam Cosgrave.

'I'm an old man now but you have made me proud,' Cosgrave told Kenny and reminded the incoming taoiseach of a little piece of history. The 31st Dáil, in which Fine Gael will be the biggest party, will meet for the first time on 9 March. It

Enda Kenny with a trainee guide dog, Nikita, in Paddy Power betting shop on Dublin's Baggot Street, where Kenny placed a charity bet on Fine Gael to win 70 seats in the general election. Photograph: Colin Keegan/Collins.

was on that date in 1932 that Fianna Fáil took over the reins of power from his father, W.T. Cosgrave, and began its long dominance of Irish politics.

Kenny won't have much time to savour his victory because the hard work of government will begin on that date.

Before it arrives, he will have to put a government together and it will be the first test of his negotiating skills and his resolve.

A coalition deal with the Labour Party is the obvious way to proceed, but there is not a lot of time to construct a programme for government.

Labour has broken its own records in this election and, while the result may not be as good as it hoped for at the beginning of the campaign, the party will have a record number of seats.

Eamon Gilmore made it clear yesterday that he is clearly interested in going into government but the question is on what terms.

Fine Gael and Labour policies are compatible on a range of issues from political reform to changes in the health service. However, there is one fundamental issue on which they have expressed very different views. That is on how to deal with the public finances.

Fine Gael has emphasised during the campaign that it favours a ratio of two to one in terms of spending cuts to taxation, while Labour wants an even split between the two.

More importantly, Fine Gael wants to meet the target set in the EU–IMF deal of getting the public finances back in order by 2014, while Labour wants to spread the process out for at least another year.

Senior people in Fine Gael are acutely conscious that the main failure of the coalition led by

Garret FitzGerald in the 1980s was that Labour got its way from the beginning on the budget targets when Dick Spring, from his hospital bed, vetoed the budget targets set by minister for finance Alan Dukes.

The result was to spread the pain of re-adjustment over too long a period and neither party were thanked by the electorate for their genuine achievements.

This time around, Fine Gael is not in a mood to water down its commitment to sorting out the public finances by 2014.

The party's Dublin South West TD and spokesman on public expenditure Brian Hayes reflected this in media comments at the weekend when he insisted that Labour would have to respect the mandate Fine Gael had received from the people.

If agreement can be reached between them on the public finances, other issues will be easily sorted.

There will be a lot of speculation over Cabinet positions and whether Labour gets the five it is entitled to on a proportional basis or the six it had when last in government.

But such a matter is a nuts-and-bolts issue and not a deal-breaker. Both parties have a strong hand. Fine Gael could try and form a government with-out Labour by looking for support from some of the Independents or even Fianna Fáil. However, a minority government would not have the stability the country requires.

There is an argument in Labour for staying in opposition to try and build the party to a position where it would be a real contender to be the biggest party at the next election.

Labour councillor Cian O'Callaghan made this point yesterday, arguing that Irish politics had now broken down along European lines with the largest party being Christian Democrat and our second-largest party Social Democrat.

'Civil war politics is now finished. Fine Gael was chosen by the people to lead the next government and Labour has been elected as the second-largest party to lead the opposition,' he argued.

However, Gilmore made the more pertinent point that these are not ordinary times and the severity of the economic crisis demands a national government composed of the two biggest parties.

Labour will have to hold a national conference to ratify any decision to go into coalition where these issues will be thrashed out.

As for Sinn Féin, the United Left Alliance and Independents, they can all look forward to making plenty of noise in the incoming Dáil.

If Fine Gael and Labour make good on their pledges of political reform, they should also get an opportunity to make a real contribution through a more powerful committee system.

Whatever happens, the next Dáil will usher in a new era in Irish politics. The election has changed the political landscape in one fell swoop, reflecting an obvious thirst in the country for a different kind of politics.

TUESDAY, 1 MARCH 2011

The Final Hours of a Student who Laid Down his Life to Defy Gadafy

Mary Fitzgerald in Benghazi

It takes just one question to find the house of the Buhidma family in Salmani, in eastern Benghazi. Ask for the home of 'shaheed [martyr] Buhidma' and you will be directed past crumbling buildings to a modest dwelling where the distraught mother and father of Abdul Kareem Buhidma grieve for their son.

Abdul Kareem was a 20-year-old economics student due to graduate later this year. Like many of Benghazi's youth, he flocked to join the anti-regime protests that erupted on 17 February. The

Rescue workers at the Cork Airport crash site, where six people died and six others were injured after a plane from George Best Belfast City Airport crashed in fog. Photograph: Daragh McSweeney/Provision.

defining battle in the fall to the opposition of this, Libya's second largest city, took place at the katiba, a sprawling military compound in central Benghazi. More than 100 unarmed demonstrators were killed in three days of clashes. One of them was Abdul Kareem.

'We went together that day to join the protests at the katiba,' recalls his brother Bilqasim, a 19-year-old high school student. 'We were not afraid . . . But then the army started attacking us. I remember bullets flying everywhere and the smell of burning. I saw Abdul Kareem crouch down briefly and when he stood up again a bullet hit him under his right eye. Some people helped me lift him into a car to go to the hospital, but he didn't make it. He died a few hours later.'

Bilqasim remains so traumatised by the killing

that he speaks in a hoarse whisper with his head bowed low. A woman in the room tells him he should hold his head high because his brother died a martyr.

His mother Aida, her eyes swollen from crying, pulls her shawl around her as her body convulses with sobs. 'I want to die too just to be with him,' she says. 'May God help us.'

Her husband Saleh, a tall man of 80 dressed in brown robes, cannot even speak about his dead son without breaking down.

Abdul Kareem's stepbrother Hussein Hamed has lived in Ireland since claiming political asylum in 1998. He ran as an Independent in Dublin South in the general election.

The family has suffered much under the Gadafy regime. Hussein, who studied in Dublin in the 1980s, fled Libya as a result of persecution due

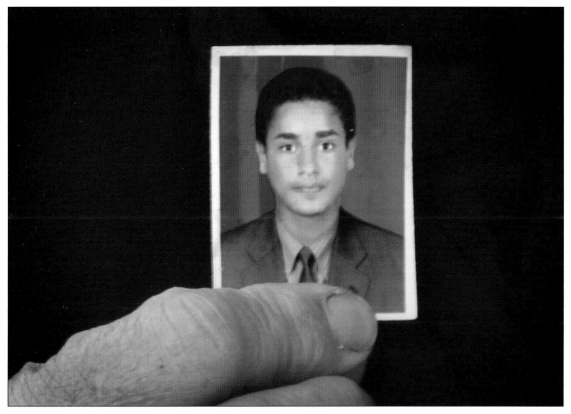

A picture of Abdul Kareem Buhidma, shot dead during protests in Benghazi in eastern Libya, is held by his mother. Photograph: Mary Fitzgerald.

to his involvement with the Muslim Brotherhood. His brother Mahmoud spent seven years in Tripoli's notorious Abu Salim prison and was tortured for suspected political activity.

The Buhidma family say they want revenge for the death of their son and brother. 'I want to catch the people who killed Abdul Kareem with my own hands,' says Bilqasim.

All pray that the protests that have swept away Gadafy's writ in Libya's eastern flank will continue towards Tripoli ousting the man who has ruled the country with an iron grip for more than four decades.

'We will bring him down,' says Mahmoud. 'And then we will punish him. We cannot live happily until we see this man, this animal, dead.'

THURSDAY, 3 MARCH 2011

O'Brien Smashes England for Six

Emmet Riordan at the Chinnaswamy Stadium, Bangalore

Crash, bang, wallop. Hello world, I'm Kevin O'Brien and I can hit a cricket ball.

Well the world certainly knows now after Ireland yet again sent shockwaves through the game with O'Brien enjoying arguably the finest innings in World Cup history at the Chinnaswamy Stadium last night as they chased down a record target of 328 against England to secure a barely believable three-wicket victory in Group B.

Kevin O'Brien celebrates reaching his century batting against England. Photograph: Graham Crouch/Getty Images.

It was brutal in its nature, the pick of England's bowlers belted to all parts of the stadium to huge cheers from both the Irish contingent of about 200 fans and the locals, who enjoy both an underdog and a big-hitter.

In total he hit six sixes, one of them the longest in the tournament so far, which measured 102 metres, and 13 fours as he scored the quickest century in World Cup history off just 50 balls.

He perished for 113 before Ireland could get over the line but in the hands of John Mooney and talisman Trent Johnston, the job got done with five balls to spare as Ireland recorded their highest one-day score.

Mooney clobbered a Jimmy Anderson full toss to the boundary fence for four to seal the victory before launching his bat so high in the air that the swooping kites were in danger of an untimely demise.

Mooney finished unbeaten on 33 from 30 balls, while Johnston made seven from four after coming in after O'Brien was run out and hitting his first delivery for four.

There were other batting heroes, with Alex Cusack proving the perfect foil for O'Brien, hitting 47 from 58 balls in a 162-run partnership for the sixth wicket, an ODI record for Ireland.

Paul Stirling (32), Ed Joyce (32) and Kevin's older brother Niall (29) all got starts after skipper William Porterfield was bowled first ball of the innings by Anderson. But when Gary Wilson was trapped leg-before by Graeme Swann to leave

After clipping the winning four to midwicket, John Mooney (left) is congratulated by Gary Wilson while Trent Johnston is given the same treatment by Niall O'Brien, in amazing scenes at the Chinnaswamy Stadium in Bangalore as the Irish cricket team beat England by three wickets in the Cricket World Cup. Photograph: Philip Brown/Reuters.

Ireland on 111 for five in the 25th over, Ireland looked done and dusted.

We didn't count on Kevin O'Brien and a bat that seemed to flash at extraordinary speed as balls clattered the boundary boards and the stands.

The umpires were even forced to change the ball as one six smashed into the concrete terracing that accommodated the local fans, who danced and cheered and waved both Indian and Irish tri-colours.

And what a contrast on an afternoon that had started in the worst possible fashion when Ireland coach Phil Simmons, having made a tactical change by bringing in all-rounder Cusack for Andrew White, then lost Andre Botha after he pulled up with a groin strain during the pre-game warm-ups.

It was a terrible blow to the North County player, who has struggled with injuries in recent years, and a serious set-back to the bowling attack after his fine display against Bangladesh, where he took three wickets for 32 in nine overs.

There was definitely more bounce in the wicket, but Boyd Rankin failed to hit the right areas yet again as Strauss and Kevin Pietersen got England off on the right note.

The big Warwickshire bowler's first four overs went for 31 runs as England and Cusack fared little better when he replaced him from the Pavilion end as Ireland haemorrhaged 77 runs off the first 11 overs.

To compound matters, there was also a scare involving Kevin O'Brien, who jarred his knee and ankle fielding a drive from Strauss in the covers. Tough as old boots, O'Brien junior was up and running after a blast of the magic spray, although after what transpired later, police may be looking for a local witch doctor.

Porterfield brought George Dockrell on in the 12th over, but when his first over went for eight the skipper must have been wondering where to turn to next.

Pietersen hit the fifth ball of Dockrell's opening over for four to bring up his half-century off 40 deliveries, amazingly the first boundary the 18-year-old conceded in the tournament.

And the new Somerset signing would make the breakthrough in his next over when Strauss waltzed across his stumps and was bowled for 34, just 124 less than his memorable knock against India here last Sunday night.

If Strauss's dismissal was poor, then Pietersen's was downright dismal as he gave away a chance of a first ODI century since 2008 when he top-edged a sweep off the last ball of Paul Stirling's first over straight into the gloves of Niall O'Brien for 59.

That left England on 111 for two, but a 167-run partnership between Jonathan Trott (92) and Ian Bell (81) brought them up to 278 for two before a late collapse again stymied England.

Mooney claimed the wicket of Bell for 81 with the last ball of the 43rd over, thanks to a smashing catch by Paul Stirling at mid-wicket, and the North County all-rounder bowled Trott for 92 in his next over to start the rot.

They would only add 49 runs and lose six wickets late on to close on 327 for eight, with Mooney finishing with four for 63, his best bowling figures for Ireland.

Four years on from the famous victory over Pakistan in the 2007 World Cup, England's total looked a world away at that stage. We never counted on an out-of-this-world batting display from one man and a team performance that must surely rank as the greatest in Irish sporting history.

WEDNESDAY, 9 MARCH 2011

The Importance of Being Enda

Enda O'Doherty

The appointment of Enda Kenny as Taoiseach in the Dáil today will mean different things to different people. For those who voted Fine Gael, it will set the seal on an almost unprecedented political landslide. For others, it will mark the beginning of a period, of as yet unknown duration, in political exile.

There is another significant yet not much considered group, however, which holds out high hopes for Mr Kenny's period in office and, indeed, aspires, through his very occupation of that office, to a recognition that has until now been denied them. I refer, of course, to the hundreds, perhaps even thousands, of Irish people called Enda.

Penny Hancook, Petra Skokova and Melanie Labrosse of Shaktimaya Bellydance juggle fire prior to the launch of eco-lanterns at James Fort, Kinsale, marking Earth Hour. Photograph: Gerard McCarthy.

Endas know what it is to be excluded, unheard, misheard, misrepresented.

'Hello, I'm Enda.'

'John, let me introduce you to Edna.'

'Ah, no, it's "Enda" actually … well, let it pass.'

There weren't too many Endas around when I was in primary school. I think I went through the entire seven years without meeting a single other one. But younger children can often accept what is given; they do not, like adolescent males, live by mockery.

Later, it seemed I never gave my name without being greeted by the sneer: 'But that's a girl's name!' There is nothing that children like more than being like everyone else. The happiest child is, therefore, the one called John Smith, or in Ireland perhaps Patrick O'Connor.

It would seem I was called Enda in the first place as some kind of by-product of my father's deep cultural nationalism. My brothers were also gifted with names that were (then) equally obscure. The association of Patrick Pearse with St Enda's School in Ranelagh, later Rathfarnham, was certainly one factor in my christening, while the name of my mother's home parish, Killanny, or Cill Éanna (Enda's church), in Co. Louth, was another.

St Enda was a sixth-century noble and warrior from Oriel in Ulster, who renounced that life for the more demanding one of austere monasticism. He is chiefly identified with the Aran Islands, in particular Inis Mór, and is sometimes spoken of as the founder of Irish monasticism.

While the pretty stories associated with the holy Enda might have impressed some, they did not always work well, I found, on hard-bitten 13-year-olds. To add to my considerable troubles, my parents were at this time about to visit another disaster on me.

Our new house, a tall, narrow redbrick on a steep city terrace, overlooked the old city mental hospital. From our bedroom in the attic we could closely observe the patients as they were led out onto the grass to take the sun on summer days. Just the kind of thing a young lad enjoys. But the street was named after the institution which it hosted.

From then on, on the frequent roll calls and checks to which a schoolchild is subjected, I was to suffer double jeopardy. 'Name?' 'Enda O'Doherty.' Titters. 'Address?' '11, Asylum Road.' Howls of derision, copy books in the air.

There are, I suppose, two possible long-term effects of being at the receiving end of such unwelcome attention at an early age. One can become invested with a lifelong timidity and prefer to linger in the background in company one does not know; or one can choose to simply ignore all unpleasantnesses and let nothing or no one stand in the way of achieving one's goals. Congratulations, Taoiseach, on so splendidly incarnating the second way.

After adolescence, of course, everything gets easier – even for Endas. Though my name puzzled work colleagues in England, their bemusement and curiosity was not unfriendly, even if this difficult two-syllable word sometimes proved beyond them. 'Eh-, Eh-,' stuttered one friendly boss. 'Do you mind if I call you Andy?'

Over the years, I have been Andy for convenience, Ends for abbreviation, Endy for affection, Elmo and Emo in error and Elbow through plain facetiousness.

But things are getting better. There are more of us around now than ever before, the Edna thing is seldom heard in Ireland at least and now that one of us is famous and set to bestride not just the Irish but the European stage, surely there can never be any confusion or mistakes again.

But what is this I hear? Could it be the voice of Sky News's Kay Burley? 'The Irish prime minister, Edna Kenny, arrived in Brussels today. . .'

'Hi, I'm Andy.'

THURSDAY, 10 MARCH 2011

Enda Enjoys Day in the Sun after 36 Long Years

Miriam Lord

'For Ireland and each other, let us lift up our heads, turn our faces to the sun and hang out the brightest colours . . .'

Enda Kenny stood with President Mary McAleese in the State Reception Room. He had just received his seal of office.

'Taoiseach! This way please! Taoiseach!' He looked up, as if surprised, then a smile flickered across his face. He turned towards the photographers.

After 36 years in politics, his time had finally come.

Taoiseach Enda Kenny.

This was probably the most peaceful part of the day for him. He had left behind the tumult of an extraordinary few hours in Leinster House; jubilant supporters cheering as he was driven from the precincts while the new deputies and their families clogged up the corridors and laid siege to the bar and restaurant.

It was a day the like of which hasn't been seen for a very long time in Kildare Street. The sense of optimism and determination and energy was irresistible. There was a festive atmosphere and a great feeling of excitement on the plinth. Lots of talk of new dawns. Proud mammies. Family photographs. Best bib and tucker. Everyone in a good mood.

The different parties gathered in the chamber for the midday start.

Fianna Fáil's 20 TDs sat in their usual spot. But they were vastly outnumbered, looking lost where

Taoiseach Enda Kenny leaving Áras an Uachtaráin after President Mary McAleese signed the Warrant of Appointment of Taoiseach and gave him his seal of office. Photograph: Alan Betson.

once they held sway. Some looked almost embarrassed.

The members of the United Left Alliance and Sinn Féin, having marched on the Dáil, didn't so much take their seats as occupy them.

That part of the chamber to the right of the Ceann Comhairle's chair will be the Occupied Left for the foreseeable future, with a tiny Fianna Fáil enclave in the middle.

The Fine Gael benches lay empty. Then, on the hour, Enda Kenny led in his 76-strong parliamentary party. They streamed in through the doors, a stirring sight, their number flowing around the bend in the horseshoe configuration of seats.

With the addition of their Coalition partners, they made a sizeable bloc.

The House rose for the prayer.

Enda Kenny glanced up at the distinguished visitors' gallery, where his wife Fionnuala sat with their three children. She nodded back to him and smiled.

We automatically looked towards the government benches. But the power, temporarily, resided across the floor. The Fianna Fáilers looked dolefully across.

Fine Gael's Seán Barrett was elected Ceann Comhairle without a vote. It fell to the youngest member of the 31st Dáil, Simon Harris, to propose his party leader as Taoiseach.

As he spoke, Fianna Fáil's Billy Kelleher turned to a colleague on his right side, and then on his left. 'Who is he? Who is he?' he mouthed to them.

Enda's nomination was seconded by Labour TD Ciara Conway.

Then, indicating that his party is adopting a new approach to parliamentary politics, Fianna Fáil leader Micheál Martin said they would not be opposing the nomination. Sinn Féin's Gerry Adams spoke his first words in the latest parliament of which he is a member, while Joe Higgins gave a long speech, suggesting the remnants of the Fianna Fáil government should have come in 'with their brows heavily stained with penitential ash'. There then followed a series of maiden speeches from Independent deputies and members drawn from the new technical group. One after another, Independents got up to speak. Enda Kenny's wait to become Taoiseach was going to be longer than he anticipated.

Luke 'Ming' Flanagan spoke above the chatter from the surrounding benches when he said his piece. If his colleagues could not have respect for the people of Roscommon–South Leitrim, whom he represents, he would make his voice heard in other ways.

'If I don't get my spake here, I'll do it in the media.' He spoke well. One observer dubbing him 'Ming the Metaphor'. As the talk went on, the Ceann Comhairle finally called on Enda to speak.

He spoke eloquently and emotionally.

He remembered his 'late father, Henry Kenny, and my mother who is watching these proceedings today. They walk with me every step of this heart-stopping journey. For me, for Fionnuala and the children, they represent the nobility, decency and very soul of the Irish people, and because they do, their spirit is with us on this important day . . .' And the Taoiseach's voice faltered and there was a catch in his throat and everyone held their breath until he took a breath and continued on.

In the gallery, Fionnuala wiped away the tears.

Cartoon by Martyn Turner.

It was a big day for the Kenny family and a big day for Fine Gael.

When the vote was taken to elect Enda as Taoiseach, Fianna Fáil abstained. The sheer weight of numbers on the Coalition side compared to the trickle of deputies on the other was astonishing.

There was applause and a standing ovation when the result of the vote was announced and Enda could finally make his way to the Phoenix Park.

Back in Leinster House, speculation mounted over who would get what Cabinet post. When it was time for the Dáil to reconvene, we watched the hopefuls who didn't make it come into the chamber: Brian Hayes, Charlie Flanagan for Fine Gael, Róisín Shortall and Jan O'Sullivan for Labour. No sign of Ruairí Quinn though, or Leo Varadkar or Willie Penrose.

Soon to be chief whip Paul Kehoe arrived with news. Could they have another half hour before reconvening? Rumour ran rife.

The main one was that Ruairí Quinn had had a 'hissy fit' and was refusing a particular job. Others speculated that Michael Ring had chained himself to a radiator in the hope of getting a ministry.

Eventually, Enda and the Tánaiste arrived with their troupe of ministers behind them.

No real surprises. A bit same old, same old, if truth be told.

The Taoiseach assigned the portfolios. No big economic ministry for Joan Burton. She got Social Protection – a very, very important job, stressed the Labour spinners afterwards. If it was that important, why didn't it go to Brendan Howlin or Ruairí Quinn? The other female minister, Frances Fitzgerald, was given responsibility for 'children'. Why didn't Gutless Gilmore go the whole hog and create a minister for knitting, with responsibility for the kitchen sink? Joan Burton has every reason to be unhappy with her lot.

And she certainly looked it yesterday evening, as she conversed in the chamber with Jan O'Sullivan and Róisín Shortall, also overlooked.

'Women in the Labour party would get more support from an underwired bra,' snorted one of their number last night, thoroughly disgusted.

Looks like Eamon Gilmore will have a second war cabinet.

Then the Ministers all got on a bus and went off to the Áras to collect their seals. Enda Kenny was one of the last to leave the chamber, but not quite.

The last to leave were four Fianna Fáil deputies. Former minister for finance Brian Lenihan, former junior ministers Dara Calleary and Billy Kelleher, along with Timmy Dooley.

They sat in the front row of their new Opposition home. Just the four of them, alone, not saying anything, just looking across the floor at where they used to sit.

They stayed while the usher came and put the cover over the national flag. Silent and looking.

Changed times.

SATURDAY, 12 MARCH 2011

I'll Tell Him About the Most Terrifying Two Minutes of My Life

David McNeill in Tokyo, Japan

Everyone who lives in Tokyo has mentally rehearsed where they might be when the Big One strikes. Inside a public park, a modern office or safely tucked up in bed underneath a sturdy roof are the preferred locations.

Strolling around in one of the city's underground shopping districts or jostling for space in crowded old buildings are not.

I found myself in the oldest section of creaking Shinagawa Station, one of Tokyo's busiest train hubs, with my heavily pregnant partner.

The quake began not with a jolt but with an almost lazy undulating rocking motion that slowly

A massive tsunami sweeps in to engulf a residential area after a powerful earthquake in Natori in Miyagi Prefecture of north-eastern Japan. Photograph: Reuters.

built in intensity until the station's roof rattled violently and glass fell onto the platform. A woman somewhere screamed, others clung to husbands, wives or children, or ran for the exits. I watched as one station attendant sprinted back and forth across the platform, waving his hands in a blind panic and shouting at commuters to stay away from the tracks. We stood frozen to the spot, hearts thumping violently and watching the roof, praying it wouldn't fall on top of our heads.

As the shaking subsided and the terror of being buried beneath tonnes of steel and concrete faded, some people began crying. It had lasted two minutes. An almost palpable sense of relief filled the crowded station, like a single, giant sigh. Then everyone began pulling mobile phones out of bags and frantically calling family and friends to check whether they were okay – crashing the network.

'*Kowakatta*! [That was terrifying],' said one

middle-aged woman. '*Dame da to omotta* [I thought we were finished],' said another.

Hundreds of people walked around on wobbly legs, dazed, their schedules knocked off kilter, the technology that cushions life in this giant metropolis rendered almost useless. Trains had stopped, phone networks were down, the power supply flickered on and off. Some commuters began struggling to find public phones, buried in hard-to-find corners of train stations.

Others headed out into the sunlight for the long walk home. On the streets as we walked the four miles towards the Foreign Correspondents' Club in Yurakucho, hundreds of office workers crowded outside buildings wearing candy-coloured safety helmets and glancing nervously towards the sky.

Fire engines and ambulances wailed; a siren sounded continuously from the local city office.

Plumes of thick black smoke billowed from the direction of Tokyo Bay.

Salarymen crowded around TVs in the upmarket Ginza district, shaking their heads and watching live reports of a tsunami washing away cars, houses and maybe towns on the Pacific coast, a few hundred miles away.

The end of the world must look something like this, we told each other. But amid the apocalyptic scenes, dozens of people were already winding down, smoking nervously, sipping coffees in cafes and babbling to friends about what had happened.

The Foreign Correspondents' Club of Japan occupies the 20th floor of an aging office building in the heart of Tokyo's business district.

The elevators were out and we walked up the emergency stairs, stepping through fallen plaster. The quake had brought half the books in the dusty library to the floor, but at the reception centre the staff, as usual, were professionalism personified. Nobody could remember a quake like it, as there was nobody old enough. My exhausted partner was given a hastily made-up bed to lie down on and I looked at her, carrying our unborn half-Japanese son, and wondered how I would tell him about this day, and what were the most terrifying two minutes of my life.

MONDAY, 14 MARCH 2011

'I Can Never Feel Safe in That Town'

David McNeill in Minamisanriku, Japan

It was once a family house. Mum would have cooked dinner on the kitchen stove and children might have played video games in the front room, facing the Pacific Ocean. Now all that is left is its bare concrete base and a few scattered belongings: the shreds of a kimono and a child's schoolbag.

Like almost everything else in this town of 17,666 people, it was washed into the sea.

'The water was 10 m (33 ft) high,' says Koichi Tsuto, who watched in horror from the surrounding mountains as last Friday's tsunami roared into Minamisanriku and took away everything he had in a giant muddy deluge.

'It was like a mountain of water,' he says, his eyes widening. Beside him, his wife, Fujiko, looks shattered, defeated. They had come to see if there was anything left but have gone away again empty-handed.

The tsunami has left this town in ruins, smashing wooden houses into matchsticks, twisting metal girders like strips of liquorice.

Cars were pushed, along with everything else, more than 2 km inland before piling to a muddy stop.

Gas cookers, children's toys, photograph albums and trucks are deposited all along the tsunami's muddy trail – and 10,000 people have simply vanished.

'I've come to look for my mother and father,' says Yuki Sugawara (25), who took two days to reach this town from Sendai city, about 50 km away.

His ruined home town is almost completely silent apart from the caw of crows and the distant hiss of the sea that erupted with such terrible, unexpected violence two days ago.

His friend from schooldays Makoto Ishida (25) is from the same town.

'I haven't been able to contact my mother or grandmother,' he says. 'I just came to see what's left.'

From the mountains that ring this once picturesque farming and tourist town, the devastation is almost total. A house, tottering on its side, somehow survived the deluge.

The post office, no doubt bustling with staff and pensioners on Friday afternoon, is recognisable only by its battered sign.

A car lies on its back in a landscape of still-smouldering steel and shattered wood. Power lines and telephone cables have disappeared.

Houses burn, as others are swept away by the tsunami that followed the earthquake off the coast of Japan.
Photograph: Reuters.

Underneath, the rescue workers say there may be bodies, those that have not been carried into the Pacific.

In one of the world's richest countries, it is a shocking sight: a once thriving town flattened into the ground, its modern infrastructure stripped bare, its people – office workers, students and farmers – reduced to walking in search of homes that are no longer there.

Minamisanriku, a town of 17,000 people, has effectively ceased to exist.

Those of its population that have survived huddle around gas heaters in a community centre about 3 km from the sea.

There is no TV or radio. A noisy generator keeps the lights on.

News comes with the papers delivered late every morning, with their thick black headlines bearing news of the latest catastrophe from the rest of the country.

Tomorrow, Tokyo will lose power for the entire day, inevitably bringing back terrible memories of the Second World War to a generation who thought such sights were gone forever.

'We didn't hear about the nuclear plant explosion till today,' says Eiko Chiba, who huddles beside her daughter on a futon. 'It's terrifying. All we can do is hope that the people in charge are doing their best.'

Ms Chiba was working in an office a few kilometres inland when the tsunami struck.

She and her friends screamed when they felt the earthquake, which was followed by a tsunami warning.

'We went up on top of the building to watch the water. It bulged at the side of the buildings then rushed in and submerged all the houses. Then it took them away.'

Her husband, a truck driver, was in Tokyo when the earthquake struck.

'I talked to him on his cellphone, but he's stuck in the city.'

With the dark and cold descending, community spokesman Jin Sasaki says the search for bodies has been called off and would begin again tomorrow.

'I've found 13 so far,' he adds. 'When we discover one, we give it to the family or take it to the local temple.'

He has heard some of what is going on in Sendai, the prefectural capital, where officials are overwhelmed searching for 115,000 missing people in this one region alone.

More than 700 people shelter in what has become a makeshift survivor centre in the prefectural offices, lying on blankets and futons in the halls and offices.

Many are from nearby Iwate prefecture, where the earthquake reportedly hit hardest.

'Most people are trying to find their families,' says government spokesman Moto Otsuki. 'Phones aren't working.'

The survivors scan bulletin boards in the prefectural office for news of their loved ones. Some will be fortunate.

Takehiro Abe is walking back from Minamisanriku on rail tracks that until last week ferried trains around the picture-postcard coast.

'I learned that my father, mother and younger brother are all safe in a refugee centre,' he says.

'I just went down to see our house, to check if anything is left, but it's completely gone. We'll have to build somewhere else – we can't come here.'

The extent of the destruction caused by the Japanese tsunami is clearly visible in the town of Minamisanriku. Photograph: AP Photo/Kyodo News.

A view of Croagh Patrick near Westport in Co. Mayo. Photograph: Michael McLaughlin.

Somewhere in the distance, a siren wails, warning of yet another aftershock and tsunami.

The few people still walking around in the dusk slowly head back towards the safety of high ground, away from the sea. *What else can the sea do to them?* they seem to be asking.

Japan is aging, its economy past its peak, its government struggling with huge debt.

How will it pay for the recovery of towns like Minamisanriku, for the hundreds of communities all along this coast struck by last week's awful events?

'Right now, we're just thinking of tomorrow and saving people,' says Jin Sasaki, 'but however long it takes, we will rebuild. People are depending on us to bring the town back.'

But Ms Chiba, huddling with her daughter and waiting for her husband to come home, will not be among the rebuilders.

'I could never go back. I can't even think about it. I can never feel safe in that town now.'

MONDAY, 21 MARCH 2011

A Grand Slap Hits the Spot

Gerry Thornley

Not so much the Grand Slam, more the Grand Slap. Slams don't come easily of course, and nothing underlined that more than Ireland's sequence of hard-earned wins in 2009. But, frankly, Saturday's 24–8 overturning of the Chariot merely underlined what a travesty it would have been if England had emulated the class of '03.

What it perhaps also demonstrated is that if any team should have emulated previous Slam winners, it was Ireland. Retaining many of the core elements of their class of '09, and adding to it, this performance finally showed what this team is capable of.

Cian Healy and Tommy Bowe celebrate after the winger scored Ireland's opening try in their 24–8 victory over England in the final round of matches in the Six Nations Championship at the Aviva Stadium in Dublin. Photograph: James Crombie/Inpho.

It was probably the performance of the 2011 Six Nations, and if Ireland had sustained this kind of intensity, focus and heads-up rugby in their previous four performances, they'd have walked it.

It was too late to win the championship, but, on a key day for head coach, management and squad, it came just in the nick of time in terms of this team's trek to the World Cup. Not alone does it send the players back to their provinces with a feel-good factor, it provides a template for the year.

As the rain teemed down, Ronan O'Gara pinned down a beaten England and 'The Fields' echoed around a throbbing Aviva on a night that had echoes of Croke Park four years ago.

And if the team were the talk of the supporters, apparently the supporters were the talk of the team. They're not robots, they're human, and the Irish

players responded to the vocal and colourful home crowd in kind.

This being a seventh win in eight over them, maybe team and crowd alike should pretend England are the opposition every week.

What was different about this performance, aside from the reduced error and penalty counts, was the intensity they brought to their game – ferocious tackling, rucking/wrestling and carrying – and a higher tempo and willingness to simply have a go. There were tap penalties, offloads and even counter-attacking.

Ireland had to run at England and make it less of a structured, set-piece game. Jonny Sexton's quick tap deep inside his half just two minutes in set that tempo as much as anything, and was carried on by some superb offloading – Jamie Heaslip to the supporting Tommy Bowe being a case in point.

When Sexton is on his game like this there's a case for hailing him as the best outhalf in Europe: he ticked all the boxes – passing, running, tackling and kicking – and was assured and ambitious in everything he did.

Then to have O'Gara to open his box of tricks as well underlines Declan Kidney's belief that Ireland really are blessed to have the two of them.

'It was always in there, but it was a balance between trying to get a lid on the fear factor and trying to lower the anxiety levels,' said the coach.

Facing a point of no return, whatever was said in camp, Ireland looked liberated. And whatever buttons Brian O'Driscoll and Paul O'Connell pressed in the build-up to the game, they were the right ones.

'There was nothing they did out there that surprised me,' said Kidney. 'We had better field position, we were a bit more patient and played with a bit more ball, until the game went to 24–3. Then we got a little bit loose and gave them balls inside our half and let them come back into it. It is thin margins. Today went our way; other days didn't.'

Who'd be a coach?

'We're learning,' added Kidney when asked about Ireland's game-plan. 'It's based on trusting the players to make decisions, and we're getting better all the time at making the decisions so allowing us to vary our play. There is a lot of talk about what is the game-plan; the game-plan is about making the right decisions out on the pitch.

'We're not physically strong like South Africa, where we can go and motor over teams. We have a different skill set to some of the other teams and I have a belief in Irish lads that they are fairly intelligent. Sometimes there is a growing process in making the right calls. Have we got it wrong in the

Ireland's Jamie Heaslip on the receiving end of some close attention from England's Simon Shaw.
Photograph: Dan Sheridan/Inpho.

past? We have. Are we getting better at it? We are. Have we a bit more to go? Yes.'

Although Ireland started 20 players in this championship – only one more than the Slam year – Kidney maintained that they have a 'broader base' now. 'We can cope with a few bangs and knocks. We need match practice to get us right for the World Cup, and that is where the four matches in August are important.'

It was a non-vintage Six Nations for many, especially compared to the relatively free-flowing Super-15, but Kidney maintained: 'It is a tough championship. It's played in different weather conditions, and each team presents a different type of defensive effort. You have to attack differently from week to week.

'I'd be happy to be involved in my rugby in the Northern Hemisphere, because I think you look at the Heineken Cup matches and you look at the Six Nations: no two of them are alike. Sometimes, alright, you can get the odd dour game, but I'd hate to go to something that looks the same every week.'

And it's on days like this you are entitled to believe no player in the world game has been more enduringly excellent over the last dozen years than O'Driscoll, defensively superb in tandem with Gordon D'Arcy, and who produced a trademark run as support trailer and left-handed pick-up for his record-breaking 25th championship try.

'Personally I'd be delighted for him,' said Kidney. 'I know he doesn't feed into the accolade, but he has been a very good captain over some difficult matches in the last 12 months. He has stayed steadfast to the team and he has left them in no doubt what this team means to him. Some of the players have fed off that.'

Magnificent for 80 minutes, O'Driscoll was pitch-perfect to the end, getting the balance right in insisting the team bade farewell from the halfway line when they returned from the dressing-room, rather than conduct an inappropriate lap of honour.

An affectionate moment as a mother giraffe shows off her new arrival at Fota Wildlife Park. The baby male was born on 11 March to Sapphire and Tadhg, bringing the Fota giraffe herd to nine. Photograph: Neil Danton.

He's not quite chopped liver yet. And, the two being inextricably linked, neither are Ireland.

My favourite Six Nations try – Brian O'Driscoll

On the weekend he set a Six Nations record with his 25th try, the Irish captain names his favourite score.

'If I had to pick one try in terms of a favourite from the 25 I've scored in the Six Nations, it would be the one against France at Lansdowne Road in 2005. We lost the match, but at the time in the game we really needed a score and so from that perspective there was a certain satisfaction.

'It started with a break in midfield, a hand-off on Freddie Michalak and then getting through the

Eddie Conlon (centre) chairs a United Left Alliance press conference in Dublin, at which the group responded to the programme for government. Also present were United Left Alliance TDs Joe Higgins (Socialist Party), Joan Collins (People Before Profit), Clare Daly (SP), Richard Boyd Barrett (PBP) and Paddy Healy, representing his brother Séamus Healy (Workers and Unemployed Action Group). Photograph: Brenda Fitzsimons.

gap. Cedric Heymans was covering across and I managed to step inside him and touch down under the posts.

'But generally I'm more concerned about the effect of the score in terms of the game than whether it looks good. I suppose that's why I'd choose the tries against England and Wales in the Grand Slam season as scores which I enjoyed the most. They were important to the team, and while they wouldn't win any beauty contests their impact means far more to me in the context of any tries I might score.

'You've also got to remember that for me to score a try so many other people are doing the groundwork, and that's something I'm acutely aware of. It's the effect a try has rather than who scored it that means more to a team.

'When your career is finished you can look back on individual records and maybe take some pleasure, but I hope I have a bit left in me so I won't dwell on it.

'You win and lose as a team and we'll very much enjoy this win as a team.'

WEDNESDAY, 23 MARCH 2011

A Damning Indictment of Lowry and O'Brien

Colm Keena

The voluminous report published yesterday by Mr Justice Michael Moriarty constitutes a damning indictment of former minister Michael Lowry and businessman Denis O'Brien, as well as a number of their associates who sought to protect them from the tribunal's inquiries.

While it is a report filled with convoluted detail and a large cast, the core issues and key findings are simple:

Michael Lowry 'secured the winning' of the 1995 competition for the State's second mobile phone licence for O'Brien's Esat Digifone.

Denis O'Brien made a number of payments to Lowry including one, for £147,000 in July 1996, when he was still a senior government minister.

The £147,000 payment went from an account of O'Brien's in Dublin to the Isle of Man to Jersey and back to the Isle of Man, where Lowry opened an account with Irish Nationwide to receive the money.

O'Brien got the money from the very first tranche of funds he received after he successfully completed a placement in the US that was to finance his Esat project.

The killer blow in the report comes on page 1,056. The High Court judge says the payments and other benefits conveyed to Lowry by O'Brien were 'demonstrably referable to the acts and conduct of Mr Lowry in regard to the [licence] process, that inured to the benefit of Mr O'Brien's winning consortium, Esat Digifone'.

The report was released unexpectedly by the tribunal, which posted it on its website. O'Brien had spent the night in Ashford Castle in Co. Mayo, where he had attended a party for more than 100 managers of his successful Digicel group, which is based in the Caribbean. He left the hotel to come to Dublin for a series of media interviews about the report. Its findings will travel swiftly around the Caribbean.

In an interview with this reporter yesterday evening, O'Brien insisted he never sought to make a payment to Lowry and that his evidence to the tribunal was the truth. Lowry was out of the country yesterday but rejected the tribunal findings, asserting they were 'fundamentally flawed'.

Michael Lowry at the Davenport Hotel in Dublin after the damning Moriarty tribunal verdict against him. Photograph: Dara Mac Dónaill.

Cartoon by Martyn Turner.

But the judge did not accept the evidence of O'Brien and Lowry. Furthermore, he said there were sustained efforts to mislead the tribunal and to prevent it learning about the financial connections between Lowry and O'Brien. These included the altering of documents by people associated with O'Brien and Lowry, documents that were then submitted to the tribunal. Financial pressure was put on O'Brien by an Omagh-based man called Kevin Phelan who, the judge says, knew that the tribunal had been supplied with altered documents.

The judge said he was satisfied that a payment of £150,000 sterling to Phelan in August 2002 by one of O'Brien's companies, Westferry, was primarily intended to ensure that Phelan would not undermine the false information that had been given to the tribunal. He said Lowry's accountant, Denis O'Connor, was involved in these dealings with Phelan.

All in all, it is a pretty sorry picture. Citizens can take some succour from the fact that Lowry gained nothing. The £147,000 payment was returned by Lowry on the date in February 1997 when the McCracken (Dunnes Payments) tribunal was established. The financial assistance he received towards buying property in Mansfield and Cheadle did not lead to any profit, though at one stage Lowry came close to gaining more than £1 million sterling.

The cost of the Moriarty tribunal may exceed a quarter of a billion euro. A large part of that was due to the misleading testimony given to the tribunal as it sought to pry into links between Lowry and O'Brien. Lowry, who topped the poll in Tipperary North at the recent election with over 14,000 first preference votes, is turning out to be one of the most expensive Irish public representatives ever elected.

The second key aspect of the Moriarty report concerns the Esat licence. The evidence in relation to the findings in this regard was less straightforward than the money-trail evidence and the associated attempts to mislead the tribunal.

Mr Justice Moriarty found that 'Lowry secured the winning of the competition for Esat Digifone'. He listed a series of events where the then minister interfered in a process that was meant to be run by civil servants. When doing so he wrote that 'each of these elements of Mr Lowry's insidious and pervasive influence on the process will now be addressed'.

The judge itemised instances where Lowry interfered in the process. Evidence supporting these findings has been heard. However, to give these events impact, Mr Justice Moriarty all but requires that the evidence given over a number of days by a Danish consultant, Michael Andersen, is dismissed.

Andersen has taken part in more than 200 licence competitions around the world, and is an acknowledged expert. He was the lead consultant to the competition won by Esat and his evidence was that the bid deserved to win. He also said that, given his experience and the fact that the civil servants involved had never run such a process before, he would have noticed instantly if there had been an attempt to favour any particular candidate.

Andersen's evidence was not challenged when he was in the witness box. All of the civil servants involved have said they were not 'overborne' in any way by Lowry.

In relation to the famous meeting between O'Brien and Lowry in Hartigan's pub on Dublin's Leeson Street in September 1995, Mr Justice Moriarty was satisfied that at the meeting Lowry conveyed to O'Brien information he had been given by the civil servant chairing the group that was then involved in assessing the licence bids. Lowry told O'Brien that the assessors had worries about Esat's finances, the judge found.

O'Brien then told Lowry that there was a proposition that Dermot Desmond might join the

A baby gorilla and his mother, Lena, in Dublin Zoo. Keepers were unable to identify the baby's gender for two weeks because his mother held him so tightly. Photograph: Conor Healy.

Esat consortium and underwrite O'Brien's finances. 'Mr Lowry provided comfort to Mr O'Brien' that notification of this to the project chairman, in breach of the competition's rules, would not adversely impact on Esat's prospects.

Desmond became involved, this was notified to the project chairman, but the letter was returned as the closing date for submissions had passed.

Desmond became a 20 per cent shareholder in Esat. He had not been mentioned in the original bid for the licence. Desmond made in excess of £100 million from his involvement.

In a statement last night, Dermot Desmond said all the civil servants involved had given evidence to the effect that there had been no political interference in the licence process. 'In the absence of any political interference in the adjudication process, any interactions which may or may not have taken place between Denis O'Brien and Michael Lowry are just side shows to the central issue of the award of the licence,' he said.

It has been a very expensive side show.

MONDAY, 4 APRIL 2011

The Leaving of Charlestown

Carl O'Brien

Sometimes, as he sits at the departure gate of Ireland West Airport near Knock, Michael wonders how his life changed so quickly. Every lunchtime on Sunday he gets on Ryanair flight FR806 to Stansted. The weekdays are a blur of long, punishing hours working as a construction manager at a site on the outskirts of London.

Then on Fridays he rushes home to Mayo to snatch a few hours with his wife and son. All too quickly, Sunday morning arrives and it begins all over again.

'It's the only option – this is the way the hammer has fallen,' says Michael (50), who has been making the weekly commute to the UK for the past year. 'I have a child who's eight. Every day he's developing and you're missing out on those crucial years. It puts enormous pressure on the family unit and your relationships. For me, the airport is an umbilical cord. It's the only way I can see my wife and son.'

Michael is not alone. On a Sunday afternoon at the departures gate, there are dozens of other commuting emigrants waiting to head back to England or further afield. Around a third of those on today's flights are commuters: carpenters, builders, engineers, therapists, computer programmers. The atmosphere is sombre, with many having said goodbye to their partners and children earlier in the morning. Many are middle-aged parents who have no choice but to leave their families to keep up mortgage payments or cover the bills. They are a new kind of displaced emigrant, caught between making a living in one country and raising their families in another.

Ross Cameron (31) is another waiting to head back to work. He's married with two children aged three and five. He's been commuting to London each week since his bathroom supply company folded almost a year ago. He misses his family terribly.

'You get home at midnight on a Friday and the kids are asleep. You don't have a drink because you want to be up in time for them in the morning. You can't head out on Saturday night with your wife because you're off to the airport first thing on Sunday. There's no downtime. The kids are adaptable, though: they get used to seeing their dad for 24 hours a week.'

George, in his late fifties, travels further still. He's on his way to Poland, via Stansted, where he works at a language school. He comes back every fortnight.

'Skype makes a big difference,' he says. 'My wife is at home and I have teenage daughters. When you can see them, it helps. It's not ideal at all. It just makes me angry to think that it has come to this.'

But it's not all downbeat. Karen Burke (25) is different from most. She's a newly qualified speech and language therapist and is heading to London for good to take up her first job. Unemployed for the past year, she's delighted to be heading abroad.

'I've been out of work since last June, which has been rubbish,' she says. 'But I'm lucky – I'm one of a handful out of 35 graduates to get jobs, and we're all in England. I've lots of friends over there. It's all very rushed – I start tomorrow at 9 a.m.'

Three miles down the road is Charlestown, Co. Mayo. Locals joke that the airport should be named after the town, given that it's far closer than Knock. It's a compact town with small retailers and wide, well-planned streets.

Charlestown, Co. Mayo, 2011. Photograph: Keith Heneghan.

As you pass the remains of a disused railway platform off the main street, you suddenly, inexplicably, cross the border into Bellaghy, Co. Sligo. Both towns lie side-by-side, the legacy of a historic grudge between two landowners.

The story goes that during the 1840s, Lord Knox, who owned the land on the Sligo side of the border, insulted Charles Strickland, the agent of the landowner on the Mayo side. Strickland's revenge was to build a brand new town cheek-by-jowl with Bellaghy, complete with a rival market and, more importantly, dozens of pubs with liberal closing times. Bellaghy declined and Charlestown thrived.

Today, Charlestown is a town of around 900 people. It's much quieter since the recent bypass diverted traffic from Dublin and Castlebar. But there's another reason the town is ghostly quiet, especially in the evenings. Unemployment and lack of job prospects mean people are leaving.

It's nothing new to these parts. The town's hinterland was ravaged by depopulation between the 1940s and 1960s and again in the 1980s. In his influential series for *The Irish Times* in 1967, 'No One Shouted Stop!', John Healy wrote of how the drip-feed of young people away from Charlestown was strangling it.

'Morning after morning in the 1940s they went in droves like cattle,' he wrote. 'There were young boys and girls, young men and women and, too often, they had no education . . . no one got mad for them because they weren't going to make money and what was here for them but the bog?'

When the boom arrived in the late 1990s, many felt the town had finally turned a corner. Many emigrants came home. Several new housing estates sprouted up around town. The Government even pledged to relocate the Department of

Community, Rural and Gaeltacht Affairs to the area. Emigration, it seemed, was a thing of the past.

Today, the word is back on everyone's lips. There are no official figures yet – census data predates the downturn – but if anecdotal evidence is anything to go by, the numbers heading abroad are growing by the day.

Healy's Café Bar on the main street, a popular haunt for young people in the area, has the hallmarks of a place furnished during the boom: dark timber floors, spot lights, tastefully decorated toilets. Barely a day goes by without someone announcing that they're leaving. Proprietor John Healy (no relation to the journalist John Healy) began to notice the phenomenon of 'emigration parties' towards the end of 2009. They're still happening.

'I have one booked in for next week,' he says. 'There was another where the lads sold a van, did an auction of the tools and had people over for the "funeral". Then they were out the door. Gone. Not so long ago, this place was buzzing. At 8 p.m. on a Saturday evening, you might have 150 young people here and they'd stay drinking till 2 a.m. That's all changed.'

Brian Colleran (33) is one of many young people from the town considering his future. He's reduced to doing a bit of part-time work on a farm, as well as working as a doorman on weekends. It can be lonely, he confides, seeing your circle of friends disappear.

'I look at lots of friends who've gone off. You see Facebook pictures of them at the beach and

Rory McIlroy shows his frustration on the 13th hole during the final round of the Masters Golf Tournament in Augusta, Georgia. Photograph: Matt Slocum/AP.

you think they're having a great time, and you must be missing out,' he says. 'You see them here one week. And the next they're booking a flight to Australia. It's sad, because you see less and less of your own age group.'

Over on the edge of town, the loss of young people is a growing concern at Charlestown Sarsfield GAA club. As a Monday night training session gets underway, trainer Steve Healy admits he is worried about the coming months.

'As of now, we've only lost a few players to places like England or Australia, so we're not that badly hit yet,' he says. 'But lots of our players are in their final year in college and finishing construction-related courses. You wonder what kind of work will be around for them. How long will they stay here? We don't know. You have to say it doesn't look good.'

Over at the grounds of the local soccer club, it's also a concern. About a third of the senior team is gone. Some of it is down to lads heading abroad, but more of it is down to players not being able to afford the day-to-day cost of training and playing.

'It's very sad,' says trainer Martin Hopkins. 'But we've just got to keep going and try to find new players.' Even with the numbers leaving, some are quick to point out that it's still no comparison to the black days of mass emigration.

Fr Thomas Johnson, the town's parish priest, remembers the 1950s, when a GAA team would start off training in the summer with a full squad, but by autumn they wouldn't have enough players to field a team.

'It's an issue, yes, but I don't think it bears comparison to those days,' he says. 'There is still work, there are lots of families. The number of children being baptised in recent years is holding steady, which is another plus.'

Emigration is just one side of how the economic downturn is affecting the town. The collateral damage caused by unemployment and a slump in retail is potentially catastrophic for Charlestown and other towns in the region.

Henry's, which sells men's clothes, is a simple shop. There are a few shelves with old-fashioned jumpers on one side; on the other side are jeans and shirts aimed at younger men. Trade isn't just slow – it's almost non-existent. On some days there are no customers at all. On a good day, there are three or four purchases. Owner Jarlath Henry spends most of the day out back doing Sudoku puzzles or listening to the radio. 'Sales are diabolical,' he says. 'How long can I keep going? To tell the truth, I'm looking for a job. I'd be gone in a flash. It's costing me to keep this place open. I've maybe another month or two.' As we speak, a stockist stops out front in a van, looking to sell clothes, but Henry waves him on.

His shop is on Church Street, one of the three main roads into the town. He points out the closed pubs and grocery shops on the surrounding streets. Rates, he says, were simply too high for many of them to keep going.

Over on the main street, Joe Mahon is feeling the pinch. His Spar is the largest shop in town and is coping with both the recession and competition from large out-of-town supermarkets. Most of his ire is directed at planning authorities. Tesco, which opened in neighbouring Swinford, had a dramatic impact in drawing trade away from Charlestown since it opened last year, he says.

'It just sucks trade away from the surrounding towns. It might employ 100 people, but it takes them away from other areas. What does that achieve? Nothing. And most of the profits go back to Britain,' he says.

Not everyone is gloomy about the town's prospects. In sharp contrast, George Cregg, a salesman and chair of the town's chamber of commerce, is a voice of relentless optimism. A returned emigrant from the US, he retains that country's can-do approach to business. His wife runs the Market Café.

'Since the bypass we've doubled in trade,' he says. 'Now, people who pass through are more likely to stop off. Before, they were always on the go and they wouldn't stop.'

His own business – delivering office supplies to companies across the region – is also thriving. 'I'm positive. If we're negative with customers, it just adds to the negativity. We have to be more positive. There is a great quality of life. We have a new government now, we should have an amnesty on negativity. It's time to get rid of the baggage we had and get on with things. We shouldn't be stuck in a rut.'

So what does the future hold for a place like Charlestown? Most agree the town is in a far better position than it was in the late 1960s, with better standards of education, a bigger population and better infrastructure. If the economy does rebound, then places like Charlestown should be in a good position to benefit.

But there are other, more immediate concerns. The town's only secondary school faces an uncertain future. The Marist Sisters announced recently that they plan to withdraw their patronage of the school within three years. If no alternative patron is found, more than 200 students will need to find alternative schools. Town leaders, though, are hopeful it won't come to that.

John Healy's brother Gerry feels prospects for Charlestown are as bad as they were in the 1950s or the 1980s. 'I lived through those recessions – but they were nothing like this,' he says. 'Then, people were more self-sufficient and had their own food. They didn't have the personal debt people have today. These young fellas, who had their vans with their names on the side of them, are gone. I don't see them coming back.'

Most aren't quite as negative. Over the longer term, local leaders say fostering and supporting small businesses will be vital to creating sustainable communities.

'We seem to be making it as hard as possible for businesses in small-town Ireland that are struggling to survive,' says local Sinn Féin councillor Gerry Murray. 'We have high rates, high energy costs. We need to tackle that. I don't think the

Government realises the scale of the problem at local level.'

There is no shortage of bright ideas to breathe new life into this part of rural Ireland. Just down the road at Ireland West Airport, the chairman, Liam Scollan, has ambitious plans to develop an industrial park in the area. It has the potential, he says, to create 300 jobs over a five-year period in tourism, renewable energy and IT.

'We've been very disappointed at the response of the Government,' he says. 'For two years, we've had definitive proposals to create these jobs. But it's as if we've been telling them about paint drying.'

Foreign direct investment in the region has been a positive, he says, but it's hardly sustainable and few have a genuine commitment to the country.

'If you look back, we were bailed out by Europe in the 1980s. We were bailed out by American multinational investment in the 1990s, and now we've been bailed out by the EU and IMF,' Scollan says. 'We need to create wealth of our own, rather than become fodder for overseas investors.'

Optimists such as George Cregg acknowledge the scale of the problem – his son will likely emigrate after college – but he feels the future will be bright if the right decisions are made and entrepreneurs are encouraged.

'I think back in the 1960s, there was a black cloud over this area. People were emigrating straight out of school. Now it's different. We're better educated. We're a different breed of people. I think we're a population which will take a chance and give it the best shot. Those people leaving now? We desperately need them to come back. I've no doubt that, in time, they will.'

To see what hard work and vision can achieve in a town like Charlestown, you head out of the town until a sprawling manufacturing plant appears on the town's outskirts.

Thirty years ago, this was a glorified shed. Tom Grady mortgaged his small farm and set up a joinery workshop. Today, Grady Joinery is a large business that produces A-rated windows and doors, which up to recently could only be imported.

At its height it employed 300 people, though numbers reduced to around half that since the downturn. But things are beginning to look up once again. Just last week, the company advertised to fill some vacancies in quality assurance and sales.

'In the town things are difficult,' says Tom's son, Arthur Grady. 'But unlike the last recession, there are good prospects. There's a vibrant airport within miles of here, much improved road network and broadband, which makes it possible for small businesses to offer their services to a wider customer base, thus grow and create employment.'

It's a long way from the scenes in Charlestown depicted by journalist John Healy, who was horrified at the complacency and apathy of the political establishment as thousands of his contemporaries emigrated in the late 1960s.

'There is in Charlestown of 1967,' wrote Healy, 'a savage echo of Synge's world, for you can stand above the town on the straggling plantation and echo the words of Maura in *Riders to the Sea*: "They're all gone now and there isn't anything more the sea can do to me."'

The series – and the resulting book, published as *Death of an Irish Town* – didn't go down well with locals who objected to the notion that their town was dying. Healy's brother Gerry, who still lives in the town, joked that he couldn't get a drink in Charlestown for six months.

Retired history professor and Mayo man, Prof. Seamus Ó Catháin, is an admirer of Healy's work, but feels the extent of emigration was exaggerated. 'The area did suffer. But remember, the GAA team of "ghosts" he wrote about went on to win the county championship in 1972. And it was trained by his nephew!' he says. 'The late 1960s were perhaps the nadir, but it grew during the 1970s. Between the 1980s and 2000, the town grew by 20 per cent. In that sense, the story of Charlestown is a positive one.'

THURSDAY, 7 APRIL 2011

Symbolism Potent as Local GAA Club Members Pass Coffin to Police Officers

Gerry Moriarty

The funeral of Constable Ronan Kerr was rich in symbolism, expressive of a society in transformation and prepared to break more of the chains of the past, powerful in its humanity and potent, too, in its denunciation of a terrible act. On Sunday, Constable Kerr's stalwart mother Nuala called on everyone to 'stand up and be counted' against the murder of her son – and that is what was manifest in Beragh yesterday.

You could tell the Protestants and the Catholics standing together outside the Church of the Immaculate Conception in the little Tyrone village. As family members took the coffin from senior members of the GAA, the Catholics blessed themselves, the Protestants bowed their heads – both acts of solidarity, sadness and respect.

The coffin, with the officer's cap and gloves on top, had just been shouldered past a guard of honour in the church grounds: two loose intermingled lines of green-uniformed colleagues of the murdered man, of red-jerseyed members of the local GAA club, the Beragh Red Knights – of which Ronan Kerr was a proud member – and of local Protestant and Catholic schoolchildren.

Also, there were the DUP First Minister Peter Robinson, breaking with a rigid doctrinal tradition to attend his first Mass, Sinn Féin Deputy First Minister Martin McGuinness, other unionist and nationalist leaders, and the four main Church leaders.

There too were Enda Kenny, the first Taoiseach to attend the funeral of a murdered

Family members carry the coffin of PSNI Constable Ronan Kerr at the Church of the Immaculate Conception in Beragh, Co. Tyrone. Photograph: Dara Mac Dónaill.

Northern Ireland police officer; Fianna Fáil leader Micheál Martin; Northern Secretary Owen Paterson; Justice Ministers from the North and South, David Ford and Alan Shatter; PSNI chief constable Matt Baggott and Garda Commissioner Martin Callinan.

Minutes earlier, Nuala Kerr and her children Cathair, Dairine and Aaron led hundreds of mourners who followed the hearse through the main street of Beragh to the church.

They managed to hold themselves emotionally together – but only just, you could see.

On the street, members of the local GAA club took the first lift of the coffin, passing on the coffin to police officers who trained and graduated with Kerr or worked in his squad in Enniskillen.

It was lost on no one that here were two forces who in the past deeply distrusted each other – as exemplified by the GAA's previous refusal to allow PSNI officers to join the organisation.

Another healing moment was reinforced when the PSNI pallbearers passed on the third lift to senior GAA figures, including Tyrone manager Mickey Harte, county team captain Brian Dooher, GAA president Christy Cooney and the Ulster GAA president Aogán Ó Fearghail.

The planning was careful, the imagery was intentional: a resolute message was being sent to people who may or may not listen.

Here was a society and an island united against a cruel murder and prepared to break with some outmoded canons to underscore that point.

In the church, Kerr's brother Aaron, with breaking voice, recited a short poem about his beloved brother, saying that the 'perfect words' escaped him to express his love for Ronan.

A book of condolence for Constable Ronan Kerr in Omagh, Co. Tyrone. Photograph: Jeff J. Mitchell/Getty Images.

Cardinal Seán Brady spoke strongly. Let no one be deceived by those 'who say that Ireland will be united or the union made more secure by war', he said. 'They are wrong. It is an illusion.'

Outside the church Paddy Joe McClean, a civil rights activist who was interned both in the 1950s and 1970s, at 78, and with all his opposition to violence and all his experience of bad times, saw some hope in the day of mourning and of people standing in solidarity.

'The right words are being spoken,' he said, 'and the so-called dissidents are going nowhere.'

SATURDAY, 9 APRIL 2011

Ireland's Lack of Civic Morality Grounded in Our History

Garret FitzGerald

A factor common to a whole range of recent Irish economic and financial failures seems to have been a striking absence of a sense of civic responsibility throughout our entire society.

The civic morality that underlies the social cohesion of many democratic societies, especially in northern Europe, has been absent in Ireland for some time.

I want to suggest that the source of this phenomenon is to be found in our history, which has been different from that of the remainder of northern Europe.

First of all, in most of northern Europe since the 17th century rulers and ruled within each state have generally shared the same faith and culture. However, most Irish people did not have that advantage, and this cultural and religious alienation from our rulers had a profound effect on the psychology of most Irish people.

We also remained, until quite recently, a largely agricultural country. By contrast, the United Kingdom pioneered the industrial revolution, which then spread to the rest of northern Europe – except to the area which became the Irish State.

As a result, Ireland did not experience the modernisation in the 19th and early 20th centuries that was the common lot of most of the rest of this area.

Moreover, for several centuries public administration of the island, a large part of its commercial life, and the owners of 95 per cent of its land, were all alien to the mass of the Irish people. For the rest, we remained a predominately peasant society.

Finally, it was only at the very end of the 19th century that a native democratic process was introduced. It was confined at first to the level of local administration, and was largely inefficient and in some important respects financially corrupt.

In such a society it is not to be expected that the alienated majority would develop the kind of strong civic sense which was able to emerge in other parts of northern Europe.

In Ireland a strong civic sense did exist – but mainly amongst Protestants and especially Anglicans.

And despite the disproportionate role awarded to the Protestant minority in the new State, that group later ceased to play a significant role in the governance of independent Ireland.

Ireland's popular Catholic Church, in opposition to the dominance of a ruling Irish minority of another faith and then to aspects of an alien UK system of government, could not be expected to instil much respect for public authority amongst the bulk of the population.

One might have hoped that all this would change with independence. Yet the Irish Catholic Church sought instead to bend the new State to its purpose, relying upon the strong personal faith of members of successive governments to secure its objectives. And it succeeded – up to a point. It secured censorship of books and films, and was successful in having contraception banned.

However, when in 1929 the Catholic hierarchy challenged the non-denominational provisions

Cartoon by Martyn Turner.

of our constitution by attempting to persuade the government to confine the appointment of dispensary doctors to Roman Catholics, it was outwitted by W.T. Cosgrave. He told the hierarchy that as guardian of a non-denominational constitution he could not implement their proposal and would have to resign from office if their proposal were to be pressed. The request was dropped.

Then in 1937, in drawing up his new Constitution, de Valera refused to make Ireland formally a Catholic state, despite Vatican pressure.

This underlying stand-off between church and state seems to have inhibited the Irish Catholic Church from advocating civic responsibility.

Instead much of its energy was concentrated on aspects of sexual morality – an area where it eventually lost credibility not only with the younger generation but with the older one as well.

The consequences of all this have been that a society with an educational system almost exclusively in the hands of the Catholic Church has been left with virtually no tradition of, or training in, civic morality or civic responsibility.

This has been particularly noticeable in the evident reluctance of the Catholic Church authorities over the years to address the evils of tax evasion.

The failure of tens of thousands of self-employed people to pay what we now know to have been billions of euro of due tax has necessitated higher payments by the honest remainder.

And because of public resistance to income tax increases, this additional revenue needed to replace the evaded taxes has generally had to come from additional taxation on expenditure, which bears on the less well-off more heavily than do taxes on income.

A further complication has been that Dublin, the political and commercial centre of the country,

Taking an outdoor bath amid the devastation caused by the tsunami in Kesennuma city, Miyagi Prefecture, Japan in March. Photograph: Yasuyoshi Chiba/AFP Photo/Getty Images.

remained in some measure alien to, and resented by, many people in the rest of the State.

In much of rural Ireland, tax continued to be seen as something imposed on the plain people of Ireland by Dublin, and evasion was thus seen by many as a weapon against what was perceived as exploitation from the capital city.

This situation has been complicated by the land reforms of the late 19th and early 20th centuries that converted a large proportion of the population into property owners. This seems to have led to a situation in which the acquisition of property became a disproportionately important goal for many people – a major factor in our property and financial crisis.

But, you may well say, while all this may help to explain Irish deficiencies in civic morality and responsibility, why has it been only in recent times

that this defect became fatal to the integrity of Irish political life?

I shall address this matter in my next article.

TUESDAY, 12 APRIL 2011

They Asked Me Why Would I Want to Live

Simon Fitzmaurice

You're in a room in Dublin. A man walks in whom you've never met. He starts to talk to you. He asks you if you have any children. You say you do. He tells you not to go home tonight. That when you leave the building you must turn right instead of left, head north instead of south. That you must keep going in an unknown direction, knowing only that you will never see anyone from your life again. The journey he is asking you to take is death.

I come from a different country to you. A different place. There are only a few of us there. My norm is very different to yours. You find it difficult to understand me. And looking at me, you must think me quite strange. I have motor neurone disease (MND).

I am in a bed in the Beacon Hospital. I came in with pneumonia and three days of no sleep and continuous coughing left me exhausted and unable to breathe. Moved into intensive care, I went into respiratory failure, collapsed unconscious and was put on a ventilator.

I now have a tube up my nose and a tube down my throat. One for feeding, one for breath-ing. Both of which prevent me from speaking. Motor neurone disease prevents me from moving my arms and legs. I communicate with my family through text messages on my phone.

A man has just walked in the door. I have never met him before and he starts to speak to me. He says his name is John Magner, consultant anaesthetist for the ICU. He tells me he has just got off the phone from Prof. Orla Hardiman in Beaumont Hospital, after I requested that he ring them to ensure that I was getting the best care for MND in the Beacon.

He tells me that Prof. Hardiman has said that they do not advocate ventilation in this country for MND patients. That it is time for me to make the hard choice. He tells me that there have only been two cases of invasive home ventilation, but in both cases the people were extremely wealthy.

Simon Fitzmaurice with his children, Jack, Raife and Arden, at home in Greystones, Co. Wicklow.
Photograph: Ruth Fitzmaurice.

My mother and my wife start crying in the corner of the room. I look at him but I cannot reply. He looks at me. 'This is it now for you. It is time for you to make the hard choice, Simon.' My mother and my wife are now holding each other, sobbing.

While he is looking at me, my life force, my soul, the part of me that feels like every part, is unequivocal. I want to live. It infuses my whole body to such an extent that I feel no fear in the face of this man. We find out two days later that the home ventilator is covered by the HSE, while the home care package needed to run it can be funded between my family and the HSE.

A day later, myself and my father are watching a movie on my laptop. Every movie watched after talking to that man feels like a vindication to me. Every moment lived is a moment lived. We are watching the movie and another man walks in the door whom I have never met. He introduces himself as Ronan Walsh, neurologist. He begins to ask me about the history of my motor neurone disease, despite the fact that I am unable to speak due to the tubes.

My father attempts to fill him in (medical details would not be his strong point). The man quickly gets down to the point: 'Why would you want to ventilate? You have motor neurone disease and you are only going to get worse. At the moment you have use of your hands, but the paralysis will grow, will get worse. Why would you want to ventilate?'

For these people the questions, 'Why would you want to ventilate?', 'Why would you want to live, having motor neurone disease, not being able to move your arms and your legs?', are rhetorical. But the irony is that they are asking the right questions.

Why would you want to ventilate, why would you want to live? I have many reasons, if they were prepared to listen. But that is not why they are there. I believe they are there because they have made a decision about my standard of living. I

think that to them, it is inconceivable that I would want to live. But not for me. For me, it's not about how long you live, but about how you live.

They ask me why I want to live and the answer is the same as given by 'mostly-dead' Westley in *The Princess Bride*, when replying to the question posed by Miracle Max, 'What's so important? What you got here that's worth living for?' 'Truue loove' is his response. That's how I feel. Love for my wife. Love for my children. My friends, my family. Love for life in general. My love is undimmed, unbowed, unbroken. I want to live. Is that wrong? What gives a life meaning? What constitutes a meaningful life? What gives one life more value than another? Surely only the individual can hope to grasp the meaning of his or her life. If not asked if they want to live, it negates that meaning.

You have motor neurone disease, why would you want to live? Motor neurone disease is a killer. But so is life. Everybody dies. But just because you die, just because you will die at some point in the future, does that mean you should kill yourself now? For me, they were asking me to take my own life. Or to endorse euthanasia. I refused.

For days they stood around, scratching their heads and wondering what to do with me. In Ireland, MND patients are not routinely ventilated. Instead, patients are sedated, helped, counselled, eased into death. They are not given a choice. Not like in other countries, including the US. Not here.

I have been in this hospital now for four months and I am going home on a home ventilator. I am one of the first people with MND to ever go home ventilated in Ireland with the help of the HSE. The HSE seems to get nothing but bad press, but they have been nothing but exemplary in their support of my move home. The nurses in the Beacon have been inspirational, guiding me through the terror of respiratory failure and the panic of recovery. I have been educated here in the vocation of caring. And the Irish Motor Neurone Disease Association

(IMNDA) has been unendingly supportive, helping us with equipment, aids and in every way possible.

As for the consultants, whom I have no doubt believed that they were doing the right thing, believed that they were delivering the hard truth, I have nothing against them. But I do wish they would open their eyes. There is no hard truth, only truth on a given day by a given person.

It is people who are hard or soft. And for every moment of hardness, there was an equal moment of kindness from a nurse or a different doctor, and I had many. A moment of kindness to a panicked, terrified patient, to the most vulnerable of people, allows that part of me that feels like every part, to take a breath.

A consultant anaesthetist, Silviu Gligor, who I had gotten to know over the long days here, came in to me yesterday. He wanted to say goodbye as I am going home in two days' time after being almost four months in the hospital. He stood there, wrestling with his emotions, clearly wanting to say something of meaning to me, not just platitudes or farewells. The silence hung about him as he tried to work out what he wanted to say. It was an emotional moment. When he finally did speak, this is what he said: 'Go home and teach your children many things.'

I do not speak for all people with motor neurone disease. I only speak for myself. Perhaps others would question whether or not to ventilate. But I believe in being given the choice, not encouraged to follow the status quo.

Change is possible. John Magner, the same consultant who told me I would have to switch off the ventilator, came in to me after four months and told me I had come a long way and that he had learned a lot.

I am not a tragedy. I neither want nor need pity. I am full of hope. The word hope and MND do not go together in this country. Hope is not about looking for a cure to a disease. Hope is a way of living. We often think we are entitled to a long

Juliette Morrison from Dundalk, Co. Louth, with her Texaco Children's Art Competition entry Raining Men. Photograph: Dara MacDónaill.

and fruitful 'Coca-Cola' life. But life is a privilege, not a right. I feel privileged to be alive. That's hope.

It's not important that you know everything about where I come from. About who I am. It's not important you know everything about motor neurone disease, about the specifics of the disease, about what it's like to have it. It's only important that you remember that behind every disease is a person. Remember that and you have everything you need to travel through my country.

Staff and members of the Quinn Employee Forum outside the Dáil. Unaware that a receiver was already being appointed to the Quinn Group, they were carrying a petition signed by over 90,000 people to the Minister for Finance. Photograph: Cyril Byrne.

FRIDAY, 15 APRIL 2011

Quinn Crushed by Weight of €4.16bn Debt Burden

Simon Carswell

At 5.30 a.m. yesterday, Anglo Irish Bank dispatched 87 people to Cavan and Fermanagh with demand notices for the repayment of more than 20 overdue and expired loans. The loans covered some of €2.88 billion of debt owing by the Quinn family.

The people included legal and financial representatives, security staff and drivers. The demand notices kick-started a sequence of well-choreographed moves that begin one of the biggest and most complex corporate restructurings (outside banking) in Irish history.

The Quinn Group's problem was that it had too much debt, which was exacerbated by the fact that the Quinn family had too much debt on top of that.

The group owes €1.3 billion to a group of banks and bondholders, while the family owes €2.88 billion to Anglo, primarily over Seán Quinn's spectacular gamble on the bank's share price that blew up in the 2008 financial crash.

Servicing debts of €4.16 billion was an impossibility when the group made cash earnings of more than €100 million a year and its insurer, Quinn Insurance – the group's one-time profit-driver – was in administration over solvency concerns.

With 2,600 jobs at risk in the Quinn Group's manufacturing businesses covering cement, glass, plastics and radiators, Anglo felt it had to move to protect the businesses and recover some debt. 'We are going to get some money back instead of the potential of this costing the State a huge amount,' said Anglo chief executive Mike Aynsley.

Now businesses and properties stretching from Derrylin, Co. Fermanagh, to Hyderabad in India and Ufa in Russia (1,200km east of Moscow) will fall under Anglo's control. It expects to recoup about €500 million selling properties. The bank has taken provisions against the remaining €2.3 billion, which is covered in Anglo's €29.3 billion State bailout.

The bank appointed a receiver over Quinn Group (ROI), the Republic of Ireland company sitting at the apex of Quinn's business empire. This is the shareholding firm owned equally by his son and four daughters.

The receiver was also appointed over Quinn Finance Holdings, which sits at the top of the corporate structure behind the family's overseas property interests.

The bank took a charge over the family's shares in Quinn Group (ROI) in 2008 in return for lending heavily to Quinn, allowing him to cover his share losses.

Yesterday's deal has various moving parts that allow the overall restructuring of a complex and interwoven corporate group.

Months of negotiations have taken place with Quinn Group's lenders, which have swelled in number from debt selling in the markets. One participant said it was 'like trying to herd wild cats'.

The restructuring will break the links between Quinn Insurance, the manufacturing businesses and the Quinn property investments. The jobs will be protected. Under the deal, trade customers and suppliers can secure insurance again to deal with the group.

The main part of the deal involves the ownership of a new Quinn manufacturing company to be split 75:25 between Anglo and the banks and bondholders.

In return, the banks and bondholders will agree a new five-year loan. A more manageable loan of about €750 million will be moved on to the manufacturing company, while about €550 million will remain with Quinn Group, the Northern Irish operations firm sitting below Quinn Group (ROI).

This debt will be repaid with cash of €80 million and a further €125 million from the disposal of assets, such as the family's hotels in Cambridge, Sofia and Krakow. The family's corporate jet and helicopter will also be sold.

Guarantees worth €464 million provided on assets in Quinn Insurance subsidiaries will be dropped by the banks and bondholders.

The reason why the joint bid from Anglo and US insurer Liberty Mutual for Quinn Insurance was named the preferred option rather than outright buyer was to allow these guarantees to be lifted. The discovery of the guarantees led the Financial Regulator to seek the appointment of administrators in March 2010 as it weakened the insurer's solvency, putting 1.3 million policyholders at risk.

The next stage in the sequence is the full sale of the insurer by the joint administrators to Anglo-Liberty. Quinn Insurance will be majority owned and controlled by Liberty, but Anglo will share half of any potential upturn in the firm.

The insurer will require cash of about €150 million from Anglo and Liberty to boost its reserves. The State's Insurance Compensation Fund may yet be tapped to cover losses at the insurance company. This may all seem peculiar given that Anglo, a dead bank, itself is being wound down over 10 years. Sources close to the Quinn restructuring say the bank would seek to sell Quinn's properties over a three-year period and exit the manufacturing and insurance business over three to five years.

The various Quinn companies were yesterday flooded with new independent directors and executives, taking control from Quinn, his family and his executives. Quinn, who started a multibillion business digging gravel out of his family farm 38 years ago, has been shut out.

FRIDAY, 22 APRIL 2011

From Big Name to No Name in Three Years

Simon Carswell

An old internal document at Anglo Irish Bank described its 'arrowhead' logo as symbolising 'security and progression' and the brand as being for 'the long haul'.

The logo lasted just over a decade. On Wednesday, the bank wiped the Anglo name and logos from over its doors, removing the signs from the bank's offices and branches around the State.

In a carefully stage-managed event, Anglo's new management, led by chief executive Mike Aynsley, sought to break from the bank's calamitous past and set out an as yet unnamed stall to maximise loan recovery and recoup as much as possible for the State.

Motorists beeped as they drove past Anglo's former head office on St Stephen's Green in Dublin city centre as the signs were removed.

The move was symbolic and may prove cathartic for some members of the public, but the bank and its loans will be here for some time to come, just in another guise.

Anglo will be renamed once the Irish Nationwide Building Society is merged, which is likely to take place during the summer. The enlarged 'recovery' bank will then be set on course to run down loans over a period of up to 10 years.

Anglo is a far different animal to what it was in 2008 when the bank was at its peak. Aynsley said it had moved from being 'a high-octane property lender to a dedicated asset-recovery bank working in the public interest'.

The board and top management team have changed. While some long-standing staff in Anglo's lower and middle ranks remain in place, Aynsley is happy with his team.

Display contractor Ken Glennon removing Anglo Irish Bank signage from the bank's former premises at St Stephen's Green, Dublin. Photograph: Matt Kavanagh.

'I am very proud of the people that we have got here – I think they are fit for purpose to support the recovery for the taxpayer.'

Staff numbers have been reduced by about 30 per cent from 1,864 in September 2008 to 1,296 at the end of last year. Some 800 staff have left the bank over that time, while Anglo has hired 200 new employees to fill gaps.

Further voluntary redundancies would be necessary, said Aynsley.

Some 250 staff will move to Anglo from Irish Nationwide, but overall staff numbers will drop to about 900 by the end of this year.

This will include about 130 employees at Anglo and about 50 at Irish Nationwide who oversee the day-to-day management of loans owned by the National Asset Management Agency (NAMA).

The bank will have transferred about €35 billion in loans to NAMA, while Irish Nationwide has about €9 billion with the agency.

The plan is for the merged NAMA units of both to be run out of Heritage House, the Georgian building a few doors up from Anglo's Stephen's Green offices.

Overall staff numbers will eventually drop to zero by 2020.

Aynsley said that about 90 staff at the bank worked in risk management, a section of the bank that has been overhauled due to the many information gaps on loans.

Costs is one area where the figures have increased rather than declined. Total operating expenses at the bank were €353 million in 2010 compared with €328 million in 2008.

Last year's expenses, however, include €89 million in one-off costs, comprising €27 million for the staff redundancies and €62 million in relation to the bank's restructuring plans, the NAMA process and the legacy matters dealing with old Anglo problems.

The €62 million has been paid to consultants and professionals.

Staff costs declined to €130 million last year from €206 million in 2008, reflecting the sharp reduction in the workforce's size.

The bank has €35 billion in loans following the NAMA transfers, and a further €500 million in commercial property loans and €2 billion in residential mortgages will be moved from Irish Nationwide in the merger of the lenders.

Under the restructuring plan, still to be approved, the €2 billion residential mortgage book will be run down or sold within five years.

The remaining loans at the nationalised bank are spread across three countries – €16.2 billion in Ireland, €10.9 billion in Britain and €7.6 billion in the US.

A potential sale of the US loan book has been considered, although the bank's preference is to hold the book to secure a better value over time. There is massive interest among potential buyers, although most are bargain-hunters looking to bag a deal at a fire sale price.

Net of provisions taken against losses on the total post-NAMA book, Anglo's loans stand at €24 billion. This matches the size of the loan book in September 2004 before the bank's lending surged during the three peak years of the property boom. In many ways, the bank is broadly reverting to its pre-bubble size.

Of the remaining loans, with a face value of €35 billion, some €16.6 billion are impaired, against which Anglo has already set aside about €10 billion in provisions to cover potential bad debts.

Like most lenders, Anglo will work with co-operative borrowers but even these clients will be subject to foreclosure actions if their debts far exceed the value of their underlying security, particularly among the property investors who didn't move to NAMA.

Aynsley said that in these cases, the bank would have to cut its losses as it must cut the losses to the State which had injected €29.3 billion into the bank. It would seize control of an underlying asset and sell it to recoup some cash, he said.

'No matter what happens, in some cases a situation is not going to get any better. In those cases, the bank just has to move to foreclose; no amount of forbearance is going to help.'

The bank is likely to draw on outside consultants to work on specialised loan work-outs such as the bank's involvement in the Quinn Group and proposed share of Quinn Insurance to try to recover some of the €2.88 billion debt owing by Seán Quinn and family.

The bank would judge debt restructuring on a case-by-case basis, said Aynsley – for example, where the term of the loan would be extended or some debt was forgiven if the bank had a better chance of recovering more money.

'I think you will do things that are commercially sensitive at this stage,' Aynsley said. 'You try to stay away from draconian measures but on the other hand you have got to be tough because you will put the market in a space where it expects debt forgiveness. Each situation is different. We won't want to be in a situation where we are making blanket decisions.'

As for the bank's new name, Aynsley said it was irrelevant given Anglo's changed role in the resolution of Ireland's worst bank.

'For a bank looking to attract customers, a brand can suck them in,' he said. 'It is not that important for a bank in wind-down.'

WEDNESDAY, 27 APRIL 2011

'It's All Undercover – it's Like Espionage'

Cian Traynor

For adopted children searching for their birth parents, the process can be frustrating, not to mention unsatisfying. New legislation aims to change that, but it needs to acknowledge the potential trauma on both sides.

To track down his birth mother, Adrian McKenna bypassed the rules with some amateur sleuthing. Since 1952, an adopted person in Ireland has no legal right to gain access to their birth certificate or other information contained in their adoption file.

McKenna's way around this was to walk into the research area of the General Register Office and search through public records of births, deaths and marriages. All he knew was his date of birth and the area he was born in. There's a way to spot the birth cert of an adoptee, McKenna explains, and through a process of elimination, he was left with one: his own.

From there he used his birth mother's name to expand the search, one sliver of information at a time, until he pieced everything together.

'By the time I was finished, I knew who her parents were, who she had married, where they lived, all the names and ages of my brothers, sisters and cousins, where they all lived and whether they were married.

'I had assembled my whole family tree, something I had never done with my adopted family.' McKenna, a 46-year-old social worker, says there are countless others resorting to the same 'rigmarole' out of frustration with having to wait up to two years just to discuss the prospect of tracing with an adoption agency.

For some, that wait is a race against time, knowing their birth parents may die before their search can lead anywhere. For others, like McKenna, it's a two-tier system where adopted people feel like second-class citizens.

That could be about to change. Legislation to help adopted children trace their parents has been promised by the new Minister for Children, Frances Fitzgerald, whose spokeswoman says work has begun on the heads of a Bill. But its feasibility remains unclear and disrupting the status quo will require careful deliberation.

'At the moment it's all undercover – it's like espionage,' says McKenna. 'And it can be very,

Adrian McKenna. Photograph: Eric Luke.

very messy. Personally I'd like to see it regulated. Good legislation wouldn't just allow everyone to rush in to get their file – when someone decides to do this, they're already emotionally wrought. There should be support there for either side.'

Though working alone, McKenna appreciated the need for a third-party mediator before he approached his birth mother. He reached out to her older sister, who had supported her through the adoption process. His birth mother had married soon after the adoption, giving her second-born the same name: Gerard. Now McKenna learned that hardship had followed and she wasn't prepared to revisit the past.

'There may have been a lot she was not dealing with well, and me appearing back on the scene was going to be difficult,' he says. 'But I never got to talk to her, so I don't know. Life had moved on for her and that was that.' McKenna says

that, while birth mothers should be notified and offered support when reunion is sought, their need for privacy shouldn't overrule the adopted person's right to access their birth cert or medical history.

'The reality is, any adopted person in this country can get access to their birth cert, find out who their natural mother is and, in the eyes of Irish law, walk up and say "I'm your son/daughter". I've supported 40 or 50 people through that process and I'm not the only one.

'That will continue, no matter what happens with the law. For us not to enact legislation to allow the rest of the process to happen is disingenuous to all of us.'

Turning up on someone's doorstep is like throwing a hand grenade into a family, says Helen Gilmartin of the Adoptive Parent's Association of Ireland. Gilmartin has helped trace people internationally, but avoids simply passing on information to the searcher, either the adopted person or the birth mother, because she feels strongly about sudden and uninvited contact. 'The person searching knows what they're doing,' she says. 'But for the person who is found, unless they're involved, it's a bolt from the blue.

'There may be women in their seventies who have never told their husband or children they had a child before they were married. One woman said she got such a fright that she slammed down the phone and didn't remember what agency it was.

'Thankfully it was just a knee-jerk reaction and it all worked out. But if anybody wants a sensible reunion you have to be considerate and careful. Otherwise the door will almost certainly be slammed in your face. How do you ever come back from that?' Gilmartin adopted four children during the 1970s and early 1980s, a time when the process was known as 'closed' or 'clean break' adoption. There was secrecy on both sides, she says, with each party undertaking never to intrude into the other's life.

Having spoken to countless young adoptees, adoptive parents and birth parents, Gilmartin appreciates the equilibrium of issues involved in tracing. There are those afraid of being perceived as disloyal to their adoptive parents; adoptive parents worried about contact coinciding with exams or fractured relationships; those who fear disruption and those who long for contact but don't know how to initiate it.

'You have to be prepared for huge emotional turmoil so timing, age and maturity are absolutely crucial,' she says. 'When someone is contacted and they've just buried a parent or lost a job, the answer could be no – but it doesn't mean no forever.'

Cartoon by Martyn Turner.

Gilmartin believes the best system currently available is the national adoption contact preference register, established in 2005 to assist adopted people and their natural families in tracing, which she feels has been under-promoted. A spokeswoman for the Adoption Authority says the new legislation proposed would see the contact register regulated on a statutory basis. Participants specify what level of communication they want – even if it's just passing on medical history – and action is only taken if both sides register. There are currently 6,372 adopted people and 2,843 natural relatives registered, resulting in approximately 500 matches. Over 42,000 people have been adopted in Ireland since 1952.

Many respondents said that, at the time of adoption, they were told they had no right to receive any information regarding their child. Because of that, many never attempted to make contact.

That's how it was for Philomena Lynott. In the three years after she gave birth to Phil Lynott in 1949, she had another two children in Britain, both of whom she was persuaded to part with while they were in care.

'They showed you that the child would have a better life elsewhere,' she says. 'At the time, I had nothing. I had gone down to six stone. You have to remember people like me we were called sinners; fallen women. I was battered, beaten and spat on.' There were no agencies then, Lynott explains, and there was an implicit understanding not to interfere in the child's life post-adoption.

'You never knew if you'd see them again but every birthday, every time you saw another child, you were thinking of them.' Because her mother was a stern 'God-fearing woman' who lived until the age of 93, Lynott kept these two children a secret, even avoiding any mention of them in her 1995 memoir, *My Boy*.

'I would have hated her to think I'd fallen so many times. I had five sisters and my father walked them all down the aisle. They were good girls. I

was the wild one. No wonder Philip wrote a song called "The Wild One".'

One day there was a phone call. Her second-born, also named Philomena, had found her. When they met, they made a pact to keep it secret until both Philomena's adoptive parents and Lynott's own mother had passed away.

Years later, when the adoptive parents of her third-born, Leslie, had died, he found a tin box containing his birth cert and was also able to trace her.

Now the three are inseparable, she says, and *My Boy* has been rewritten to include her previously unspoken difficulties and the 'happy ending' that followed. Now 80, Lynott has a better understanding of 'closed' adoption's legacy after holding book signings around the country.

'People are coming up to me in tears,' she says. 'Some found their birth mothers but haven't been accepted because the shame lingered on, or their family would have been mortified. That's still happening. I'm getting heart-rending letters. But I think people should reach out to each other if they can. Many a lady has gone to her grave wondering what happened to her babies, [feeling] unable to do anything about it.'

SATURDAY, 30 APRIL 2011

Will and Kate Show is Testament to Abiding Allure of the Royals

Maeve Binchy

Well, everyone mellows a bit in 40 years. The edges blur. You see more innocence and hope and harmless lunacy than arrogance and triumphalism. It was a day when two people got married and two billion other people watched them. It was a day when millions dressed up, got over-excited and partied to celebrate young love.

Prince William and his wife Kate Middleton kiss on the balcony of Buckingham Palace in London following their wedding at Westminster Abbey. Photograph: Chris Ison/PA.

And it wasn't all in England. A man from Eircom who came to sort out the broken-down broadband said that every house he had visited was glued to a television. It was on in the bank and the customers dawdled so that they could see more.

The streets and shops in Dalkey were emptier than on any other Friday. There were many households where ladies gathered, each wearing a hat and carrying a bottle. And why not? It was not a question of wanting to be English, nothing to do with losing our identity, changing our allegiance. It was all about watching a big, glittery show. A well-choreographed parade. With fine horses and gold carriages and flags and marching bands. If that's how you look at it then it's a morning well spent.

The best bit is that we know the cast. The Duke of Edinburgh, who always looks irritated and

as if he's on the verge of imploding, looked just the same. But he is going to be 90 next birthday. He has a silly sort of sword, which would be handy to lean on, but he never uses it even though it's hanging from his waist. He walks upright on his own. Queen Elizabeth is 85 and well able to climb into a glass coach and leap out of it without assistance. These are sturdy people; Ruritania doesn't seem to have affected their stamina.

It was so different watching a royal wedding from my own home. For years, I have been going to Westminster Abbey or St Paul's Cathedral and climbing almighty scaffolding to get to a seat on the top of a specially constructed press section. I was at Prince William's parents' wedding and his aunt Anne's and his uncle Andrew's. Not a good fairy at the feast, I fear I brought them no luck. All three marriages ended in divorce.

In a way I wish I had been in London. I miss the magic of the English losing all their reserve, their fear of having a conversation with you in case you might go home with them. Street parties are so much the opposite of the British way of life, which is based on people keeping themselves to themselves. And yet when they did sit down they loved the chance to get to know their neighbours. I remember with great affection those parties at trestle tables with beer and cider and something roasted on a spit.

But hey, what do I know really? Everything's changed since I started being a royal wedding watcher in 1973. For William and Kate's wedding the guests arrived in buses as if they were going to a football match. Years back it was a long line of Bentleys. There was constant reference to the fact that the couple had lived together already for some years. At the time of Diana's wedding her uncle had to tell the world that she was a virgin. At those long-ago marriages Elton John and his partner David would not have been ushered politely into the Abbey. Nor would there have been a rake of red hats – one token Catholic would have covered it.

Of course it's not perfect. Hereditary power is never a good thing. But it's a lot better in a few decades than it used to be. Yes, they still made her change her name to Catherine. They didn't invite poor Fergie, who would have loved a day out. They left Tony Blair off the list. Tony who saved their bacon when Diana died.

But in the end, the bride was beautiful, the groom was handsome, the little pages and flower girls were adorable. It all went like clockwork. The somewhat tarnished image of royalty was forgotten for a day anyway.

Woody Allen always has a useful phrase. And when asked in a movie whether he was mellow, he replied, 'I'm so mellow I'm almost rotten'.

I know what he means. It's not a bad place to be.

SATURDAY, 7 MAY 2011

Ireland's Future Depends on Breaking Free from Bailout

Morgan Kelly

With the Irish Government on track to owe a quarter of a trillion euro by 2014, a prolonged and chaotic national bankruptcy is becoming inevitable. By the time the dust settles, Ireland's last remaining asset, its reputation as a safe place from which to conduct business, will have been destroyed.

Ireland is facing economic ruin.

While most people would trace our ruin to the bank guarantee of September 2008, the real error was in sticking with the guarantee long after it had become clear that the bank losses were insupportable. Brian Lenihan's original decision to guarantee most of the bonds of Irish banks was a mistake, but a mistake so obvious and so ridiculous that it could easily have been reversed. The ideal time to have reversed the bank guarantee was a few months later when Patrick Honohan was appointed governor of the Central Bank and assumed *de facto* control of Irish economic policy.

As a respected academic expert on banking crises, Honohan commanded the international authority to have announced that the guarantee had been made in haste and with poor information, and would be replaced by a restructuring where bonds in the banks would be swapped for shares.

Instead, Honohan seemed unperturbed by the possible scale of bank losses, repeatedly insisting that they were 'manageable'. Like most Irish economists of his generation, he appeared to believe that Ireland was still the export-driven powerhouse of the 1990s, rather than the credit-fuelled Ponzi scheme it had become since 2000; and the banking crisis no worse than the, largely manufactured, government budget crisis of the late 1980s.

Rising dismay at Honohan's judgement crystallised into outright scepticism after an extraordinary interview with Bloomberg business news on 28 May last year. Having overseen the Central Bank's 'quite aggressive' stress tests of the Irish banks, he assured them that he would have 'the two big banks, fixed by the end of the year. I think it's quite good news. The banks are floating away from dependence on the State and will be free standing'.

Honohan's miscalculation of the bank losses has turned out to be the costliest mistake ever made by an Irish person. Armed with Honohan's assurances that the bank losses were manageable, the Irish Government confidently rode into the Little Bighorn and repaid the bank bondholders, even those who had not been guaranteed under the original scheme. This suicidal policy culminated in the repayment of most of the outstanding bonds last September.

Disaster followed within weeks. Nobody would lend to Irish banks, so the maturing bonds were repaid largely by emergency borrowing from the European Central Bank: by November the Irish banks already owed more than €60 billion. Despite aggressive cuts in government spending, the certainty that bank losses would far exceed Honohan's estimates led financial markets to stop lending to Ireland.

On 16 November, European finance ministers urged Lenihan to accept a bailout to stop the panic spreading to Spain and Portugal, but he refused, arguing that the Irish Government was funded until the following summer. Although attacked by the Irish media for this seemingly delusional behaviour, Lenihan, for once, was doing precisely the right thing. Behind Lenihan's refusal lay the thinly veiled threat that, unless given suitably generous terms, Ireland could hold happily its breath for long enough that Spain and Portugal, who needed to borrow every month, would drown.

At this stage, with Lenihan looking set to exploit his strong negotiating position to seek a bailout of the banks only, Honohan intervened. As well as being Ireland's chief economic adviser, he also plays for the opposing team as a member of the council of the European Central Bank, whose decisions he is bound to carry out. In Frankfurt for the monthly meeting of the ECB on 18 November, Honohan announced on RTÉ Radio 1's *Morning Ireland* that Ireland would need a bailout of 'tens of billions'.

Rarely has a finance minister been so deftly sliced off at the ankles by his central bank governor. And so the Honohan Doctrine that bank losses could and should be repaid by Irish taxpayers ran its predictable course with the financial collapse and international bailout of the Irish State.

Ireland's Last Stand began less shambolically than you might expect. The IMF, which believes that lenders should pay for their stupidity before it has to reach into its pocket, presented the Irish with a plan to haircut €30 billion of unguaranteed bonds by two-thirds on average. Lenihan was overjoyed, according to a source who was there, telling the IMF team: 'You are Ireland's salvation.'

The deal was torpedoed from an unexpected direction. At a conference call with the G7 finance ministers, the haircut was vetoed by US treasury secretary Timothy Geithner who, as his payment of $13 billion from government-owned AIG to Goldman Sachs showed, believes that bankers take priority over taxpayers. The only one to speak up for the Irish was UK chancellor George Osborne, but Geithner, as always, got his way. An instructive, if painful, lesson in the extent of US soft power, and in who our friends really are.

The negotiations went downhill from there. On one side was the European Central Bank, unabashedly representing Ireland's creditors and insisting on full repayment of bank bonds. On the other was the IMF, arguing that Irish taxpayers would be doing well to balance their government's books, let alone repay the losses of private banks. And the Irish? On the side of the ECB, naturally.

In the circumstances, the ECB walked away

Katriva Pagagova and Silvia Trstenovioova from Slovakia at the OMC (Organisation Mondial Coiffure)
European Cup and the Irish Hairdressing Championships at the RDS in Dublin. Photograph: Alan Betson.

with everything it wanted. The IMF were scathing of the Irish performance, with one staffer describing the eagerness of some Irish negotiators to side with the ECB as displaying strong elements of Stockholm syndrome.

The bailout represents almost as much of a scandal for the IMF as it does for Ireland. The IMF found itself outmanoeuvred by ECB negotiators, their low opinion of whom they are not at pains to conceal. More importantly, the IMF was forced by the obduracy of Geithner and the spinelessness, or worse, of the Irish to lend their imprimatur, and €30 billion of their capital, to a deal that its negotiators privately admit will end in Irish bankruptcy. Lending to an insolvent state, which has no hope of reducing its debt enough to borrow in markets again, breaches the most fundamental rule of the IMF, and a heated debate continues there over the legality of the Irish deal.

Six months on, and with Irish Government debt rated one notch above junk and the run on Irish banks starting to spread to household deposits, it might appear that the Irish bailout of last November has already ended in abject failure. On the contrary, as far as its ECB architects are concerned, the bailout has turned out to be an unqualified success.

The one thing you need to understand about the Irish bailout is that it had nothing to do with repairing Ireland's finances enough to allow the Irish Government to start borrowing again in the bond markets at reasonable rates: what people ordinarily think of a bailout as doing.

The finances of the Irish Government are like a bucket with a large hole in the form of the banking system. While any half-serious rescue would have focused on plugging this hole, the agreed bailout ostentatiously ignored the banks, except for reiterating the ECB-Honohan view that their losses would be borne by Irish taxpayers. Try to imagine the Bank of England's insisting that Northern Rock be rescued by Newcastle City Council and you have some idea of how seriously the ECB expects the Irish bailout to work.

Instead, the sole purpose of the Irish bailout was to frighten the Spanish into line with a vivid demonstration that EU rescues are not for the faint-hearted. And the ECB plan, so far anyway, has worked. Given a choice between being strung up like Ireland – an object of international ridicule, paying exorbitant rates on bailout funds, its government ministers answerable to a Hungarian university lecturer – or mending their ways, the Spanish have understandably chosen the latter.

But why was it necessary, or at least expedient, for the EU to force an economic collapse on Ireland to frighten Spain? The answer goes back to a fundamental, and potentially fatal, flaw in the design of the eurozone: the lack of any means of dealing with large, insolvent banks.

Back when the euro was being planned in the mid-1990s, it never occurred to anyone that cautious, stodgy banks like AIB and Bank of Ireland, run by faintly dim former rugby players, could ever borrow tens of billions overseas, and lose it all on dodgy property loans. Had the collapse been limited to Irish banks, some sort of rescue deal might have been cobbled together; but a suspicion lingers that many Spanish banks – which inflated a property bubble almost as exuberant as Ireland's, but in the world's ninth largest economy – are hiding losses as large as those that sank their Irish counterparts.

Uniquely in the world, the European Central Bank has no central government standing behind it that can levy taxes. To rescue a banking system as large as Spain's would require a massive commitment of resources by European countries to a European Monetary Fund: something so politically complex and financially costly that it will only be considered in extremis, to avert the collapse of the eurozone. It is easiest for now for the ECB to keep its fingers crossed that Spain pulls through by itself, encouraged by the example made of the Irish.

Irish insolvency is now less a matter of economics than of arithmetic. If everything goes according to plan, as it always does, Ireland's government debt will top €190 billion by 2014, with another €45 billion in NAMA and €35 billion in bank recapitalisation, for a total of €270 billion, plus whatever losses the Irish Central Bank has made on its emergency lending. Subtracting off the likely value of the banks and NAMA assets, NAMA Wine Lake (by far the best source on the Irish economy) reckons our final debt will be about €220 billion, and I think it will be closer to €250 billion, but these differences are immaterial: either way we are talking of a government debt that is more than €120,000 per worker, or 60 per cent larger than GNP.

Economists have a rule of thumb that once its national debt exceeds its national income, a small economy is in danger of default (large economies, like Japan, can go considerably higher). Ireland is so far into the red zone that marginal changes in the bailout terms can make no difference: we are going to be in the Hudson.

The ECB applauded and lent Ireland the money to ensure that the banks that lent to Anglo and Nationwide be repaid, and now finds itself in the situation where, as a consequence, the banks that lent to the Irish Government are at risk of losing most of what they lent. In other words, the Irish banking crisis has become part of the larger European sovereign debt crisis.

Given the political paralysis in the EU, and a European Central Bank that sees its main task as placating the editors of German tabloids, the most likely outcome of the European debt crisis is that, after two years or so to allow French and German banks to build up loss reserves, the insolvent economies will be forced into some sort of bankruptcy.

Make no mistake: while government defaults are almost the normal state of affairs in places like

Greece and Argentina, for a country like Ireland that trades on its reputation as a safe place to do business, a bankruptcy would be catastrophic. Sovereign bankruptcies drag on for years as creditors hold out for better terms, or sell to so-called vulture funds that engage in endless litigation overseas to have national assets such as aircraft impounded in the hope that they can make a sufficient nuisance of themselves to be bought off.

Worse still, a bankruptcy can do nothing to repair Ireland's finances. Given the other commitments of the Irish State (to the banks, NAMA, EU, ECB and IMF), for a bankruptcy to return government debt to a sustainable level, the holders of regular government bonds will have to be more or less wiped out. Unfortunately, most Irish government bonds are held by Irish banks and insurance companies.

In other words, we have embarked on a futile game of passing the parcel of insolvency: first from the banks to the Irish State, and next from the State back to the banks and insurance companies. The eventual outcome will likely see Ireland as some sort of EU protectorate, Europe's answer to Puerto Rico.

Suppose that we did not want to follow our current path towards an ECB-directed bankruptcy and spiralling national ruin, is there anything we could do? While Prof. Honohan sportingly threw away our best cards last September, there still is a way out that, while not painless, is considerably less painful than what Europe has in mind for us.

National survival requires that Ireland walk away from the bailout. This in turn requires the Government to do two things: disengage from the banks, and bring its budget into balance immediately.

First the banks. While the ECB does not want to rescue the Irish banks, it cannot let them collapse either and start a wave of panic that sweeps across Europe. So, every time one of you expresses your approval of the Irish banks by moving your savings to a foreign-owned bank, the Irish bank goes and replaces your money with emergency borrowing

A helicopter spreads water across a gorse fire outside Pontoon, Co. Mayo, where warm, dry and windy weather helped to fan the flames of the fires. Photograph: Eamonn Farrell/Photocall.

from the ECB or the Irish Central Bank. Their current borrowings are €160 billion.

The original bailout plan was that the loan portfolios of Irish banks would be sold off to repay these borrowings. However, foreign banks know that many of these loans, mortgages especially, will eventually default, and were not interested. As a result, the ECB finds itself with the Irish banks wedged uncomfortably far up its fundament, and no way of dislodging them.

This allows Ireland to walk away from the banking system by returning the NAMA assets to the banks and withdrawing its promissory notes in the banks. The ECB can then learn the basic economic truth that if you lend €160 billion to insolvent banks backed by an insolvent state, you are no longer a creditor: you are the owner. At some stage the ECB can take out an eraser and, where 'Emergency Loan' is written in the accounts of Irish banks, write 'Capital' instead. When it chooses to do so is its problem, not ours.

At a stroke, the Irish Government can halve its debt to a survivable €110 billion. The ECB can do nothing to the Irish banks in retaliation without triggering a catastrophic panic in Spain and across the rest of Europe. The only way Europe can respond is by cutting off funding to the Irish Government.

So the second strand of national survival is to bring the Government budget immediately into balance. The reason for governments to run deficits in recessions is to smooth out temporary dips in economic activity. However, our current slump is not temporary: Ireland bet everything that house prices would rise forever and lost. To borrow so that senior civil servants like me can continue to enjoy salaries twice as much as our European counterparts makes no sense, macroeconomic or otherwise.

Cutting Government borrowing to zero immediately is not painless, but it is the only way of disentangling ourselves from the loan sharks who are intent on making an example of us. In contrast, the new Government's current policy of lying on the ground with a begging bowl and hoping that someone takes pity on us does not make for a particularly strong negotiating position. By bringing our budget immediately into balance, we focus attention on the fact that Ireland's problems stem almost entirely from the activities of six privately owned banks, while freeing ourselves to walk away from these poisonous institutions. Just as importantly, it sends a signal to the rest of the world that Ireland – which 20 years ago showed how a small country could drag itself out of poverty through the energy and hard work of its inhabitants, but has since fallen among thieves and their political fixers – is back and means business.

Of course, we all know that this will never happen. Irish politicians are too used to being rewarded by Brussels to start fighting against it, even if it is a matter of national survival. It is easier to be led along blindfold until the noose is slipped around our necks and we are kicked through the trapdoor into bankruptcy.

The destruction wrought by the bankruptcy will not just be economic but political. Just as the Lenihan bailout destroyed Fianna Fáil, so the Noonan bankruptcy will destroy Fine Gael and Labour, leaving them as reviled and mistrusted as their predecessors. And that will leave Ireland in the interesting situation where the economic crisis has chewed up and spat out all of the State's constitutional parties. The last election was reassuringly dull and predictable, but the next, after the trauma and chaos of the bankruptcy, will be anything but.

FRIDAY, 13 MAY 2011

OMG! This is the Best Thing in the World

Karen Fricker in Düsseldorf

Jedward bounced, strutted and cartwheeled to qualification last night in the second semi-final of the 56th Eurovision contest.

The twin brothers, John and Edward Grimes,

gave a terrifically energetic performance of their song 'Lipstick', which, combined with the act's stunning stage design, had the audience in the Esprit Arena singing, clapping and cheering along.

'OMG! This is the best thing in the world!' said the pair. 'We want to thank all the countries who voted for us, our fans, our mentor Caroline, the songwriters and RTÉ. We can't wait to perform again on Saturday. Go Team Jedward!'

Before the performance in the arena's press centre, Jedward's manager Louis Walsh expressed uncertainty about their chances of qualification.

'I just want them to get through tonight,' he said.

While acknowledging that the reaction in the past number of weeks to Jedward had been 'incredible', Walsh called Eurovision 'just another chapter' in a career that he predicted would be 'global'.

While it was he who put Jedward forward for the Eurovision contest, Walsh underlined the central role that Caroline Downey Desmond – their mentor in the RTÉ selection process for Eurovision – has played in bringing their act together, and in shepherding the singers through the maelstrom of attention that has come their way since arriving in Düsseldorf.

Overall last night, Europe's voters and expert juries came out clearly on the side of the up-tempo entries: Sweden, Estonia, Romania, Denmark, and Moldova together with Ireland all qualified for the final, with energetic, and in some cases anthemic, numbers.

Quirkier qualifiers included Bosnia and Herzegovina's catchy, folksy 'Love in Rewind', written and performed by 49-year-old Dino Merlin, and Ukraine's high-concept 'Angel', which features artist Kseniya Simonova making pictures in sand with her hands as Mika Newton sings. Austria and Slovenia also qualified.

Jedward celebrate after qualifying for the final of the 2011 Eurovision Song Contest in Düsseldorf. Photograph: Wolfgang Rattay/Reuters.

The highest-profile act not to qualify last night was Israel's Dana International, who was returning to the contest having won in 1998 with 'Diva' (she also composed and co-wrote Israel's 2008 entry, which placed fifth).

Dana International is transsexual and her victory 13 years ago is considered a landmark in the public visibility and acceptance of gay, lesbian, bisexual and transgendered people. Her song this year, 'Ding Dong', however, did not capture the public's attention.

Jedward will be the only pair of identical twins singing on Saturday night: Daniela and Veronika from Slovakia, who perform as the act Twiins, were also relegated.

Last night's 10 winners will perform alongside the 10 acts chosen on Tuesday and the performers from the five automatic qualifying countries: France, Spain, Germany, Italy and the UK.

Most major bookmakers last night were still tipping France to take home top honours on Saturday, with Ireland placing second in most polls.

RTÉ said today the audience watching the semi-final on RTÉ Two peaked at 1.135 million viewers between 9.45 p.m. and 10 p.m. when Jedward were performing.

Jedward came a respectable eighth, with 119 points, in the final on 14 May, against 221 for the winners, Azerbaijan.

THURSDAY, 19 MAY 2011

Sombre Remembrance of the War Dead in the Hush of Islandbridge

Mary Fitzgerald

The silence that accompanied the laying of wreaths — one poppy, one laurel — by a British queen and an Irish president at the Irish National War Memorial Gardens yesterday conveyed more than any number of words.

In the hushed surroundings of the Sir Edwin Lutyens-designed gardens, whose fortunes — a little like the relationship between Ireland and Britain — have ebbed and flowed over time, Queen Elizabeth and President Mary McAleese honoured the Irish who died in the First World War.

The story of how almost 50,000 Irishmen perished in the trenches of that war had, until quite recently, suffered something of a blotting out in the annals of Irish history. But their memory lived on in yesterday's sombre commemoration, which stood as testament to the efforts of Mrs McAleese and many others determined to ensure that the sacrifice of Ireland's war dead be remembered.

The ceremony under overcast skies echoed another landmark moment in 1998 when the Queen and Mrs McAleese unveiled a tower on the site of the 1917 battle of Messines Ridge in memory of the Irish who had gone to war under the Union flag and never came back. That was the first public event undertaken jointly by an Irish and a British head of state.

As the Queen entered the gardens accompanied by Mrs McAleese at about noon yesterday, her eyes were drawn towards the altar-like granite structure referred to as the War Stone, which is engraved with the words: 'Their Name Liveth for Evermore'.

She later viewed the nine-metre Guillemont Ginchy cross, which takes its name from two towns captured by the 16th Irish Division during the Battle of the Somme. The wall behind the cross is inscribed with the following: '*I ndíl-chuimhne ar 49,400 Éireannach do thuir sa Chogadh Mhór 1914–1918* – To the memory of 49,400 Irish men who gave their lives in the Great War 1914–1918'.

Opening the ceremony, the officer in charge of the cadet guard of honour announced the Queen's name in Irish — 'Banríon Eilís a Dó' — to the more than 500 attendees assembled along neat rows of garden chairs. A strong breeze buffeted a large Tricolour that stood at half-mast. Behind it, the Union flag flew alongside the three divisional

Queen Elizabeth II and President Mary McAleese after laying wreaths at the Garden of Remembrance in Dublin. Photograph: Maxwell Photography.

flags of the British Legion and the light-blue standard of the United Nations.

Those present included politicians from north and south of the Border, Army veterans, church leaders, senior judges, foreign ambassadors, representatives of the Orange Order and leaders of the Ulster Defence Association (UDA). The mayors of Messines and nearby Heuvelland were also in attendance.

All stood to attention as a Defence Forces band played 'God Save the Queen', with many attendees singing along. Later, as the Queen and then President McAleese placed their wreaths before stepping back and bowing, the only sound was the drone of an Army helicopter circling overhead and the clicking of scores of camera shutters.

A minute's silence was then observed, broken by a muffled drum roll, followed by a Defence Forces piper playing the Thomas More air 'Oft in the Stilly Night'. As the Last Post was sounded, some attendees dabbed at their eyes. The Tricolour was then raised to full mast, accompanied by a drum roll. The reveille followed, segueing into 'Amhrán na bhFiann', which several present sang with gusto.

The Queen and the Duke of Edinburgh were then escorted from the cenotaph to view the Guillemont Ginchy cross and illuminated manuscripts, created by stained-glass artist Harry Clarke, containing the names of all the soldiers commemorated.

The Queen greeted several of those present, including Northern Ireland First Minister Peter Robinson, SDLP leader Margaret Ritchie, Ulster Unionist leader Tom Elliott, Alliance Party leader David Ford and Minister for Finance Michael Noonan.

As the Queen and the President were making their way out, Mrs McAleese spotted Kevin Myers

Queen Elizabeth II meets students at Trinity College Dublin, following her visit to the Long Room. Photograph: Maxwell Photography.

in the line and said to the Queen: 'This is the journalist who kept the flame of this place alive for so many years. He fought the good battle and, like so many good battles, it was worth fighting.'

Myers regularly wrote in *The Irish Times* about the heroism of the Royal Dublin Fusiliers and the 10th and 16th Irish divisions in the Great War. When the Queen nodded approvingly in his direction, he blurted out 'Your Majesty'.

Speaking afterwards to RTÉ, he said: 'The reaction has been even more moving and touching than I had expected and I had expected to be moved and touched by today's events. There is a simplicity here and an honesty and an integrity which stand alone . . . Words are not being uttered but they do not need to be uttered. The spirit is there, it is within the occasion and it is visible in the goodwill, palpable in the air, and I think words

are not necessary on an occasion like this but both peoples have been enhanced by what has happened here today.'

THURSDAY, 19 MAY 2011

'What Were Once Hopes For the Future Have Now Come to Pass'

Stephen Collins and Mark Hennessy

Queen Elizabeth has spoken of the painful legacy of history that affects Ireland and Britain, but said that while people should bow to the past, they should not be bound by it.

Speaking at a State dinner in her honour at Dublin Castle last night, concluding the second day of her visit to the Republic, the Queen said it was impossible to ignore the weight of history.

'Indeed so much of this visit reminds us of the complexity of our history, its many layers and traditions, but also the importance of forbearance and conciliation; being able to bow to the past but not being bound by it.

'It is a sad and regrettable reality that through history our two islands have experienced more than their fair share of heartache, turbulence and loss. The events have touched us all, many of us personally, and are a painful legacy. We can never forget those who have died or been injured, or their families.'

The Queen extended her 'sincere thoughts and deep sympathy' to all who had suffered as a consequence of the troubled past.

'With the benefit of historical hindsight we can all see things we wish had been done differently or not at all but it is also true that no one who looked into the future over the past centuries could have imagined the strength of the bonds that are now in place between the governments and the people of our two nations.'

Queen Elizabeth began her short speech in Irish saying: '*A Uachtaráin agus a chairde,*' which drew a round of applause from the guests.

She said she and her husband, Prince Philip, were delighted to be here to 'experience at first hand Ireland's world famous hospitality'. England and Ireland were so much more than just neighbours; they were firm friends and equal partners.

The Queen referred to the ceremony at Messines, in Belgium, in 1998, when she and President McAleese dedicated a tower to the memory of the Irish soldiers who died in the First World War. She also pointed to the successful establishment of a powersharing administration in Northern Ireland, and applauded the work of all those involved in the peace process.

'What were once hopes for the future have now come to pass,' she said.

The Queen was responding to a speech by President McAleese, who said the visit was the culmination of the success of the peace process. It was an acknowledgment that, while none of us can change the past, we can change the future, she said.

'It is only right that on this historic visit we should reflect on the difficult centuries which have brought us to this point. Inevitably where there are the colonisers and the colonised, the past is a repository of sources of bitter division,' Mrs McAleese said.

'The harsh facts cannot be altered, nor loss nor grief erased, but with time and generosity, interpretations and perspectives can soften and open up space for new accommodations.

'Yesterday, Your Majesty, you visited our Garden of Remembrance and laid a wreath there in honour of the sacrifice and achievement of those who fought against Britain for Irish independence. Today at Islandbridge, just as we did at the Island of Ireland Peace Park at Messines in 1998, we commemorated together the thousands of Irishmen who gave their lives in British uniform in the Great War,' said the President.

There were 172 guests at the dinner, including figures from the worlds of politics, sport, the arts and religion. British Prime Minister David Cameron was there, as were Northern First Minister Peter Robinson and his wife, Iris, who had not been seen in public for more than a year, following a controversy over her private life.

Nobel Prize-winning poet Seamus Heaney and his wife, Marie, rugby player Brian O'Driscoll and his wife, Amy Huberman, also attended. Mr Cameron said the visit was 'hugely successful and very significant'.

In a statement last night, Sinn Féin president Gerry Adams said the import of the Queen's remarks would be judged by the actions of her government. 'I believe that her expression of sincere sympathy for those who have suffered as a consequence of our troubled past is genuine.'

Queen Elizabeth II and President Mary McAleese at the Irish National War Memorial Gardens in Dublin, where they laid wreaths. Photograph: David Sleator.

FRIDAY, 20 MAY 2011

Local Royal Gaybo Presents Show Fit for a Queen as Chosen Few Relish Special Encounter

Miriam Lord

It was a performance fit for a queen when Dublin celebrated Her Majesty's final night in the capital city by giving her a send-off to remember.

Queen Elizabeth left the stage of the convention centre with the 2,000-strong audience on their feet and loud cheers and applause ringing in her ears.

The show may have been laid on by her loyal subjects in the British embassy, but it was a thoroughly Irish celebration of music, dance and the spoken word.

Local royalty was represented in the form of broadcaster Gay Byrne, who compèred the 45-minute show with his usual aplomb.

'It's a celebration that would have been beyond the imaginings of your parents and mine,' he told the lucky holders of the gilt-edged invitations, before confessing that the Queen's visit was something he thought he would never see in his own lifetime.

There was a certain hint of smugness about the audience, possessed as they were of the hottest tickets in town.

But future bragging rights come at a price, and for the glammed-up guests of Her Majesty's foreign office, it meant a long wait before they got to see the Queen.

The show didn't begin until seven in the evening, but the people attending had to muster down the road from the conference centre in the 02 Arena to clear security before they were bussed to the venue.

There were few exceptions. Even the Lord Mayor of Dublin, Gerry Breen, resplendent in his gold chain of office, had to take his turn through the airport-style scanners.

The members of the Government were more fortunate. They all pitched up in the foyer within 10 minutes of each other, clogging up the red carpet and drawing out the lovely music of the RTÉ chamber orchestra.

In fact, the evening was rather like a works outing from Leinster House – the place was teeming with TDs and Senators, party advisers and constituency stalwarts of the ruling parties.

When they finally cleared off in the direction of the pre-show VIP reception, a team of cleaners raced into the spot they had vacated and hoovered like mad.

There was a lot of 'style' according to those in the press pack who know about fashion, but even us more slovenly souls could see that the Celtic Tiger bling, mercifully, is gone.

This being a gig organised by our newly minted very best friends from the UK, the Queen arrived at the conference centre before President Mary McAleese.

She stepped from her Range Rover (would somebody not get the woman a step to help her alight safely, it's a hell of a drop to the tarmac for an 85-year-old woman?) bang on the dot of 6 p.m.

Her Majesty wore another creation by designer Angela Kelly – a delicate teal lace coat dress, trimmed with teal satin edging. No hat or tiara this time, but we were relieved to see the diamond

Cartoon by Martyn Turner.

Dressed in a teal lace coat dress designed by Angela Kelly, Queen Elizabeth II received a standing ovation from President Mary McAleese, Lord Mayor of Dublin Gerry Breen and over 2,000 other guests who gathered at the National Convention Centre in Dublin's docklands for what was described as an indoor garden party, hosted by British ambassador Julian King and his wife Lotte Knudsen. Photograph: Carl de Souza/Getty Images.

count was satisfied with yet another enormous brooch.

The Taoiseach and his wife Fionnuala – wearing a beige silk-knit suit – arrived with the Garda Commissioner Martin Callinan and his wife Marion. They were welcomed by the British ambassador Julian King and his wife Lotte Knudsen.

The crowd looked down from the balconies as the VIP guests arrived, applauding the Queen when she arrived and applauding even louder when President Mary McAleese made her entrance. The depth of the welcome for her was testament to the great job she has been doing this week.

Her Excellency looked stunning in a gold suit dress, set off dramatically by towering metallic navy stilettos.

The group went to see a fashion show before the main event. As a team of high-stepping models moved down the runway to face her, the Queen beamed at the sight of their day-glo hats and fascinators.

When one model sashayed towards her wearing what looked like a twig broom on her head, Her Majesty pointed and giggled and made a comment to the ambassador.

But it was an elegant cream Grace Kelly-style cape and dress that seemed to impress her most.

Among the audience was supermodel Erin

O'Connor, while Enda Kenny managed to make it inside for the final seconds of the show. Probably by design rather than by accident.

One word writ large could describe the audience – establishment. They looked a very comfortable bunch, among them TD Luke 'Ming' Flanagan, looking very much at home as he gazed down from the balcony, cupping a glass of red wine in his hand.

Former taoisigh Albert Reynolds and Bertie Ahern were in attendance – Bertie wearing a fetching pink shirt and a black tie with pink stripes. He was accompanied by his daughter Georgina, elegant in blue.

We spotted a good number of the social partners, David Begg chief among them. Henry Mountcharles was there, along with Michael Colgan of the Gate, John and Moya McColgan, celebrity chefs Richard Corrigan and Rachel Allen, playwright Sebastian Barry, Jack Charlton and Eddie Jordan.

Broadcaster Maura Derrane looked stunning in crimson, while Amanda Brunker and Lorraine Keane delighted the photographers from the social pages.

The show was stunning. From Mary Byrne, who sang U2's 'All I Want is You', to the Chieftains, to composer Micheál Ó Súilleabháin and singer Eimear Quinn.

Olivia O'Leary brought the house down with her take on the royal visit and Ireland's attitude to it. It was funny, warm and incisive and struck the right tone.

Westlife thrilled the ladies in the audience and Riverdance was stunning.

When it was over, the Queen made her way to the stage. When she mounted the steps, the crowd gave her a standing ovation.

She had a great chat with Mary Byrne.

Everyone left on a high.

'Tonight's a great crescendo,' said billionaire businessman Denis O'Brien.

'She has grown in our affections,' said Michael Noonan.

A Politician of Rare Vision, Intelligence and Energy

Denis Coghlan

Garret FitzGerald lacked political guile and cunning. That, along with a modest lifestyle, was probably his greatest attraction because it differentiated him so plainly from his immediate political rival, Charles Haughey. Any taoiseach who appeared in public wearing different coloured socks needed minding. And the public warmed to this absent-minded professor image. Behind the image, however, lay a sharp intellect and driving ambition.

You don't become party leader or taoiseach without purpose. His project involved nothing less than the transformation of society in the Republic. This political ambition placed him in the camp of Declan Costello and an up-and-coming minority within Fine Gael that supported a 'Just Society'.

Elected to the Dáil in 1969, his energy in debate and at question time antagonised colleagues who were part-time, Law Library politicians. Joe Leneghan famously remarked that, in the Dáil chamber, he was 'up and down like a whore's knickers'.

The scale of the challenge FitzGerald posed to the established order became clear when, in 1972, he published *Towards a New Ireland* in which he considered the kinds of political and administrative changes required on both sides of the Border to bring about that objective. He argued that EEC membership would help to end domination of Irish trade by Britain and provide the State with extended and healthier marketplaces that would generate national confidence.

Promotion of liberal Catholicism through changes in the laws on censorship, contraception and divorce would, FitzGerald suggested, help to reassure unionists. The special position accorded to the Catholic Church in the Constitution should be removed. A requirement to speak Irish to secure employment should change. And the prospect of a 'special relationship' with Britain, involving a future federal Ireland, should be pursued.

This agenda was unacceptable to many within a deeply conservative Fine Gael party, and Liam Cosgrave regarded it as a challenge to his leadership. Exiled to the Department of Foreign Affairs from 1973 to 1977, FitzGerald performed exceptionally well, escaped blame for the economic downturn and was well positioned to become party leader when the Fine Gael/Labour Party government eventually fell. On becoming leader of Fine Gael, he appointed key individuals who promoted talent over time-servers and encouraged new ideas.

In the process, divisions between the liberal and conservative wings widened.

Efforts to prevent the rezoning activity of some Fine Gael councillors, who were combining with their Fianna Fáil counterparts in reaching dubious planning decisions, were shrugged off. It was a harbinger of things to come. A lack of forcefulness, or political ruthlessness, in FitzGerald's make-up appeared to be an integral part of his DNA. He hated direct, personal challenges. His academic background, his fascination with ideas and a tendency to lecture were ridiculed by political opponents. 'That was fine in practice,' they parodied, 'but does it work in theory?'

Both of his governments were dominated by economic crises.

His first one lasted only a matter of months. Dependent on votes from Independent TDs, it fell

Cartoon by Martyn Turner.

following a huge political miscalculation and a lack of consultation involving an attempt to tax clothing and children's shoes.

The second one, also involving a coalition with the Labour Party, struggled on for four years against virulent Fianna Fáil negativity before reductions in public spending and other cutbacks finally sundered the parties. Interminable cabinet meetings at which little was achieved became the stuff of gossip.

A New Ireland Forum was established to explore the various forms of association that might emerge on the island. Unionists refused to participate and Haughey promoted Irish unity as the only acceptable outcome. When Margaret Thatcher delivered her 'Out, Out, Out' response to the various options, FitzGerald was publicly humiliated.

But he kept his nerve and, with perseverance and a great deal of hard work behind the scenes, the Anglo-Irish Agreement was secured in 1985. The agreement provided a mechanism for consultation between the Irish and British Governments regarding the governance of Northern Ireland. It was repudiated by Ulster Unionists and the Democratic Unionist Party but it eventually led to the peace process and the Downing Street Declaration of 1993.

Earlier, efforts to provide for divorce by way of a constitutional referendum were opposed internally and eventually defeated. Similarly, he was wrong-footed and outmanoeuvred on the issue of abortion when a contentious amendment was made to the Constitution.

The economic gloom that pervaded the State towards the end of this second coalition government and the negative politics espoused by Haughey provided a fertile element for the formation of the Progressive Democrats. FitzGerald may not have anticipated the threat posed by these disaffected Fianna Fáil politicians. In any event, that misjudgement cost Fine Gael dearly in the subsequent election and FitzGerald resigned as party leader.

Paradoxically, his contribution to public life as a columnist, broadcaster and academic may outweigh his achievements as a politician. Away from the pressures and economic difficulties of government, he encouraged politicians and public servants to engage in best practice. He was scathing of vote-buying at election time and of the handling of the economy and the national finances since 1997. A gradual loss of competitiveness since 2001 was of particular concern and it was an issue he returned to repeatedly in this newspaper.

FitzGerald's recollections of the time he had spent in government and the importance of decisions taken there developed a rosy hue in later years. But fundamental attitudes persisted: politicians and public services existed to serve the public; the creation of a just society was a challenging goal; and the ideas contained in *Towards a New Ireland* remained a work in progress.

Denis Coghlan was on the political staff of The Irish Times *from 1973 to 2002.*

SATURDAY, 21 MAY 2011

Sterling Show as Royals Win Over Traders at English Market

Barry Roche in Cork

Cork may well have to write to Meath to ask for an exchange of nicknames after the Rebel County gave a right royal welcome to Queen Elizabeth II and Prince Philip when they paid a short but highly successful visit to the city yesterday.

Gardaí estimated that about 30,000 people came into Cork city centre to witness the first visit to the city by a member of the British royal family since Queen Elizabeth's great grandfather Edward VII came in 1903.

They were rewarded when tight security was

relaxed just a little to allow the Queen go on an unscheduled walkabout.

Emerging from the English Market, Queen Elizabeth crossed a sun-splashed Grand Parade and made her way up to the corner of Washington Street, chatting with groups of teenagers including some with special needs, who had lined the street to catch a glimpse of her.

Of course, Cork earned its soubriquet as the Rebel County not, as some think, for the daring deeds of War of Independence guerrilla fighters such as Tom Barry and Liam Lynch, but for its support in the 1490s for the Yorkist pretender to the British throne, Perkin Warbeck.

But yesterday, it appeared that the Queen was willing to overlook Cork's mutinous indiscretions when she breezed into the English Market and put in a sterling 20-minute performance where she won over traders with her interest and informality.

Fishmonger Pat O'Connell spoke movingly of how proud his late mother Kay, who established the business in 1962, would have been on such a day before revealing how he unintentionally set Queen Elizabeth laughing merrily.

'I told her it's almost 30 years to the day since I got married and that was the last day I was this nervous of a morning and she just laughed – she was very relaxed, extremely friendly with a good sense of humour – it's the most exciting day we've had in the market.'

Tom Durcan presented Queen Elizabeth and Prince Philip with a hamper of local produce from

Queen Elizabeth II meets fishmonger Pat O'Connell at the English Market in Cork.
Photograph: Maxwell Photography.

the vendors in the market and revealed that while neither of them commented on the local delicacies of tripe and drisheen, Prince Philip was very taken with the spiced beef.

'He was asking me about the spiced beef and how you cook it so I explained – I think they enjoyed the visit,' said Durcan, whose eight-year-old nephew, John St Ledger, presented Prince Philip with a bound copy of Diarmuid and Donal O'Drisceoil's history of the market.

The Lord Mayor of Cork, councillor Michael O'Connell, presented the Queen with a specially commissioned brooch by Cork silversmith Chris Carroll depicting Cork's Butter Market and finished off with 18 carat gold, and garnets and diamonds to represent the Cork colours.

'I had met her in Dublin on Thursday night and her parting words to me then were as if she had been in Cork all her life – "I'll see you in the market tomorrow",' quipped O'Connell, adding that she really enjoyed the visit and the warm welcome accorded her in Cork.

Olive stall owner Toby Simmonds, who has lost his London accent after living for nearly 20 years in Cork, told how Queen Elizabeth and Prince Philip were very taken with his wide selection of olives – including some unusual looking white ones.

'She asked me did I grow my own olives so I told her we had tried but it didn't work out too well and then she asked me about the white olives and I explained that they were actually buffalo mozzarella and she just commented on how cosmopolitan Cork was.'

Among the other traders who met Queen Elizabeth was ABC bread shop owner Liverpool-born Sheila Fitzpatrick, whose great-great grandmother, Bridget Melia, left Crossmolina in Co. Mayo as an Irish speaker and started a market stall in Liverpool.

'I was used to seeing her image on stamps and coins,' she said. 'So it's a bit surreal to see her in front of you but she was very gracious and warm and I was delighted to meet her. It was such a positive experience and a sign things have moved on as they should do and it's wonderful.'

SATURDAY, 21 MAY 2011

It is Fitting Queen Should Visit as FitzGerald Bowed Out

Stephen Collins

There was something providential about the fact that Dr Garret FitzGerald, one of our greatest political leaders, died during the hugely successful, and surprisingly emotional, State visit of Queen Elizabeth to Ireland.

FitzGerald did more than any other political leader in this State's history to build bridges between Ireland and Britain and between the people who live on this island. The Queen's visit and her subtly moving speech in Dublin Castle have finally put the seal on the kind of relationship between the two countries for which FitzGerald had worked all his political life.

More than half a century ago he had a vision of a pluralist and tolerant Ireland with North–South relations on a sound footing and good neighbourly relations with Britain. Huge obstacles had to be overcome before that came to pass. The vicious terror campaign of the Provisional IRA was the most difficult, but other seemingly intractable problems had to be dealt with as well.

In death FitzGerald is receiving the accolades he deserves, but during his political life he faced fierce opposition as he tried to bring the country along with him. He was a politician who had the courage to lead public opinion rather than follow it and he paid an electoral price for that. Ultimately, though, so much of what is good about Ireland today – its tolerance, the outward-looking attitude of the majority of its people as expressed in involvement in the EU, and the good relations with Britain – reflect the goals he set for the country back in the early 1960s.

Breaking out of the narrow, backward-looking version of nationalism that developed such a grip on the country in the first half of the 20th century was no easy task. Like Seán Lemass, the Irish leader he most admired, FitzGerald was determined that this country should look outwards and take its place among the nations of the world.

Joining Europe was a liberation which allowed most of us to break free from the shackles of the past and the obsession with Anglo-Irish relations. Explaining why more than 80 per cent of Irish people voted to abandon the narrow concept of sovereignty and join Europe in 1972, Conor Cruise O'Brien observed: 'There were quite a few people who, in their hearts, were frightened at the idea of being locked up alone in the cold, clammy, dark with Kathleen Ní Houlihan and her memories of the dead.'

Unfortunately the Troubles fuelled the bloodthirsty side of Kathleen Ní Houlihan and it took courage for FitzGerald and like-minded politicians to chart a way out of the mindless cycle of violence.

Queen Elizabeth hit the nail on the head in a key passage of her speech. 'So much of this visit reminds us of the complexity of our history, its many layers and traditions, but also the importance of forbearance and conciliation. Of being able to bow to the past, but not be bound by it.'

Hopefully, the visit will not just have a positive impact on the present, but will also enable us to look at the past in a more clear-sighted way. The popular view of the past is still too often viewed through the narrow prism of Irish republicanism with its emphasis on oppression and violence. That in turn fuels the ignorant ideology of those still committed to violence for its own sake.

The Queen's acknowledgment of the various traditions on this island should help us to open our eyes to our own past, which is far more complex and varied than the republican myth would allow. While we have come to recognise the validity of the unionist tradition on the island, there is still a reluctance to give proper recognition to the proud tradition of democratic nationalism, which has actually done far more to shape Irish democracy than the actions of violent republicans.

The visit of President Obama will provide another opportunity to focus attention on the democratic Irish tradition, as the President is expected to pay tribute to Daniel O'Connell, one of the truly great men of Irish history.

O'Connell was a towering figure who inspired Irish Catholics and gave them the courage to seek freedom and justice. What made him remarkable was that he did not restrict his ambitions to the emancipation of his own people, but campaigned tirelessly for universal liberty. The abolition of black slavery was one of the causes dear to O'Connell's heart. In the general election of 1832 that followed Catholic Emancipation and the Great Reform Act, O'Connell led the first organised mass political party in Europe. All his party's candidates had to take a pledge to support not only the repeal of the Act of Union, but also a programme of political reform that included the abolition of negro slavery.

At the first meeting of the World Anti-Slavery Convention in 1840, the New York delegate James Canning Fuller declared: 'There is a charm in the name Daniel O'Connell all over the universe. Mr O'Connell could do more for the suppression of slavery in the United States than any other man.'

It was this reputation that prompted the great black abolitionist Frederick Douglass to visit Ireland in 1845 and speak alongside O'Connell at a number of anti-slavery public meetings. 'My sympathy is not confined to the narrow limits of my own green island,' declared O'Connell at one of those meetings. 'My heart walks abroad and wherever the miserable is to be succoured and the slave is to be set free, there my spirit is at home and I delight to dwell in its abode.'

Years later Douglass reflected that the death of O'Connell had been a great blow to 'the cause of the American slave'. He expressed regret that the Irish leader had been succeeded 'by the Duffys, Mitchels, Meagher and others, men who loved liberty for themselves and their country but were utterly destitute of sympathy with the cause of liberty in countries other than their own'.★

Since the establishment of the independent Irish State in 1922, the Duffys, Mitchels and their successors, who rebelled in arms against British rule, have been given the pride of place in official history, while O'Connell, Parnell and Redmond have been airbrushed from the popular version of events.

Surely it is time, now that we have been able to welcome the Queen, to properly acknowledge the leaders of the past who left us a great legacy of democratic values and institutions. A true appreciation of our past would be of inestimable help in shaping a better future, free of the stain of politically motivated violence.

★*Quotation from* Liberator, *Patrick Geoghegan's recent biography of O'Connell.*

SATURDAY, 21 MAY 2011

Recollecting Many a Moment with Garret the Family Friend

Caroline Walsh

J ust Garret. There was something perfect about the title of Garret FitzGerald's last volume of autobiography, published by Liberties Press last year.

There was the entirely appropriate allusion to the *Just William* books by Richmal Crompton about a mischievous English schoolboy because, even as a world statesman and towering intellectual, Garret remained a boy at heart. But the title was remarkable in another way because there was nothing 'just' about Garret in the sense of ordinariness that that word implies. He was a person who was uniquely himself in every way.

We were, like other friends of the family, in the Irish Museum of Modern Art on Wednesday night at Crash Ensemble's concert performance of Gerald Barry's opera *The Intelligence Park*, libretto by Garret's son-in-law Vincent Deane. But Vincent wasn't there. Word filtered through that Garret was in what turned out to be his final hours, lovingly cared for as always by his family as he always cared for them.

The old Box Brownie-type snaps of his own childhood in the 19th-century house Fairy Hill, outside Bray, where he grew up, the youngest of a band of brothers, give the key to why family was the lifeblood that fuelled him – and it wasn't just his own family. It was the families of his friends and the friends of his children, John, Mary and Mark too – and he even brought the whole crew on holidays.

The first one I went on was to Croix-de-Vie in the Vendée in France the summer after the Junior Cert. Arriving by train to a nearby station late at night with a friend of John's slightly older than myself, William Earley, with whom I'd travelled from Dublin, we were met by Garret and his wife Joan with flasks of soup – two flavours – to warm us up.

There were days in Schull and, in recent years, various houses in the south of France, especially the one in Cogolin in the hills above St Tropez. Most likely the waiter who took the order for the 20 or so members of the household on a trip to St Tropez – everyone ordering various coffees and patisseries, with Garret orchestrating the order – is still talking about what hit him.

The south of France conjures up glamour – and for sure there was style on those holidays. But what really characterised them were loads of children, everyone having shopping, cooking and wine-buying duties, and making sure there were enough

Cabinet members Richard Bruton, Brendan Howlin, Alan Shatter, Michael Noonan, Pat Rabbitte, James Reilly, Jimmy Deenihan and Attorney General Máire R. Whelan using a bus, as opposed to State cars, to get to the 1916 commemoration at Arbour Hill. Photograph: Matt Kavanagh.

episodes of *The West Wing*. One abiding memory of Garret is standing in the kitchen in Cogolin as we set in to do the washing-up and Garret looking around and saying, 'How is it that you can never find a dishcloth when you need one?'

If people were leaving to make a ferry in Cherbourg, or heading to the Chunnel, and Garret thought they were being overcautious about how long it would take, the map would be out and all routes explored. 'Sure you could easily stay another night' – and people often did.

Garret's love of being at the heart of a big household in France probably dated back to his

French exchanges in the 1930s in Le Bercail, home of the boisterous family of a Madame Camus, a widow with 12 children, members of which he stayed in touch with all his life.

At home there were the picnics in Wicklow, often at Powerscourt Waterfall. When he was taoiseach at the height of the Troubles, the security detail came too. Once when Garret and the family came to our terraced house in Ranelagh for supper in the 1980s, our small son Matt spent the entire evening running from the front of the house to the back, fascinated by the armed Special Branch officers.

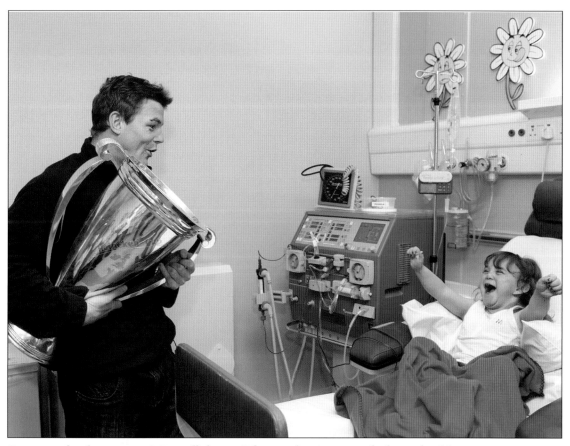

Leinster rugby player Brian O'Driscoll shows off the Heineken Cup to Michaela Morley (6), from Mayo,
a young patient at the Children's University Hospital in Temple Street, Dublin.
Photograph: Shane O'Neill/Fennell Photography.

When Garret called to the house one night when a school project on the Berlin airlift was under way, he happily got stuck in, all the while eating Arrowroot biscuits spread with butter. We could all have done a PhD on the subject by the time he left.

His interest when our daughter Alice was doing her masters in economic history on the Whitaker/Lemass years was typical. Not content with giving her a lengthy interview himself, he rang his pal T.K. Whitaker, central player of the era, and got him to give her an interview as well. No wonder rafts of young people loved him.

With a flotilla of grandchildren from Doireann,

the eldest, through Iseult, Aoife, Réachbha, Sorcha, Ciara, Garret, Erinne, Laoise down to Méadhbh – and on to his great-grandson – there were endless opportunities for parties, which Garret loved.

The questions at the children's parties in the 1960s when the family lived on Eglinton Road would leave you scratching your head with the pencil provided. 'How many stones in the pyramids' wasn't a statistic most of us carried around in our heads – and that was before Google. But it was the fun of it all: Garret, ringmaster of the mixer dance, the Paul Jones, where changing partners when the music stopped sometimes brought you face to face with your heart's desire – and sometimes not.

On top of the boundless enthusiasm, the innate generosity of spirit and the sheer lovability, there was a profound practicality. When Joan died in June 1999, I wrote the paper's obituary and Garret amazed us by writing his column about her too.

His logic was impeccable: who knew Joan better than him? And he was a journalist, after all, well able to turn out 1,000 words instantly.

With typical warmth, he rang the house early the next morning, delighted that two big tributes to Joan graced that Saturday's *Irish Times*.

And he could be so funny too, writing in that piece on Joan: 'I am not sure that she ever actually rang me as often as 28 times in one day, as has been suggested, but on occasion it may have come close to that.'

Realising now fully the great luck of knowing Garret for 50 years, I'm grateful to my mother, Mary Lavin, as it was through their friendship this gift came. My lifelong friendship with his daughter, Mary, was another great consequence.

Once, after yet another teenage party at the FitzGeralds', when I boldly didn't go straight home but on to the home of another guest for a coffee, Mother, then a widow, rang Garret who got out of bed and came over at once. The two of them began touring all potential locations until they found me and I got into the back of the car, as if en route to the scaffold. Mother said I'd be packed off to boarding school in the morning.

'Ah now Mary, that's too harsh . . .' said Garret and, with one bound, I knew I was free.

When in 1982 I was sent as a reporter to Kinsealy to interview Maureen Haughey, speaking loyally about her husband she gave out about the way in the media it was always 'Garret is good. Garret has a halo'.

And that's just it. We loved Garret because he was good – and he made us want to try to be good too. It's the best legacy any human being could leave another.

TUESDAY, 24 MAY 2011

Hours of Waiting a Distant Memory in Presence of Hero

Kathy Sheridan in College Green

Nothing quite prepares a person for the sight of the President of the United States wandering so close. Or the impish look in his eye as he glad-hands his way through the wheelchair enclosure and coolly takes the phone from Jessica Walls to say 'Hi' to her mother Glynis, minding her business in her Skerries kitchen, cooking spaghetti bolognese. No point in pretending to be objective.

Just surrender and swoon. 'I was 10 yards from him,' crooned Liz O'Donnell. And? 'What a beautiful man. He's gorgeous, he walks like a Kenyan – they have such elegant body movement . . .'

Psychologist Maureen Gaffney raised the tone just a tad by quoting Edmund Burke. 'Obama is a natural aristocrat. He is emotionally pitch perfect. Burke called it the natural aristocracy – people of unbelievable vigour, zest and character . . .'

Suddenly the interminable hours of standing and waiting and – for some of us, a shambolic series of confused and confusing US security demands – were a distant memory. The news that two floors of the Burlington were taken up with US Secret Service folk and their dogs was no surprise. They were tripping over each other around the city.

'Ah, it's a bit like childbirth,' sang a middle-aged Clare woman, 'you forget all the pain when you get this – God, I don't know – this MIRACLE put in front of you.'

She wasn't talking about Enda Kenny. But as a lawyer muttered sagely, 'Following Jedward is no small thing . . .'

Voice hoarsely reminiscent of campaigning from the back of a lorry circa 1975, the Taoiseach roared words that appealed to the spirit of hope and

President Barack Obama is greeted by excited well-wishers in College Green, Dublin. Photograph: Eric Luke.

optimism. 'If there's anyone out there who still doubts that Ireland is a place where all things are possible; who still wonders if the dream of our ancestors is alive in our time; who still questions our capacity to restore ourselves, reinvent ourselves and prosper . . . Today is your answer . . .'

The crowd loved it – mostly. About five minutes into the speech, as he was mentioning how 'the Irish harp glittered above the heart of the English Queen' and how we have the kind of wealth 'that can never be accumulated in banks or be measured by the markets', the crowd began to chant 'Obama!' A man close by muttered, 'He should have stopped about two minutes ago.'

In essence he was speaking the same inspirational language as Obama would minutes later – except that Obama was the man the crowd had come to hear. This, as a man told his small daughter, is 'what you'll be telling your grandchildren

about . . . that you saw Barack Obama with your own big, brown eyes'.

And here he was, having made it back from Moneygall despite a host of Twitter jokes suggesting he would be late because he was stuck in a round in Hayes's bar. Gazing out from his bullet-proof glass screens to a 50,000-strong crowd crammed in the reserved area in College Green, the American President had them from the moment he announced he was Barack Obama 'of the Moneygall Obamas. And I've come home to find the apostrophe that we lost somewhere along the way'.

From somewhere in the crowd came the roar, 'I've got it here!'

'Is that where it is?' asked the President. 'Some wise Irish man or woman once said that broken Irish is better than clever English,' he went on, to loud applause. 'So here goes: *Tá áthas orm bheith in*

Barcelona coach Josep 'Pep' Guardiola is given the bumps after his side's stunning victory over Manchester United in the Champions League final at Wembley Stadium in London. Photograph: Glyn Kirk/Getty Images.

Éirinn – I am happy to be in Ireland! I'm happy to be with so many *a cháirde'*. First the Queen of England; now the US President.

'God, the Irish language is going to power ahead after this,' said Maureen Gaffney. Liz O'Donnell marvelled at how he pronounced all the syllables in '*orm*'. He and Michelle were feeling very much at home, he said, 'even more at home after that pint that I had . . . Feel even warmer'.

A man nearby muttered wearily about the 'Paddywhackery'. But it was 'charming', argued his wife. 'But he's saying nothing,' insisted the husband. 'Oh give us a break – he's feckin' beautiful,' retorted the wife. The husband, sadly, had no answer.

Meanwhile, Obama was having a dig at the folks in the US who take 'a lot of interest in you when you're running for president. They look into your past. They check out your place of birth. Things like that . . .'

There was a yarn about his craving for a slot in Chicago's St Patrick's Day parade and how the organisers wouldn't believe Obama was a Gaelic name and slotted him into the back – inches ahead of the garbage workers. 'Bet they're looking at TV today and feeling kind of bad . . .' he said, to rapturous applause. 'Go Bulls!' yelled someone, probably apropos Chicago. 'Go Bulls – I like that. We got some Bulls fans here,' said the president.

There was the usual rhetoric about 'a proud, enduring, centuries-old relationship'; about being 'bound by history and friendship and shared values'.

A reference to his grandfather's grandfather, Falmouth Kearney of Moneygall, who left during the Great Hunger, 'as so many Irish did, to seek a new life in the New World . . . It's a familiar story because it's one lived and cherished by Americans of all backgrounds. It's integral to our national identity. It's who we are, a nation of immigrants from all around the world . . . But standing there in Moneygall, I couldn't help but think how heartbreaking it must have been for that great-great-great grandfather of mine, and so many others, to part. To watch Donegal coasts and Dingle cliffs recede. To leave behind all they knew in hopes that something better lay over the horizon.

'They had nothing to sustain them but their faith – their faith in the Almighty, but also a faith that America was a place where 'you could be prosperous, you could be free, you could think and talk and worship as you pleased, a place where you could make it if you tried . . .'

As he spoke about the Irish poet who wrote 'In dreams begin responsibility', the skies that had threatened rain all day cleared almost miraculously.

And when he finished with the words that 'America will stand by you . . .' we stood in wonder, until someone – an economist? – behind yelped, 'Tell that to Geithner'.

'Your best days are still ahead,' said Obama. '*Is féidir linn*! Yes we can!'

As the crowds broke up, they walked lightly to the rhythm of upbeat American marches, and it wasn't just the women. 'That crowned a perfect week,' said Fine Gael TD Andrew Doyle as he headed home. 'I detest hero worship but I don't mind worshipping such a hero,' said Cathal Grennan, a corporate lawyer.

Obama's Waffle Feeds Irish Taste for Fantasy

David Adams

Only a fine line separates a great orator from a flimflam merchant. And much as I admire the man, Barack Obama proved the point with his speech the other week at College Green, Dublin.

So patronising was he that halfway through I found myself wondering what kind of brief his two Irish-American speech-writers had been given: 'Let's just tell these people whatever they want to hear'?

There has always been something rather pathetic about Ireland marketing itself as a casualty of colonialism and competing for victimhood status with former British colonies in the developing world. When in fact, as an integral part of the UK, Ireland was at least as much coloniser as colonised, given the role it played in helping establish and maintain the British Empire.

Excluding African-Americans, whose horror story is on a different plane altogether, this is nothing compared to the brass neck of an American claiming a role in a victims of colonialism pageant, as Obama did at College Green.

His Kenyan antecedents certainly qualify. But his American ones, those he chose to stress, emphatically do not. Simply put, only Native Americans can legitimately claim to have suffered directly from colonialism in America; and how they suffered. All others – excepting slaves – were and are the interloping beneficiaries of it.

Aside from that, there was nothing Obama said about the Irish contribution to the US that couldn't, far more accurately in many cases, be said about a host of other races: the Scottish, Welsh, Italians, Spanish, Chinese, French, 'Germans' (a blanket term in early America for all those of

A tufted duckling meets its fate — by becoming a meal for a heron in Dublin's Herbert Park.
Photograph: Paul Hughes.

Nordic extraction) and, most particularly, the English and Jews of innumerable national origin.

In large part, but not entirely, the problem with his speech lay not so much with Obama as with his audience. If he had made similar complimentary remarks in London, Madrid or Munich they would have been warmly applauded and then shrugged off as a typical piece of political hyperbole. But in Ireland – where history is little more than self-serving delusion at the best of times and where the very essence of a historian's job, revisionism, is considered the greatest professional sin he or she can commit – they were taken as gospel.

Never mind the overblown rhetoric of Enda Kenny, the overwhelmingly gushing media commentary was proof enough of how eagerly Obama's speech was imbibed as yet more testimony to the exceptionality of the Irish. How needy and fawning are we to crave this sort of nonsense? How lacking in self-awareness must we be to actually believe it?

Naturally enough, given our nature, no one thought to tackle the obvious question that Obama's eulogistic meanderings raised: how come, if we're so successful and wonderful abroad, we always manage to make such a pig's ear of things at home?

Perish the thought, but might Irish exiles have been the major beneficiaries of immersion in other societies, rather than the reverse? Where Obama was severely at fault was in adding yet another piece of flannel to the 'most oppressed, yet most talented and decent people ever' Irish self-view. Thanks to his well-meaning waffle about 'finding common cause in repression', the Irish now believe that their far-off cousins stood shoulder to shoulder with African-Americans in their struggle for civil rights.

A tiny few undoubtedly did, as part of a relative sprinkling of courageous white Americans from every background, most notably Jewish.

However, the overwhelming majority didn't, and were as racist and bigoted as anyone else. Moreover, the idea that the Irish in America sat just one rung above African-Americans on the social scale, which is used to excuse such racist attitudes as are acknowledged, is truly risible.

Read about the experiences of the Chinese, or Jewish-Americans, or the treatment of the Native Americans, to discover just how ridiculous and downright insulting that proposition is – as a good starting place, I would suggest *The American Future* by Simon Schama, who like me is a big fan of the US.

The two American presidents of Irish origin who Obama's speech-writers name-checked were an interesting choice, Ronald Reagan and John F. Kennedy. There have actually been at least 12 or 13 Irish-American presidents, some of whom were first or second generation Irish, though usually only JFK gets the nod here at home. That all of the others were of Scots-Irish (i.e. Protestant) descent can surely have no bearing on their invariable omission – at least not with Obama's speech-writers, raised as they were in the broad-minded 'American way'.

My apologies to Obama for being so critical, but the sort of one-eyed historical/mythological mix that he delivered has done and continues to do enormous damage in Ireland.

Thankfully, just of late we seem to have embarked upon what will be a long, tortuous journey towards accepting that we are no better or worse than any other race of people, and indeed have been a lot more fortunate than most.

Can we afford another flimflam merchant, however well-meaning, at this critical juncture in our trek to maturity?

Is féidir linn: we've already more than enough of them to contend with.

MONDAY, 6 JUNE 2011

'It's Fun to Watch a Dinner Party Disintegrating Around the Host'

Rosita Boland

Come Dine With Me has finally arrived in Ireland – almost seven years after the wildly popular reality television programme based on rotating dinner parties first aired on Channel 4 in Britain.

For those who are not familiar with *Come Dine With Me*, it sees four (sometimes five) strangers in the same town hosting a dinner party by turn in their house over four or five consecutive nights. They receive a catering budget of £125 for the night (€125 for Irish contestants), which they can add to as they wish.

Guests are encouraged to poke around the house on arrival while the host is busy in the kitchen. The host's bedroom is usually scrutinised, often with deeply strange objects left around to be accidentally-on-purpose discovered.

Hundreds of contestants around Britain have appeared on more than 1,000 episodes of CDWM, as it's known, since 2005. But the one constant presence in all of them has been the distinctive, sarcastic, gleeful voiceover commentary of Dave Lamb. From show to show, through kitchen disasters, drunken guests, rude guests, flirting hosts and incontinent pets, Lamb has unflinchingly narrated the story of each dinner party.

Dave Lamb, whose sardonic behind-the-scenes comments add zest to **Come Dine With Me.**
Photograph: Alan Betson.

Dinner itself must include starter, main course, dessert, sometimes preceded with canapés, and always served up with copious amounts of alcohol. More recent series have also featured after-dinner 'entertainment'. This can range from the host attempting to sing or doing stand-up, to friends juggling fire in the back garden, teaching dance moves, reading your tarot cards or, well, anything really. Guests score their host out of 10 on the food and how much they enjoyed the evening. The contestant with the highest score at the end of the week wins £1,000, or €1,000, as is the case in Ireland.

Come Dine With Me has been franchised around the world, and there are some intriguing cultural insights to be observed in the way different countries have translated the original title of the show. In Finland, it's called *Rate My Dinner*; in

Hungary, it's *Dinner Battle*; in Germany, *The Perfect Dinner*; in France, *The Almost Perfect Dinner*; *Without a Napkin* in Slovenia; *Half-past Seven At My Place* in Sweden; *Eight O'Clock At My Place* in Norway; *Dinner Takes All* in the US; *Soiree* in Russia; *Cooked* in Poland; and the most accurate description of the show from any country, *Tastes Differ*, in the Netherlands.

Six weeks of the Irish series have recently been filmed: two in Dublin, and one each in Cork, Galway, Limerick and Waterford. The first to be broadcast will be from Cork, beginning tonight and running over five successive evenings.

Dave Lamb has also done the voiceover for the Irish shows, a fact that is certain to delight fans of the series on this side of the water. Contestants come and go, but Lamb's acerbic commentary is a consistently entertaining highlight and a draw in itself.

The diners, all from Cork, in the first episode of the Irish **Come Dine With Me.** *Photograph:* **Come Dine With Me.**

Over for the day in Dublin from Brighton, where he lives, Lamb is sitting at a table set for 12 in a hotel. Sadly, there's no dinner party planned here; it's a conference room. So what's the real background story to the filming of the series? Do people bad-mouth each other off-camera at 3 a.m.? Have they ever had to drop contestants? Does he write his own scripts?

'The success of the show has exceeded all expectations,' he says. 'Perhaps it's because hosting a dinner party is something a lot of people do. So it's fun to watch from a safe place as a dinner party disintegrates around the host.

'The crew film hours and hours. They have to know what the story is going to be, and how the show's attitude to each character will be, so they gather a huge amount of material,' Lamb says. 'They usually start at 7 a.m. in someone's house, and they'll go out shopping with them, watch them cook, and then they have to stay until the night finishes. Sometimes it can be 3 a.m. or later.'

A feature of the show is the contestants on their way home in the back of a black cab, holding up score cards for the evening. 'A lot of time can be taken up with the cab rides,' he explains. 'Because there's only one cab, and they all take turns – and everyone is usually hammered and they need several takes.'

Can he offer any insight into why people drink so much while being filmed for national television?

Lamb shakes his head, looking genuinely baffled. 'You would think they wouldn't. But they always do.'

Over time, the focus has moved quite a lot from showcasing the food to the frequent poor behaviour of the guests. 'The producers pay a lot of attention to the casting,' he confirms. 'It has become more personality-driven and how you deal with conflict.'

Lamb is never on-location himself, and sees only the edited half-hour versions that will go out on air. He doesn't write the scripts, but he does ad lib lines here and there, which tend to stay in. The scripts and his asides make it abundantly clear to viewers when a contestant is making a fool of themselves.

'I enjoy the gap between how people perceive themselves and how they are perceived by others. People quite often also are playing the game. Up until they've hosted their own night, they can be charming, and then after they've done their night, they turn nasty.'

So has any contestant ever complained to him about the way the show was edited and what he said about them as a result? He laughs. 'There may be complaints, but they don't get passed on to me. I've never met any of the people on the shows.'

That was, except for this very day, when he met 10 of the Irish contestants from Cork and Dublin, who took part in the first two shows to air.

'Yes, but they've not seen the shows yet,' he points out with relief, adding, 'I quite often try to make the commentary less cruel.'

So what, if any, cultural differences did he notice between the dinner parties here and in the UK?

'There weren't as many conflicts [in Ireland]. People all seemed really up for it, and to have fun. And the entertainment was quite different.'

The after-dinner entertainment has become a fixed part of most evenings now, something the contestants themselves, rather than the producers, have pushed for. What kinds of entertainment can we expect to see in the coming weeks?

'Eurovision seems to be big here. There was a Eurovision night, where every course was themed on a song, and there were Eurovision charades afterwards.'

But for him, the oddest 'entertainment' was the man with the horse. 'One guy finished his night by saying he had a horse outside and "let's go and see if we can find it",' Lamb recounts with puzzlement. How do you explain what 'Horse Outside' is to someone who thinks a rubber bandit is a type of elastic? Especially when this contestant apparently did have a real horse outside.

And no, in case you were wondering, Lamb has never done an ad-hoc running commentary when he goes out to dinner in friends' houses.

FRIDAY, 10 JUNE 2011

What if They Thought I was a Silly Old Fusspot?

Lara Marlowe

Wednesday morning this week started like any other day, with a pot of tea and a stack of newspapers on the balcony and Spike the cat resplendent on the other deck chair watching birds. It hadn't registered that on the other side of the Atlantic, tens of thousands of Irish teenagers were sitting their Leaving Cert exams.

I moved inside to answer emails. The heat and a squawking catbird drove Spike in soon after. There was a blur of telephone calls and interviews. I was reporting two stories at once: the fall of New York congressman Anthony Weiner and the rise of the new editor of the *New York Times*, Jill Abramson. As I worked, I watched my Blackberry for replies to interview requests.

At 11.32 a.m., that rare and serendipitous thing happened: unexpected good news. Seán Flynn, *Irish Times* education editor, sent me a congratulatory email. My article in praise of cats, published as an Irishwoman's Diary a year ago, was the first question on the Leaving Cert higher level English paper.

For some reason, my first thought was of Frank McNally's recent Irishman's Diary about his pleasure at discovering that his use of the expression 'to lose the run of oneself' was quoted in the *Oxford English Dictionary*. This, I thought, was a comparable achievement. It felt like *une consécration*, not in the English meaning of dedicating someone or something to a purpose, but in the French sense – from the *Petit Robert* dictionary – of 'confirmation, ratification, validation'.

Thirty-five thousand Irish teenagers had been, quite literally, my captive audience that morning. My pride swelled when I saw that texts by Colum McCann and Kevin Barry – real writers they, award-winning writers – appeared in the same exam. Not bad for a girl from California. Surely now they must grant me Irish citizenship . . .

I played my own little Oscar awards ceremony in my head.

'I'd like to thank Fionnuala Mulcahy of *The Irish Times* for requesting this article . . .' I studied the harp on the upper left-hand corner of the exam paper, the only national symbol that speaks of heaven. 'Coimisiún na Scrúdaithe Stáit' it said. I owed a debt of gratitude to the anonymous civil servant who deemed my article worthy.

No, we journalists are not only as good as our last article, the Leaving Cert examiners told me. The written word – even newspaper print – remains. This round-about honour, for a piece I'd written on a quiet Sunday afternoon, seemed a vindication of slow journalism, of articles that cannot be researched on the internet, that take time to write and time to read.

My thoughts turned to those thirty-five thousand young people scrunched over their texts, wearing school uniforms. I tried to imagine how my article must read to them, what I would have thought had I read it decades ago. It was too far a stretch of the imagination.

Matilda Lee, aged 3, from Milltown in Dublin, enjoying gardening at Bloom in the Phoenix Park. Photograph: Brenda Fitzsimons.

I hoped it wasn't a chore for the students who based their answers on my text, that it brought them luck. Question A (i) filled me with trepidation: 'From reading this article what impression do you form of both the personality and lifestyle of Lara Marlowe?' Crikey.

What if they thought I was a silly old fusspot, with my cat and dead writers and terrace in Georgetown? How easy it is for animal-lovers to appear eccentric . . .

When my article was originally published, with a photograph of Spike, I sensed a special pride in the way he swaggered around the apartment. On Wednesday, I found him napping on the bed, his usual daytime occupation. 'Hey Spike! We're on the Leaving Cert!' I told him over and over. He smiled, like Julie Manet's cat in Image 1 on the examination. Later he would be the surly alpha male of Image 2, Steinlen's *Summer: Cat on a Balustrade*.

The theme of the exam paper was mystery. The objective, neutral and detached journalist in me knows I commit the sin of anthropomorphisation each time I see my mood reflected in Spike's. But there's another, simpler part of me that still wonders at the inexplicable, joyous connection between animals and humans.

SATURDAY, 11 JUNE 2011

On Video Nasties

Róisín Ingle

Something great happens. I rent *The Social Network* from the video shop. This is a big deal. I've mostly given up watching movies. I find it increasingly difficult to drag myself out to the cinema and I happen to live with someone who hits his own internal snooze button before the opening credits have rolled. I say: 'This is great, isn't it? I love just watching a film together,' and he answers with a snore that rattles the Spire.

When I mention *The Social Network* he indicates that perhaps this is a film he might stay awake for, so, full of optimism, I go to the video shop. I enjoy the way that they are still called video shops in the way I like saying I've 'video-taped' something on telly when I've actually done no such thing. I've merely pressed a magic button on my remote control and within a matter of weeks I have 162 episodes of *Peppa Pig* at my fingertips. In case of emergencies.

I used to be on nodding terms with the people at the video shop. I would ring them up and have lengthy conversations about the latest Almodóvar when all I really wanted to know was whether they still had a copy of *10 Things I Hate About You* or whether Andrew McCarthy had been in anything lately. They told me about Fellini and I pretended to know what they were talking about. I went to the cool video shop back then. Now I go to the other one.

The guy I rent *The Social Network* from . . . well, I don't know him from Adam Sandler as it has been so long since I darkened these doors. But he's cool and aloof and enigmatic in that video-shop-guy way and I get nostalgic for my once weekly visits.

Cool and aloof. I think it's in the job description. A lot of video-shop dudes – there seems to be rather less video-shop dudettes now that I think about it – come off as though the call from Woody Allen is due any day now and they've got a Tarantino-esque script burning a hole in their man bag. It's as though answering your questions about *Legally Blonde 2* is demeaning. Which is why I used to always ask them: 'That Witherspoon one. You've got to love anything she's in really, haven't you? She just doesn't know how to pick a bad movie.'

I am almost giddy going to pick up *The Social Network*. If he doesn't fall asleep or at least only falls asleep near the end, this could mean the revival of my whole movie life. Renting the film I expect a bit of chat from video guy about how fantastic the

Broadcaster Miriam O'Callaghan after receiving an honorary Doctor of Letters degree at the University of Ulster in Derry. The citation described her as 'the ultimate multi-tasker — humanity and compassion are the central elements of her journalism'. Photograph: Trevor McBride.

film is because that is what every person on the planet seems to think. But he just scans my movie without even a glance.

'You're probably wondering what took me so long to get around to watching it,' I say as an opener. I've been missing this video-shop banter. He doesn't answer. I tell him that I don't get out to the cinema much on account of having children and he couldn't look more fascinated if I started talking about the funny thing they said the other day. Or read him my shopping list. Hey ho.

I don't leave anything to chance. I make sure I put the movie on just after dinner. I turn all the lights on full blast. I make my boyfriend sit in the most uncomfortable chair in the house and I open

the window so a chill breeze whips around the room. I can do no more. My fate is in the hands of Zuckerberg/Eisenberg and the Winklevoss twins lookalikes.

I swear to God, Zuckerberg/Eisenberg is only back from being dumped by his girlfriend and blogging about it while simultaneously creating Facemash before my companion is snoring like a hippo. After an hour I stop poking him in the ribs, which made no difference to his snooze but made me feel better.

It is weeks before I try again. I am in Portadown for the Drumcree Church Fête where I buy a bag of toy medical supplies for 60p and briefly attend an exhausting auction. Later I rent the Witherspoon vehicle *How Do You Know*.

This is a question but there is no question mark in the title, which I take as a sign of the film's cleverality and not a sign it's missing other vital components. Enjoyability, for one thing. (It turns out Witherspoon is capable of picking turkeys. Must inform video-shop dude.)

Not that I saw the whole thing. Around the time Witherspoon decided to shack up with Owen Wilson, I decided to lie down on the sofa and there are three witnesses to my snore-fest that my boyfriend's father said could have rattled the hut on Drumcree Hill.

And so it has come to pass. I am just another annoying person who falls asleep in the middle of a film. It doesn't matter that this one was rubbish. It can only be a matter of time before I start stockpiling Werther's Originals and marvelling at modern 'video-taping' technology. Too late.

SATURDAY, 11 JUNE 2011

Forty Years A-Cartooning

Kathy Sheridan

Some of us are old enough to remember when his cartoons had to be collected off the bus arriving into Sheriff Street from deepest Kildare. And how, on disconcertingly one-sided phone calls, he would often settle for two words when other freelancers would use a hundred (90 of them probably buttering up the commissioning editor).

What was he doing in Kildare with that posh English accent anyway? Was he some kind of weirdo, arty, recluse? Martyn Turner always played by his own rules. It's not that he wouldn't know how to butter up an editor; it's that he wouldn't. It's not that he is monosyllabic, although he can be – just not with people he respects or enjoys. He is no recluse either, although he likes to portray himself as one.

He has been contentedly married for nearly 43 years to Jean, a humorous librarian turned champion Irish Setter breeder, whom he met when he was 17, 'two days after England won the 1966 World Cup'. He is a besotted grandfather to their son's two little boys. He plays golf with the same bunch of people, loves the banter and is passionate about the game. (His riff on the notion that it's a game played by capitalists but organised by communists is highly persuasive, even for golf-haters.)

In the Turners' second home in southwest France, there's even a neighbouring French gardener who likes him enough to pass fat, flavoursome vegetables through what a grandson calls 'the magic hedge', for fear the 6ft 7in vegetarian might fade away for lack of nourishment.

He is a man 'who never wasted words but has a lot going on behind the eyes', says Prof. John Horgan, who once commissioned Turner cartoons for this newspaper's education supplement. Horgan expeditions to the Turner home 'involved being assaulted by the monstrous breed of Irish Setters who would nearly be as tall as Martyn himself when they stood on their hind legs and would want to lick your face . . . The things you'd put up with for the sake of Martyn and Jean's company are

Cartoon by Martyn Turner.

At home in his studio, Turner's lair. Photograph: Brenda Fitzsimons.

quite surprising,' he says affectionately. Definitely no weirdo recluse then.

So, Jean, what was so impressive about the 17-year-old Martyn Turner? 'Eh, I think he was 18 . . .' But what quality stood out? There's a strangled laugh. 'He's very tall.' Anything else?

'He has remained a child. I think everyone would know what I mean by that. Yes,' she says thoughtfully, 'he has many child-like qualities.'

It's a recurring theme. Turner himself remembers a psychiatrist on *The Pat Kenny Show* explaining how, as we attain adulthood, we assume things and stop questioning. 'Except Martyn Turner,' the psychiatrist said; he was the perpetual child who sees that none of the emperors have any clothes. 'A very tall child who gets paid for it,' Turner adds, with a lugubrious laugh. 'I just think of it as seeing events and attitudes and situations at their simplest, and seeing what gives.'

So what gives about Turner's vision? Horgan describes it as a 'capacity to put two unrelated contemporary things together to create something extraordinarily rich'. He still laughs at the one depicting Charles Haughey with Margaret Thatcher, in which Haughey is thinking: 'This relationship will last at least until she retires.'

This writer cherishes an original 1995 Turner on her wall, in which two unrelated contemporary events are ingeniously combined: an eruption over Finola Bruton's smoking and Michael Lowry's first dodgy ethics run-in. Apart from representing a neat piece of political history, the cartoon also represents Turner's many quiet kindnesses. I found it in the letter box soon after returning home from a distressing assignment.

Turner himself mentions a cartoon of Dick Spring standing in a lost-and-found, asking: 'Have you seen the run of myself?'

'I love that cartoon,' Turner says. The twist is that it wasn't one of his own. 'I don't like my cartoons.' The reason he keeps going, he says, is so that he can have another go tomorrow.

But they have to keep on coming anyway. It's how he has made a living for 40 years, turning out five – four since he hit 60 – a week for *The Irish Times* since 1971. That's 40 years of pressure to find a fresh gag every working day, then a way to express it as art, all in a few hours.

'There is a routine, and at some stage in the routine, something emerges. It could happen when I'm swimming, or walking, or when I'm going to make a cup of tea. The trick is not to think too much but to wait for something to come out of the ether . . . The harder you think deliberately about something, the less likely you are to come up with something that isn't what everyone else is thinking.'

The routine is to start at 7 a.m. by tuning in to *Morning Ireland*, then to read the paper, then listen to Pat Kenny, then *News at One*.

'By the end of the one o'clock [news] I'll have something to do. Though really it's more of a concept at that stage. Last Saturday, for example, I knew I wanted to do something about cucumbers and I was also trying to think of a handy way to shut ministers up, but I didn't know how to turn it into a cartoon till I worked it out: you stick them in ministers' mouths.'

The trick is to try and draw it as he thought of it in that one-hundredth of a second, to simplify, not to wreck it by over-refining it.

Turner says he thinks in words rather than pictures, 'which is why my average cartoon has about 200 words in it. I should really be an editorial writer on Twitter – everything within 140 characters . . . I'm not trying to make people fall over laughing – and I succeed in that quite well, I think – but I am trying to get them to look at something in a different way.'

Turner claims not to be a very good caricaturist – there are about five good ones in the world, he says – so he 'doesn't actually get a likeness . . .

What I try to do is create a sense of how I feel about the person. If there's any magic involved in what I do, that seems to work quite well. So when you look at what I've done on Haughey, or Bertie, or Brian Cowen or Garret, you can know instantly what I think about them without adding any words.'

He doesn't know them personally, so is creating a political rather than a personal view of them, 'which is why they're not strictly caricatures; they're a person representing that particular character. It's not a personal attack on him . . . most of the time.'

Despite the fact that John Bruton ended up with scary panda eyes, Turner says he was very difficult to draw. 'Very bland. Same with Michael Noonan. I was told one day that I'd drawn him as a half-boiled egg and I realised that's exactly what he looked like. The only thing about John Bruton was his laugh, so trying to find a way to get his laugh visually finished up with that completely inane grin.'

It took months to 'get' Bertie Ahern. 'Then one day it clicked. I always drew him in an anorak, even though he wasn't wearing one any more, and a schoolboy tie. It just looked right. He added the rest himself – he was stupid enough to wear yellow trousers.'

Brian Cowen, Alan Dukes and Barack Obama all shared the scruffy cigarette signifier (Turner doesn't like smoking) in one way or another.

Dukes told him that it didn't stop him smoking, but he kept thinking he should be putting a cigarette in his ear so that people would know who he was.

The discovery that Cowen was a smoker was a boon. 'I'd say I did three or four cartoons based on it when he was going down, until he eventually finished up as a pile of cigarette ash.'

But that Enda Kenny chap is a challenge. 'I've kind of given up on him. He's just sort of stuck with the way he is. It doesn't really look like him but it doesn't matter because, repetitively, you'll eventually realise he's Enda Kenny.' Is it because he's unmarked? 'He is – for a person who's 60, he's amazing, because he looks about six. That's pretty incredible. I just try and draw him as young as I possibly can. That's the way it's turning out'. The point at which Kenny should start worrying is when he starts to look like a baby.

Turner has an underlying political ideology, 'but none that transposes to any known political party. I think I'm just an ageing hippy who thinks everyone should love each other and get on with it and be nice . . . You don't like people exploiting other people, or taking advantage of other people, so that kind of rules out most of the economic systems of the world.'

He 'suffers' from 'isms', he says. His vegetarianism was triggered when he ran over a rabbit 40 years ago. He argued with himself: if he was a carnivore he would take the rabbit corpse home and eat it; otherwise he would bury it. He buried it and decided he no longer wanted people to do his 'dirty work' for him – killing animals, doing something he wouldn't do. 'And then if you extend that to other things, like why do I oppose the war in Iraq – well, it's because I wouldn't go and do it myself and I wouldn't expect my children to go and do it.'

He defended a Danish newspaper's decision to publish the Muhammad cartoons on the basis of press freedom. 'If you look at the countries where there aren't political cartoonists, ask yourself, would you like to live in one of those countries?'

He is only vaguely aware of occasional storms that break over his own cartoons, probably because

David Norris with Moore Street stallholder Catherine Kennedy while canvassing in Dublin for the Seanad elections. Photograph: David Sleator.

no one could possibly guess his email address. But he is no effete artist.

This is a man tempered by deep, private tragedy – not for public consumption – but utterly without self-pity. He was the child of London East Enders, whose father was a warehouseman-turned-dustbin salesman and whose 'incredibly intelligent' mother had to leave school at 12 or 13 to help her father in his rag-and-bone scrapyard.

It was she who pushed her bright boy to apply for one of two coveted scholarships at Bancroft's public school in Woodford. He got in, but 'loathed every minute of it'. Why? 'Because I was one of two poor boys in a school of rich idiots.' He became a surreptitious 'golf professional' for a day and a half, until his mother whacked him and sent him back to school.

Nonetheless, Bancroft's was a life-changer. Those years not only changed his accent – 'from East End of London to this sort of vaguely posh accent I have now' – they also transformed him from extro-vert to introvert, a painful process intensified by the constant rows that preceded his parents' divorce. 'I used to go and hide . . . So I kind of got used to not being in the middle, to keeping out of the way. I still like that – being on the fringe of things, watching what's going on, not really getting involved.'

It was the need 'to get as far away from London as possible, from school, family, the whole thing, to start again I suppose' that landed him at Queen's University, Belfast, in 1967 to study geog-raphy. After a term there, he discovered that his grandmother had been born in Belfast. 'I thought we were all Protestants and Jews, and it turned out we were Belfast Catholics as well.'

In the meantime, he had found Jean, while looking for a summer job in Cologne after leaving school. She happened to be working alongside his sister in the British Council library there. He was just 20, still a student, when they married. A qualified librarian by then, she had got a job in Queen's and he credits her early earning power and budgeting skills with enabling him to pursue his

cartoon commissions and edit the 'neither republican nor unionist' *Fortnight* magazine with Tom Haddon. 'If I'd known how broke we were, I would prob-ably have got a teaching job or something.'

The move south to Kildare came with *The Irish Times'* offer of the political cartoonist's job in 1976, a 'loose' arrangement which never developed into a permanent staff position.

The upside of the arrangement was independ-ence. It has allowed him to work for many prestigious publications around the world, as well as *The Irish Times*. He has also turned out numer-ous wonderfully titled books and calendars. The downside of the loose arrangement manifested itself when *Irish Times* contemporaries began to take comfortable early-retirement packages to the south of France, he says with a wry laugh. Luckily, Jean still manages the business side of things.

These days, they spend as much time as they can in France. Some day, if he can afford to, he'd like to retire there. And next week, the grandchil-dren are coming.

Would he have had things differently? He cracks up laughing. 'I'm as happy as Larry. I'm a round peg in a round hole. I can't imagine doing anything else. I can't imagine thinking in any other way. I kinda like being cynical, being an outsider. I don't want to go anywhere, or do those TV or radio things people are supposed to do. You have your friends, and that's it.'

SATURDAY, 11 JUNE 2011

He Made it Easy For Us to Forget He Was Dying

Miriam Lord

Brian Lenihan made it easy for us to for-get he was dying. Minister for Finance in the middle of a massive economic crisis. He had cancer. He wanted to do

Former Minister for Finance Brian Lenihan jesting with reporters and photographers in a corridor of Government Buildings just before presenting his first budget to the Dáil in October 2008. Photograph: Maxpix.

his job. What he didn't want was sympathy.

He made one demand of his opponents: 'Aggressive intervention!' They were not to hold back.

They didn't. The minister made it easy for them to forget.

Yes, the future was uncertain, but Brian Lenihan was aware of two things. He knew that with time, and no small amount of pain, the country would recover. And he knew he had time, and no small amount of pain, but the diagnosis was terminal.

He was 50 years old – it was Christmas 2009 – when he found out. But he was back at his desk at the beginning of the new year. *Noblesse oblige.*

A lot of people had good cause to curse a politician and his party and their politics for bringing the country to this sorry state. But they were genuinely heartbroken when they learned of Brian's devastating medical condition.

The Lenihans have been with us for as long as we can remember, with their unique brand of political soap opera. Never dull, often controversial, always different.

People who never met him felt they knew Brian. You couldn't fall out with him. He was the cut of his father, charming, likeable, with those doleful panda eyes and that wheezy-blustery way of speaking.

Given his pedigree and academic brilliance, he could have been awfully pompous, but he wasn't, this Belvo boy who went to Trinity and Cambridge and the King's Inns. Naturally, he took silk. He was fluent in several languages. But like his dad, Brian made that easy to forget.

He liked a drink and late nights. He wasn't afraid of journalists and argued his corner. He loved to gossip and could be hilariously indiscreet. And he could never fathom why nobody believed he didn't dye his thicket of jet-black hair.

He could be conceited too, with that pedigree. He was far from perfect.

Up to a few weeks ago, the sight of him beetling across the Dáil canteen was a welcome sight. He was great company.

Yet, by this stage, we all knew he was very ill. He didn't talk about it. At the outset, he had gently chivvied tearful staff: 'No need for that sort of carry on!' Brian wanted to be leader of Fianna Fáil. But when the opportunity came at the chaotic end of the last government, he botched it.

During that infamous Galway Fianna Fáil think-in last year, we sat in the hotel lobby and had a long conversation.

There had been much talk about him mounting a challenge. We could see he was still thinking about making a move, trying to talk himself out of it, but not convincing either of us.

Finally, he put down his glass of red wine. 'For f★★★'s sake, I'm dying!' he blurted out. But he did it anyway.

Brian had the generosity to make it easy for us to forget. And it makes the shock of his passing all the deeper today.

TUESDAY, 28 JUNE 2011

The Florida Philosophy

Isabel Conway

It attracts thousands of retirees with its beaches and golf courses, but can Florida really turn back the clock? Its residents seem to think so.

'Age.' The platinum blonde in tight raspberry capri pants, waving impressive sculpted nails, fingers adorned with rings the size of golf balls, shrugs. 'As far as I am concerned, 80 is the new 60 or maybe even 55, at a push.'

It is early afternoon inside Galleria, an upscale shopping mall in Fort Lauderdale, a pleasant waterfront city of towering retiree condominiums, north of Miami.

People who appear to be middle-aged or younger are snoring gently in the deep leather sofas put there to take the exhaustion out of shopping. Senior citizens, escaping the blinding June heat outside for the cool of the mall, are hopping in and out of demonstration massage chairs, barely listening to sales pitches.

Glamorous and sprightly elderly women are mulling over halter-neck beach dresses. A man with a shock of jet-black hair and enough wrinkles to put him in the octogenarian age bracket dances across the menswear department of Neiman Marcus, politely asking me which shirt he should choose: would it be psychedelic palms or the red and purple checks? A tough choice, so he opts for both.

The nation's headquarters for retirees, Florida's major industry is the 'age wave'. Targeting here is relentless, from law and accounting firms specialising in estate matters, to clinics treating conditions from stiff necks and arthritis to cosmetic surgery and impotence.

Then there are the 'early bird' senior dinners, the happy hours, the casino incentives for elderly gamblers, the cut-price furniture and clothing for those magically entering the twilight years zone. Inevitably, also, there are the many funeral homes.

Retirement communities in Florida continue to attract people from all over the US and abroad, notably Scandinavia, drawn by affordable luxury homes that have fallen in price since the property slump. Sunshine, beautiful beaches, golf courses, highly organised age-related services and a more affordable cost of living are the main attractions.

Property promotional bumph describes Florida as a hotbed of physical activity. Vigorous oldsters are depicted swimming, cycling, playing tennis,

Florida pensioners, all in their eighties, enjoying the pool at Forest Trace. Photograph: Isabel Conway.

jogging – not so much growing old gracefully as staying young forever.

So, is it a myth – that lure of rejuvenation, turning back the clock, a madly optimistic hormonal silliness, a place where people come to believe that 80 is indeed the new 55?

'No,' replies Fort Lauderdale-based Dr Bruce Szamier, a former Harvard medical professor specialising in inherited eye diseases.

Today he works as a yacht broker too, though he is still involved in science and eye research. Not for a moment considering retirement, the tanned 70-year-old is soon to re-marry.

'People keep going much longer down here,' he says. 'They stay younger and more active. Maybe it's the climate, but it is also far easier to live in condo [condominium] developments where you don't have to mow the lawn or worry about roof repairs. You pay a maintenance fee and it is taken care of.

'There are all sorts of other perks, like a golf course on your doorstep, a swimming pool, social outlets. You can easily find company. If you are an active person, there is just so much to do here in Florida.'

A 'luxury resort adult community' called Forest Trace, west of Fort Lauderdale city, became home more than five months ago to Jack and Evelyna Cantwell. He is a retired top advertising executive, second-generation Irish with roots in Cork and Kilkenny. She is an English-born, prolific inventor, related to the Dyson (vacuum cleaner) inventing dynasty.

Amy Quinn from Bray (centre) with supporters at Dublin Airport, as the Irish Special Olympics team arrived home from the World Summer Games in Athens. Photograph: Sasko Lazarov/Photocall Ireland.

They decided to move into this more secure environment after, as Evelyna (84) puts it, Jack suffered a couple of 'nonsenses' (bad turns) and she had several minor strokes and a fall.

They sold their condo where they had been happy for 12 years since moving from Philadelphia to Florida, deciding that a mild and unobtrusive level of security and care was an inevitable next stop. They did not want to be 'a bother to the children, worrying about us and if we were alright'.

This is the best of both worlds. At Forest Trace, which has more than 300 apartment units in a purpose-built series of buildings, they enjoy their complete independence and privacy in a spacious two-bedroom flat with its own fully equipped kitchen and fabulous views over 70 acres of grounds and a large lake, knowing there is unobtrusive surveillance from staff and a 24-hour on-site medical call-up.

Imagine a five-star hotel with all the amenities that conjures up: spacious meeting rooms, a library, a beautiful dining room with free seating and dining from mid-afternoon to evening, a lobby where a pianist is tinkling away, landscaped lavish greenery on the other side of the windows but occupied exclusively by senior citizens. That's Forest Trace.

Residents who are 100 years old or more are not uncommon here, still enjoying the flagship entertainment and even going on stage to sing along with Broadway and cruise-ship entertainers at night.

Younger residents include Morganna King, who played Marlon Brando's wife in the film *The Godfather*, and an aunt of the judge featured in the *Judge Judy* television show.

The complex has an assisted living wing for those who need a higher level of care but are still below nursing home dependency. That later, and sometimes inevitable, step is designed to be achieved seamlessly.

Evelyna Cantwell, elegant and quick-witted, a renowned bio-chemist whose inventions have ranged from an ultrasound scanner for examining burns and other skin problems to oxygenating products for preserving cut flowers, earned herself the title in syndicated US newspapers of 'mother of invention' and continues to work on new projects at Forest Trace.

Jack (89), cheerful and outgoing in a bright pink Ralph Lauren shirt and yellow tie, 'drags her out of bed every morning before 7.30 a.m. to swim' in the large heated pool, which forms part of resort-style amenities that include steam and sauna rooms, fitness centre and beauty parlour.

'People here really celebrate life,' says Jack, showing off the impressive building and grounds. 'People aren't waiting for death, they enjoy every day that comes.'

Michelle Slagel, marketing manager at Forest Trace, says it offers one of the best and cheapest deals anywhere: from $2,700 (€1,900) a month for a large one-bedroom apartment for one person with an add-on of $500 for a partner sharing, inclusive of two meals with menu choice per day, all activities and entertainment, which is pretty much non-stop, including outings, clubs, sports, shopping, golf and a daily happy hour with two free cocktails.

'We try to give our guests the best quality of life, what they miss is their youth and you can never give that back. But you can make growing older a lot easier and also fun . . . laughter and looking forward to stuff means so much,' Slagel says.

Dublin-born staff member Paula Mullen, who runs the shop at Forest Trace, says: 'I was broken-hearted visiting Ireland and seeing how bad some retirement homes were in comparison. There was absolutely nothing only depressing "waiting-for-death" options, and older people needing more security, back-up and companionship were not being catered for at all.'

Beverly Abramowitz (81), lately arrived at Forest Trace and still unpacking her cases after a solo trip around China, adjusts her bling gold glasses, fixes her pretty lace-trimmed blouse and declares: 'Age . . . don't give into it, stay healthy, eat properly, take exercise and live and laugh. That's been my philosophy and whenever I hear old people "acting old" and complaining I just walk away.

'Stay positive and you stay young . . . that's the secret. It's the philosophy down here in Florida where a lot of us come and it works.'

SATURDAY, 2 JULY 2011

Irish Team's Hoop Dreams Alive After Semi-Final Win

Damian Mac Con Uladh in Athens

'I'm so proud of her. It's brilliant, she's brilliant, they're all brilliant,' said Dublin woman Ann Byrne, her eyes welled up with emotion, after her granddaughter Sarah Byrne and her fellow Irish basketballers had beaten Italy 24–16 at the Special Olympic semi-finals yesterday.

Around her on court four of the Olympic indoor complex the atmosphere was electric, as it had been throughout the match, in which 14-year-old Sarah was the star performer and team lynchpin.

Like all events involving any of the 126 Irish athletes, the game was attended by many from the tight-knit and passionate Irish delegation – made up of 49 coaches, 400 family members and 200 volunteers – as well as other Team Ireland athletes.

No matter whether they win or lose, the delegation's support for their athletes in Athens is total, in recognition of the huge individual achievement for each member of the team in making it to an international sporting event.

And the feeling is that every performance in Athens, whether it brings in medals or not, only serves to strengthen the Special Olympics movement at home, to encourage even more athletes to compete among themselves and allow their abilities to shine.

'It's all about participation. The medals are only a bonus,' says Pam Beacom, whose daughter Aisling has picked up two in swimming.

If the Irish have brought one thing to the Athens games, it's that deep sense of community that made the 2003 games in Dublin the resounding success they were.

The 200 Irish volunteers, who each had to raise €3,250 to participate and give up two weeks of their time, are highly regarded for their diligence and helpfulness.

Although they were excused from their duties during last week's two-day general strike, all the volunteers showed up at their posts, most organising taxis paid for out of their own pocket.

At the healthy athletes programme run in conjunction with the games, Tipperary volunteer Mary G. Ryan-Strappe and her colleagues have opted to work flat-out on double shifts, so great has the demand been for their expertise.

But behind the glowing praise for the general organisation of the games and the state-of-the-art venues, some parents believe the welfare of the athletes has not always been to the fore, blaming the Athens organising committee for a number of shortcomings.

'It's been a test of endurance,' said one mother, citing the 17-hour ferry journey without cabins that the Irish team took from Rhodes, their host town, and the 'ridiculously long' opening ceremony that ended so late that it left athletes with less than two hours' sleep before their first day's sporting events.

The Irish delegation also senses the games haven't engaged Greeks in the same way that the 2003 games engaged Ireland.

Special Olympics Ireland head Matt English says 'it's obvious that the city of Athens hasn't embraced it the same way as the whole of Ireland did in 2003'.

The coverage in the print media has been minimal, with little interest shown in the event.

Even Prime Minister George Papandreou failed to turn up to the opening, despite being scheduled to speak, but that didn't stop one newspaper, *To Vima*, from reporting he was present.

Nor has there been any live daily coverage on state broadcaster ERT, which was so jealous of its exclusive rights to film the opening ceremony that it prohibited media from other countries from doing so.

Many Greeks, shocked that the 2011 games cost €35–€40 million more to stage than those in Ireland and Shanghai in 2003 and 2007, respectively, wonder why it came to Athens at all.

SATURDAY, 2 JULY 2011

Healy-Rae Saga Gives North Even More Reason to Look Down on Us

Donald Clarke

There are times when you pray the world isn't watching us. Last week was such an occasion. The scandal that bubbled up around Michael Healy-Rae is not likely to evolve into our own latter-day Watergate. But it should make decent Irish people – however innocent – cringe with refracted embarrassment.

As you should be aware, Healy-Rae, an unpretentious politician of the populist stripe, has agreed to pay for €2,600 worth of suspicious phone calls made from Leinster House. Big deal. Over the last five years, Westminster politicians have had to apologise for charging duck houses, ivy

A man with a neck . . . Michael Healy-Rae talks to reporters about the €2,600 bill run up by someone using a Leinster House phone, making 3,636 calls that helped him win a reality TV programme. At the time, his father Jackie was a TD in Leinster House. Photograph: Bryan O'Brien.

repairs and moat refurbishment to their unfortunate taxpayers. Moreover, at time of writing, Healy-Rae has not been directly implicated in the making of the calls. Why worry?

Well, at least those British politicians got something worth having from their duplicity (worth having for ducks, anyway). The telephone calls were made – oh, I can barely bring myself to write the words – in order to help Michael, scion of the great cap dynasty, win some reality TV jamboree entitled *Celebrities Go Wild*. State representatives of the Bongo Bongo Islands rarely find themselves caught up in such pathetic scandals.

The news comes a few weeks after the release of a fascinating poll concerning the attitudes of Northern Irish people towards a united Ireland. That survey found that some 52 per cent of

Catholics in the North wanted to remain within the United Kingdom.

Jeez. Who'd blame them? We'll be eating our young next.

This writer has always had something of a split personality when it comes to cross-Border matters. Raised in south Belfast (to a Protestant family, not that it's any of your business) until the age of 11, I have spent most of the succeeding years in the Irish Republic.

On visits to the North, I have, thus, gained a certain perspective on middle-class unionist attitudes to those living south of Newry. Many Northern Protestants, of course, regard the South as a beacon of progress and stability. But a strong strain has always viewed the nation as a bit of a joke.

Chris Martin of Coldplay performs on the final day of the Oxegen music festival at Punchestown Racecourse in Co. Kildare. Photograph: Dara Mac Dónaill.

Trains don't run on time. Heroin-addled car thieves wait on every street corner. Government employees use their phones to propel eccentric politicians towards victory in preposterous television shows.

Ironically, this view was at its most prevalent during the years of the economic boom. To that point, the State's relatively sluggish economic performance was seen as confirmation that Southerners were not fit to be trusted with the controls of a pedal car.

The explanation for this fantastic (in all senses) surge in wealth was simple: every penny sitting in every Irish bank account came from 'the Common Market'. It seems that, each weekend, European officials would travel over from Brussels and drive around the country handing out fivers to every gap-toothed yokel (that's to say every citizen of the State) in every poorly maintained, rat-infested hovel (that's to say every house outside the six counties).

Being simple folk – children really – the Southerners would then spend the cash on magic beans, pinwheel hats and rosary beads. Eventually, the European money would run out and they (you) would all have to go back to eating rotten potatoes and having too many children.

If you were feeling in robust form, you might have pointed out that Northern Ireland was, by some reckonings, the most subsidised corner of western Europe. You'd have been wasting your lazy breath. It was hard work, carbolic soap, early nights and Presbyterian thriftiness that turned the North into the economic powerhouse it clearly wasn't.

The funny thing is that such views were not the preserve of the Protestant community. I can remember, sometime in the early 1990s, standing outside a pub in Soho and listening to a huddle of Northern pals, all inclined to vote for Sinn Féin or the SDLP, as they explained that 'the Free State' was a motley-clad jester of a nation.

The conversation was triggered by the news that, faced with an administrative backlog, the Republic was planning to hand out driving licences without the formality of a test.

'What kind of country does that?' they sneered in chewed vowels. The implication was clear. Once a united Ireland arrived, the Northerners would potter down the road and knock this displaced Albania into some sort of working order.

There are, in these times of economic meltdown, more important things to worry about than the smug noises being emitted by Rosemary and Edwin McCausland at their local golf club. But it's hard not to care a little that so many Ulster Protestants will be eating such great helpings of I-Told-You-So pie. The antics of Healy-Rae's supporters will only add relish to their dish.

Let's hope they were all looking elsewhere last week. Wasn't Wimbledon on the telly?

FRIDAY, 8 JULY 2011

Unlocking an Answer You Won't Find on Google

Karlin Lillington

Last week, I sat outside in the California sunshine at Google headquarters in Mountain View – aka the Googleplex – and talked to some googlers about whether it was pure chance, or a set of specific factors, that has made Silicon Valley the world's centre for technological innovation.

The context of the conversation itself, I think, provides some of the answer. Although I was scheduled to interview one of Google's engineers at 3:30, I had been invited to take a tour of the Googleplex at 2 p.m.

You could easily spend hours meandering around and talking to people in divisions working on search, where Google corners the market, then advertising, and then there's Google's mobile platform, Android, and its web browser and operating system, Chrome – plus all the various apps and services.

And there's always the legal end of things, as Google has had its share of controversy on privacy issues in particular, with the EU currently rattling sabres.

But that wasn't the plan – if there was one in any formal sense. Google has a reputation for being slightly disjointed and quirky at times, especially in terms of organisation, and that was certainly the case here. I arrived at two and had a friendly, albeit brief, walkabout with a very nice young woman who had been at Google for all of five months.

Then she had to go to meetings, and so I was handed to someone in the communications division, who suggested we go sit down at a picnic table, out past the life-sized model of a T Rex skeleton covered in plastic flamingos, the volleyball court and outdoor vegetable garden.

I assumed this would be for some kind of briefing or the continuation of the tour, but instead I was thrown the musing question about Silicon Valley innovation: why here, in this place? Oh, OK.

We'd only just begun to chat about this when we were joined by another googler who had worked in the Dublin office and said he had wanted to connect at some point either before or after the scheduled interview. So he sat down and jumped into the chat. The more, the merrier.

I had absolutely no idea why we were all sitting there having this conversation, interesting and enjoyable though it was.

Caoimhghín Ó Caoláin TD, Minister for Arts, Heritage and the Gaeltacht Jimmy Deenihan, and Labour TD Eric Byrne get walking in Merrion Square to publicise the Houses of the Oireachtas hill walk taking place in Waterford in July. Photograph: Bryan O'Brien.

For my part, I noted that the question is one that comes up all the time. For example, only two months ago, Stanford president (and adviser to the UCD/TCD Innovation Alliance) John Hennessy tackled the question before an audience at Trinity.

As he noted then, everybody who comes to visit Stanford asks this question, usually phrased as an inquiry about concocting the exact recipe for Silicon Valley, so it can be duplicated back home.

What national region or country would not want to copy a system that turns out so many of the world's top technology companies, and which

takes in the bulk of US venture capital every year? In the first quarter of this year, for example, Silicon Valley took in $2.49 billion (€1.74 billion) in venture investment for 212 companies.

The second-largest region was New England, which lagged well behind at $639 million for 90 companies, and the investment declines steeply after that.

Hennessy also noted that, of course, there was a factor of chance that came into play very early on. You had the can-do mentality that came with California's pioneer territory, inherently pro-entrepreneurial. Stanford, the university that churns out tech companies, was located in the heart of the region, along with the University of California at Berkeley, which has a very strong engineering and computer science department.

Then there were some early companies that grew to be huge – such as Hewlett-Packard in the 1930s and microchip pioneers Fairchild Semiconductor, which would spin out Intel (with Fairchild itself spun out of William Shockley's pioneering Semiconductor Laboratory in Mountain View). Spin-outs of spin-outs of spin-outs, the classic valley story.

And there's the weather. Neither too hot nor too cold, right on the edge of San Francisco Bay, with easy access to the sea, the mountains and one of the world's most beautiful cities.

Yes, chance brought some of these factors together, but mostly the valley slowly evolved over the last 100 years or so. Trying to duplicate such organic growth is unlikely ever to succeed in whole.

Still, as the googlers noted, you can have successful regions – the Boston and Cambridge areas of Massachusetts, New York's silicon alley, and Austin, Texas, are just some examples, with many other US and international locations as well.

As we talked, it occurred to me that all these people – the young googlers, sharp and confident – were part of the answer. None were native Californians; all had come from other states. They fitted or adapted quickly to the odd, energetic, forward-thinking work culture of the valley.

Work is hard, but work is fun. They liked the weather, they liked the energy, they liked the

A woman mourns over one of 613 coffins of newly identified victims of the 1995 Srebrenica massacre in a hall at the Srebrenica-Potočari Memorial and Cemetery in Bosnia. Photograph: Sean Gallup/Getty Images.

opportunity and the quirky, loose management style that exemplifies so many valley companies. They liked the ability to work between offices in other states and other countries.

And then to come back to the valley, where many will spin out the next generation of valley innovation.

MONDAY, 18 JULY 2011

Clarke Realises Open Dream

Philip Reid at Royal St George's, Sandwich

The coronation was belated, but arguably all the sweeter for the wait. And, in truth, who really saw this coming? In one of those uplifting deeds which sport, in all its glory, throws to the unsuspecting hordes on only the rarest of occasions, Darren Clarke won this 140th edition of the British Open over the quirky links of Royal St George's with a grace and display of shot-making that equalled any of those great champions who had gone before him.

On a grey day with a constant wind coming in off the English channel to accentuate the challenge, Clarke – a 42-year-old Ulsterman who had watched without the slightest touch of envy as two other players from his part of the world claimed Major titles over the past 13 months – took his turn to achieve destiny with a final round of 70 for a winning aggregate total of 275, five-under-par, which left him three strokes clear of runners-up Phil Mickelson and Dustin Johnson.

'It's been a dream since I was a kid to win the Open, like any kid's dream is,' said Clarke, after a day when he kept his composure and finished a job that was only half-done on Friday when he shared the midway lead and only three-quarters complete on Saturday evening when he finished with a one-shot lead over Johnson. Yesterday, there was no denying him, with even a traditional final-round

charge from Mickelson failing to deflect him from his appointed course.

Clarke's victory completed another extraordinary time for Irish golf, enabling him to join Graeme McDowell and Rory McIlroy – the past two winners of the US Open – in an elite group of Major champions. And, with Pádraig Harrington's three Major title successes, going back to his breakthrough win in this championship in 2007, it means Irish players have won 6 of the last 17. Surely a golden generation in the sport.

In terms of emotion and sentiment, this win was hugely popular: in the grandstands, on every hillock on this corner of England and, most certainly, in the locker-room, where his peers have often wondered how he had gone through an honour-laden career without a Major. That sense of wonderment is now no more.

In fact, Clarke revealed after his round that among those who had sent messages of support were Tiger Woods – who is currently sidelined with a knee injury – and McIlroy, who was paying his mentor back for advice sent to him on the night before his own win in the US Open at Congressional.

Clarke's arrival at the top table of golf is a testament to his self-belief and perseverance, having overcome personal trauma – with the death of his wife, Heather, to breast cancer in 2006 – to use a wonderful talent that first surfaced as an 11-year-old when his father, George, a former soccer player with Glenavon and Dungannon Swifts, and mother, Hettie, took out family membership at Dungannon Golf Club. Now, some three decades later, he has enrolled in a champions' club that dates back to 1860.

Oh, how those past masters would approve of the new champion, a player with a beautifully repetitive swing. And, on this occasion, an ability to use the putter – so often his Achilles' heel in the past – with touch and feel.

For sure, there were times yesterday when Clarke must have wondered if this would be his

Darren Clarke celebrates a famous victory after finally securing his first major championship title when he kept his nerve in testing conditions to win the British Open at Royal St George's, Sandwich, finishing five-under, three clear of Americans Dustin Johnson and Phil Mickelson. Photograph: Eddie Keogh/Reuters.

day, most especially when Mickelson – playing with a sense of freedom that has been so absent on his past visits to the famed links courses that play host to the Open – went on a front-nine charge that included three birdies and an eagle by his seventh hole, at which stage he moved level at the top of the leaderboard.

Unfazed, however, Clarke stuck to his task. And, in truth, the roars that greeted the Northern Irishman's play were louder than anyone's. On the 564 yards par-five seventh hole, Clarke provided his answer to those who wanted to usurp him: there, he hit a perfect drive and, with 198 yards left to the pin, hit an eight-iron approach that landed 16 feet from the hole. He rolled in the eagle putt with authority.

In the lead again on his own, Clarke never relinquished it. Mickelson's charge – covering the front nine in a mere 30 strokes – petered out on the homeward run as he missed some short putts and eventually signed for a 68, for 278.

Clarke could keep a much closer eye on his other principal opponent, as Johnson was playing alongside him. Johnson's threat effectively disappeared on the 547 yards par-five 14th, where the long-hitting American – who had seen Clarke lay-up with his own approach shot – went for the green in two only to see his iron shot pushed to the right. It was last seen sailing above the out-of-bounds white stakes.

There and then, Clarke knew all he had to do was to get home safely. And he did, even if he finished bogey-bogey. The main thing was that he had kept any calamity off his card and his 70th stroke of the round and his 275th stroke of the championship was no more than a tap-in from an inch.

British Open champion Darren Clarke at his local bar, the Bayview Hotel in Portballintrae, Co. Antrim, after lengthy celebrations of his win. Photograph: Colm O'Reilly/Pacemaker Press.

The sound of the ball rolling into the tin cup provoked raucous roars from the huge galleries, acclaiming golf's newest champion. 'You never really think you're safe until you're on the 18th green with a couple of shots ahead. You never know what's going to happen and I got a couple of good breaks that went my way. Yesterday (Saturday) I played as good as I could play from tee to green and I didn't really get anything out of it. Today (Sunday) I played not bad; I played okay. But I got a couple of good breaks but also at the same time hit lots of great putts which burnt the edges and didn't go in. So it sort of balanced out.'

Of his breakthrough win and how he managed to keep his emotions in check in getting the job finished, he explained: 'I'm just older, just a little bit older and allegedly a little bit wiser. But I certainly had a few thoughts going through my head when I was walking onto the green on 18 because, at that stage, I could have four putts from there.

'Even I figured I could manage to get down in four from the edge of the green there. But the few thoughts, thinking about the past, and then making a speech, I can only be as normal as I am. So if I didn't feel a little bit emotional it wouldn't quite be right.'

Mickelson, whose front-nine assault seemed likely to gatecrash Clarke's coronation, was among those to express sincere congratulations: 'I'm really happy for him. He is one of the first people that called us, Amy and I, a couple of years ago (after Mickelson's wife was diagnosed with breast cancer).

Dominique Strauss-Kahn and his wife, Anne Sinclair, arrive at a New York State Supreme Court hearing on charges of his sexual assault of a maid in his hotel room. The charges were later dropped but Strauss-Kahn resigned as head of the International Monetary Fund and his chances of getting the Socialist Party of France's nomination for the French presidency vanished in a welter of accusations about his allegedly abusive treatment of women. Photograph: Mario Tama/Getty Images.

He's been through this and we couldn't have had a better person to talk to. It was fun to make a run at him . . . but I couldn't be happier for him.'

TUESDAY, 19 JULY 2011

Church's Solicitor Guarded Every Angle

Patsy McGarry

A name that crops up with conspicuous frequency in the Cloyne report, when it comes to 'restraint' on the part of Catholic Church authorities in co-operating with State inquiries into child sex abuse allegations, is that of solicitor Diarmuid Ó Catháin.

This is the same Ó Catháin who advised Cardinal Desmond Connell when in 2008 he initiated High Court action against his successor as Archbishop of Dublin, Diarmuid Martin. That was an attempt to restrain Archbishop Martin from handing over documents to the Murphy commission, which the cardinal deemed confidential to himself personally. Cardinal Connell later dropped the action and the documents were handed over.

This is the same Ó Catháin who attended a controversial meeting in Limerick on 30 March 2006, as a member of the interdiocesan case management advisory committee of Cloyne and Limerick dioceses. Set up in 2005, this committee advised then bishop of Cloyne John Magee and then bishop of Limerick Donal Murray on handling allegations of clerical child sex abuse.

At that meeting, Ó Catháin and two priests representing Limerick diocese met 37-year-old Peter McCloskey, who alleged that in 1980 and 1981 he was repeatedly raped by a priest in Limerick. Bishop Murray later issued a statement saying he 'completely accepts the truth' of McCloskey's allegations.

Deirdre Fitzpatrick, then of the One in Four group, accompanied McCloskey at the meeting and recalled he was 'very distressed and disappointed' afterwards.

She was critical of Ó Catháin for suggesting the diocese could sue McCloskey for costs should he proceed with court action. Three days later, on 1 April 2006, McCloskey died by suicide.

Ó Catháin was solicitor for Cloyne diocese. Msgr Denis O'Callaghan was child protection delegate there. Both were on the interdiocesan case management advisory committee of Cloyne and Limerick dioceses, set up in 2005. This, the report said, 'was not appropriately constituted' as Msgr O'Callaghan and Ó Catháin's other roles 'made it virtually impossible for them to give the sort of independent advice which the bishops needed'.

A member of this committee said the meetings were dominated by Msgr O'Callaghan, Ó Catháin and the priest delegate from Limerick. 'It was not permissible to express a contrary opinion,' he told the commission.

The Cloyne priest delegate from 2008 to June 2010, Fr Bill Bermingham, told the commission Ó Catháin 'did not agree with the procedures and policies underlying the [Bishops' 1996 Framework] document', as the report put it.

Minister for Children, Frances Fitzgerald, speaking outside the Dáil after she laid the Cloyne report before the Oireachtas. Photograph: Cyril Byrne.

Ó Catháin told the commission he had reservations about the mandatory reporting element of the document the bishops had adopted 'despite his expressed views to the contrary'. He said he saw no conflict in his being a member of the case management advisory committee while acting as solicitor for the diocese in clerical child sex abuse cases.

An indication of Ó Catháin's approach can be gleaned from the case of Fr Drust. An allegation was made in 2002 by 'Ula' that she had been sexually abused by the priest between 1967 and 1971. In 2003 gardaí sought a statement from Bishop Magee. Ó Catháin told the commission he explained to a Garda sergeant investigating the case that 'if a matter was discussed in confidence with a bishop, the bishop could not disclose the confidence without first getting, obtaining, the consent of the person who had reposed the confidence'. He told the sergeant, as he recalled it for the commission, he believed 'it was in the interests of the common good that Magee should not be asked to make a statement'.

When, later, the sergeant met Bishop Magee, he was assured of total co-operation. It was not to be the case. Through a solicitor, Bishop Magee declined to make a statement or to supply a copy of Ula's handwritten account. His solicitor said the document was 'a church document and hence confidential'. Bishop Magee would not make a statement 'in consideration for the public good and the maintenance of the confidentiality of the church'.

In the case of Fr Brendan Wrixon, accused of abuse by 'Patrick', Bishop Magee gave two accounts of a meeting he had with the priest on 22 September 2005. An accurate account, where the priest admitted guilt, was sent to Rome and a fictional one, where he denied the allegations, was for diocesan records. When asked by the commission why he prepared two accounts, Bishop Magee said he had inquired from Msgr O'Callaghan and Ó Catháin about his correspondence to the Vatican and 'was assured it was a privileged relationship and . . . would not be discoverable . . .' He found out later this was not so. According to the report,

Ó Catháin told the commission he had 'no recollection of Bishop Magee consulting him directly about this issue . . .'

In the summer of 2008, the case management committee reacted vigorously to draft findings of the church's child protection watchdog – its National Board for Safeguarding Children – that child protection practices in Cloyne were 'inadequate and in some respects dangerous'. On 9 July 2008, it sent a forcefully-worded letter to the board saying: 'If you issue this report in its present form or include its distortions in your forthcoming annual report, we shall have no choice but to seek remedies in either ecclesiastical or secular courts or both.' Among the signatories were Msgr O'Callaghan and Ó Catháin.

WEDNESDAY, 20 JULY 2011

A Day of Humble Pie for Murdochs but Responsibility is Another Question

Mark Hennessy

Comedian Jonnie Marbles, little known outside his own sittingroom, yesterday did Rupert Murdoch a favour when he hit him with a shaving-foam pie, but it would have been better for the billionaire publisher had he acted two hours earlier.

Marbles, who launched his attack as Murdoch and his son James neared the end of their evidence to a House of Commons committee, was quickly brought to heel by security, with the aid of a 'great left hook' from Murdoch snr's wife, Wendy.

James Murdoch and others rushed to the defence of the 80-year-old, but Murdoch stayed utterly calm. It was his best moment of the afternoon – the culture, media and sports hearing will not go down as his finest hour.

Father and son came with a plan to atone for the sins of *News of the World*. Rupert Murdoch would open with a detailed statement; expressing respect for MPs, a public contrition and a firm purpose of amendment.

But committee chairman John Whittingdale, a Conservative MP, ruined the game-plan, denying him permission for the statement – a decision that irked his son, who is known for having a temper.

James Murdoch, who indulges in management-speak, attempted the apologies: 'These are not the standards that our company aspires to around the world'. It sounded exactly what it was: pre-prepared.

His father, never before seen by the public in this way, leant across and touched his son's arm and said: 'This is the most humble day of my life.' He knew this would become the day's TV soundbite. However, he was exposed by Labour MP Tom Watson, who showed Murdoch to be a distant emperor who had failed to mind a far-off satellite.

Again, and again, Murdoch snr was shown not to have command of the detail. His son frequently tried to intervene, but was rebuffed by Watson, with faux-politeness: 'I will come back to you, Mr Murdoch'. The younger Murdoch, whose own career could soon be decided by shareholders, bristled.

Repeatedly, the junior Murdoch was at pains to emphasise he had taken control in London in December 2007, when there was no suspicion of the cancer eating away at the newspaper as the police had completed their investigations.

Murdoch snr, denying blame for the past, insisted he was the man to sort it out, emotionally drawing on the memory of his father Keith, who exposed the horrors of the Gallipoli campaign in 1915.

The Marbles moment meant Murdoch finally did get to read his statement, expressing hope that 'we will come to understand the wrongs of the past, prevent them from happening again' and restore the nation's trust in the company, and in journalism.

Later, Rebekah Brooks called foul when MPs charged that she was too close to British prime minister David Cameron during her time as chief executive at the company.

'The truth is that he is a neighbour and a friend but I deem the relationship to be wholly appropriate and at no time have I had any conversation with the prime minister that you in the room would disapprove of,' she said.

She continued the afternoon's theme of denial, saying though she had used private investigators for 'legitimate' use during her time as editor, she did not know private investigator Glenn Mulcaire, who was jailed in 2007 for hacking.

WEDNESDAY, 20 JULY 2011

This is a Republic, Not the Vatican

Enda Kenny

On 20 July 2011, Enda Kenny addressed the Dáil on Church–State relations in terms that were unprecedented and unheralded. The Irish Times published what he said, in this lightly edited version, as an article on the opinion page.

The revelations of the Cloyne report have brought the Government, Irish Catholics and the Vatican to an unprecedented juncture. It's fair to say that after the Ryan and Murphy reports Ireland is, perhaps, unshockable when it comes to the abuse of children.

But Cloyne has proved to be of a different order.

Because, for the first time in Ireland, a report into child sexual abuse exposes an attempt by the Holy See to frustrate an inquiry in a sovereign, democratic republic – as little as three years ago, not three decades ago.

And in doing so, the Cloyne report excavates the dysfunction, disconnection, elitism – the narcissism – that dominate the culture of the

Martyn Turner's take on Enda Kenny's Dáil speech on the Vatican.

Vatican to this day. The rape and torture of children were downplayed or 'managed' to uphold instead, the primacy of the institution, its power, standing and 'reputation'.

Far from listening to evidence of humiliation and betrayal with St Benedict's 'ear of the heart', the Vatican's reaction was to parse and analyse it with the gimlet eye of a canon lawyer. This calculated, withering position being the polar opposite of the radicalism, humility and compassion upon which the Roman Church was founded.

The radicalism, humility and compassion which are the very essence of its foundation and purpose. The behaviour being a case of *Roma locuta est: causa finita est.*

Except in this instance, nothing could be further from the truth.

Cloyne's revelations are heart-breaking. It describes how many victims continued to live in the small towns and parishes in which they were reared and in which they were abused. Their abuser often still in the area and still held in high regard by their families and the community. The abusers continued to officiate at family weddings and funerals. In one case, the abuser even officiated at the victim's own wedding.

There is little I or anyone else in this House can say to comfort that victim or others, however much we want to. But we can and do recognise the bravery of all of the victims who told their stories to the commission.

While it will take a long time for Cloyne to recover from the horrors uncovered, it could take the victims and their families a lifetime to pick up the pieces of their shattered existence.

A day post-publication, the Tánaiste and Minister for Foreign Affairs and Trade met with the Papal Nuncio to Ireland, Archbishop Giuseppe

Leanza. The Tánaiste left the archbishop clear on two things: the gravity of the actions and attitude of the Holy See; and Ireland's complete rejection and abhorrence of same.

The Papal Nuncio undertook to present the Cloyne report to the Vatican. The Government awaits the considered response of the Holy See.

I believe that the Irish people, including the very many faithful Catholics who – like me – have been shocked and dismayed by the repeated failings of church authorities to face up to what is required, deserve and require confirmation from the Vatican that they do accept, endorse and require compliance by all church authorities herewith, the obligations to report all cases of suspected abuse, whether current or historical, to the State's authorities in line with the Children First national guidance, which will have the force of law.

Clericalism has rendered some of Ireland's brightest, most privileged and powerful men, either unwilling or unable to address the horrors cited in the Ryan and Murphy reports.

This Roman clericalism must be devastating for good priests, some of them old; others struggling to keep their humanity, even their sanity, as they work so hard to be the keepers of the church's light and goodness within their parishes, [their] communities [and within] the human heart.

But thankfully for them, and for us, this is not Rome.

Nor is it industrial-school or Magdalene Ireland, where the swish of a soutane smothered conscience and humanity and the swing of a thurible ruled the Irish-Catholic world.

This is the Republic of Ireland 2011.

A republic of laws, of rights and responsibilities; of proper civic order; where the delinquency and arrogance of a particular version, of a particular kind of 'morality', will no longer be tolerated or ignored.

As a practising Catholic, I don't say any of this easily.

Growing up, many of us in here learned we were part of a pilgrim church. Today, that church

needs to be a penitent church. A church, truly and deeply penitent for the horrors it perpetrated, hid and denied. In the name of God. But for the good of the institution. When I say that through our legislation, through our Government's action to put children first, those who have been abused can take some small comfort in knowing that they belong to a nation, to a democracy where humanity, power, rights, responsibility are enshrined and enacted – always, always for their good. Where the law – their law – as citizens of this country, will always supersede canon laws that have neither legitimacy nor place in the affairs of this country.

This report tells us a tale of a frankly brazen disregard for protecting children. If we do not respond swiftly and appropriately as a State, we will have to prepare ourselves for more reports like this.

I agree with Archbishop Martin that the church needs to publish any other and all other reports like this as soon as possible.

I must note the commission is very positive about the work of the National Board for Safeguarding Children, established by the church to oversee the operation by dioceses and religious orders. The commission notes that all church authorities were required to sign a contract with the national board agreeing to implement the relevant standards and that those refusing to sign would be named in the board's annual report.

Progress has been in no small measure [due] to the commitment of Ian Elliott and others. There is some small comfort to be drawn by the people of Cloyne from the fact that the commission is complimentary of the efforts made by the diocese since 2008, in training, in vetting personnel and in the risk management of priests against whom allegations have been made.

Nevertheless, the behaviour of Bishop Magee and Monsignor O'Callaghan show how fragile even good standards and policies are to the weakness and wilful disregard of those who fail to give the right priority to safeguarding our children.

But if the Vatican needs to get its house in

order, so does this State. The report of the commission is rightly critical of the entirely unsatisfactory position which the last government allowed to persist over many years.

The unseemly bickering between the minister for children and the HSE over the statutory powers to deal with extra-familial abuse, the failure to produce legislation to enable the exchange of soft information as promised after the Ferns inquiry, and the long period of confusion and disjointed responsibility for child protection within the HSE, as reported by the commission, are simply not acceptable in a society which values children and their safety.

For too long Ireland has neglected its children.

Just last week we saw a case of the torture of children, within the family, come before the courts. Just two days ago, we were repulsed by the case of a Donegal registered sex offender and school caretaker – children and young adults reduced to human wreckage – raising questions and issues of serious import for State agencies.

We are set to embark on a course of action to ensure the State is doing all it can to safeguard our children.

Minister [for Justice Alan] Shatter is bringing forward two pieces of legislation – firstly, to make it an offence to withhold information relating to crimes against children and vulnerable adults; and secondly, at long last, to allow for the exchange of 'soft information' on abusers.

As Taoiseach, I want to do all I can to protect the sacred space of childhood and to restore its innocence, especially our young teenagers, whom I believe to be children, because regardless of our current economic crisis, the children of this country are, and always will be, our most precious possession of all.

Safeguarding their integrity and innocence must be a national priority. This is why I undertook to create a Cabinet ministry for children and youth affairs. The legislation Children First proposes to give our children maximum protection and security without intruding on the hectic, magical business of being a child.

Cardinal Josef Ratzinger [the current Pope Benedict] said: 'Standards of conduct appropriate to civil society or the workings of a democracy cannot be purely and simply applied to the church.'

As the Holy See prepares its considered response to the Cloyne report, as Taoiseach, I am making it absolutely clear that when it comes to the protection of the children of this State, the standards of conduct which the church deems appropriate to itself cannot and will not be applied to the workings of democracy and civil society in this republic.

Not purely, or simply or otherwise.

Children . . . First.

MONDAY, 25 JULY 2011

Norway Mourns its Dead and Vows to 'Never Give Up its Values'

Derek Scally in Oslo

With calm defiance Norway will this morning face down the man, one of their own, responsible for the worst massacre in its post-war history that has killed 93 and injured 97.

Anders Behring Breivik (32), who describes himself as a conservative Christian, has admitted carrying out the twin attacks he described yesterday as 'terrible but necessary' but will plead not guilty.

As Norway struggles to deal with a massive breach of trust, Prime Minister Jens Stoltenberg vowed that his country would 'never give up its values'.

'Our answer is more democracy, more openness, and more humanity – but never naivety,' he told a memorial service in Oslo.

At noon today, the country will observe one minute's silence in memory of the dead.

People place flowers in front of Utøya island, where 69 people were murdered when a gunman, Anders Behring Breivik, dressed as a policeman, opened fire at a youth camp run by Norway's Labour Party. Photograph: Fabrizio Bensch/Reuters.

In an Oslo courtroom, meanwhile, reporters will get their first glimpse of the man who hopes his attack will trigger a 'revolution' against multiculturalism and what he sees as the growing threat of radical Islam in Norway and around Europe.

Norwegians were determined yesterday to deprive him of that satisfaction.

'I believe Norway will emerge stronger,' said Andreas Lubiana (24) outside Oslo cathedral.

A manifesto reportedly written by Breivik and circulated on the internet yesterday suggests the author saw the attacks as the bloody means to a singular end: a court case offering him 'a stage to the world'.

The 1,500-page document, including many passages plagiarised from other texts, describes his lengthy campaign against 'cultural Marxists, multiculturalist traitors and Muslims'.

'He wished to attack society and the structure of society; he wants a revolution,' said his lawyer, Geir Lippestad. 'But he feels that what he has done does not deserve punishment.'

Breivik has told police he acted alone, but police have said they are still hunting for possible accomplices. Eye witnesses from the island report seeing a second gunman.

Investigators said yesterday evening that they had located the last victims' bodies in a lake around the island of Utøya, an hour's drive from Oslo.

Oslo-born Breivik told police he went to the island on Friday afternoon, two hours after detonating a powerful bomb in Oslo's government quarter at 3.26 p.m.

Police said he travelled from Oslo by car, carrying a handgun and an automatic rifle and arrived on the island by ferry. Dressed as a police officer, he gathered the mainly teenagers attending a summer camp around him before opening fire with a machine gun.

Eye-witnesses report him moving methodically around the small island, shooting everyone in sight. His shooting spree continued for 90 minutes; many victims were shot in the water as they swam for safety.

Survivor Thorrbjørn Vereide (22) told yesterday how Breivik lured a group of young people out of hiding.

'He said: "It's safe to come out, you will be saved, I'm a policeman." We were in a gang of 30 to 40 and followed his instructions when he began to shoot,' said Mr Vereide. 'When he was finished there were five or six of us left standing. We ran away to a cave.'

More than 20 coroners, dentists and DNA experts have been mobilised to identify the dead

before a list of names is released.

Yesterday afternoon a special investigation team raided a house in eastern Oslo, linked to the gunman, and detained several people before releasing them without charge.

Meanwhile, police in the village of Sundvollen, near the island of Utøya, explained it took them nearly 45 minutes to reach the island after the alarm was raised because they didn't have a suitable boat. They waited for a special unit from Oslo who landed on the island and a further 50 minutes to locate the gunman. He was caught without a struggle.

By that time several local residents had mobilised their boats and rescued several dozens of youths from the island, where they were attending a summer camp run by the youth wing of Norway's ruling Labour Party.

As Oslo gets back to work today many government ministries, including Mr Stoltenberg's

Brian Coleman from Belmullet, Co. Mayo, now living in London, watches the action at the Galway Races through his 100-year-old opera glasses. Photograph: Brenda Fitzsimons.

own office, stand in ruins after a powerful detonation blew out windows in a four-block radius.

Police and soldiers maintained a cordon around the ruined buildings last night while Oslo residents kept a silent, candlelight vigil at the nearby cathedral.

In his manifesto titled '2083 – A European Declaration of Independence', Breivik described the European Union as a 'coup d'état in slow motion'. He attacked the Irish government's handling of the two Lisbon Treaty referenda as 'powerful testimony to the evil nature of the European Union'.

To back up his arguments, he drew on a 2007 essay by EU critic Anthony Coughlan that EU integration 'would lead to a "gradual coup by government executives against legislatures, and by politicians against the citizens who elect them"'.

Muslim groups yesterday criticised Norwegian media for jumping to conclusions on Friday that the attacks had an Islamist background.

In an editorial, the daily *Aftenposten* warned of double standards in public debate. 'We have warned many times against holding Muslims collectively responsible for terror. This principle applies also the other way.'

MONDAY, 25 JULY 2011

Don't They Know Rock 'n' Roll is Different for Girls?

Ann Marie Hourihane

I grow old, I grow old. Amy Winehouse was born on 14 September 1983, less than a week after the voting in the abortion referendum, one of the formative cultural experiences of my generation. She died on Saturday. I'm angry with her and of course I've no right to be.

Old people tend to develop their own unsolicited and totally unscientific theories about things.

My unsolicited and totally unscientific theory is: class A drugs are not an equal-opportunity employer. They are harder on women than they are on men. In drug-taking couples it is the woman who is more damaged, who has more trouble coming off, who hits the alcohol the hardest in compensation, who is never the same.

Amy Winehouse and her ex-husband Blake Fielder-Civil are the most public and most recent example of this. We oldies have seen it, unfortunately, several times, and much closer to home. And because we are not members of Amy Winehouse's family, we do not altogether blame Blake Fielder-Civil for her addictions. Although he has said publicly – perhaps boasted – that he introduced her to heroin and crack, he hardly introduced her to bulimia and self-harm.

It's different for girls, in a way that we don't yet understand. Maybe it's physiological, maybe it's social. If you want to see girls who look like Amy Winehouse, just watch the anorexic women walking, very carefully, around our psychiatric hospitals. These young/old women are her sisters in self-destruction.

This is not, of course, to say that women aren't able to give up drugs and alcohol. Many of the greatest rehab successes are wonderful women – look at Betty Ford herself. But Betty, although in the public eye, was not incapable in public. Amy was in the spotlight, stumbling through her Serbian set. Amy was in the spotlight, stumbling through a lot of the last five years, in her blood-stained ballet slippers. Amy, a breakthrough act for many young female artists. Lady Gaga sent her condolences yesterday. Lily Allen, Adele, they all owe her something.

Tony Bennett, with whom she recently recorded a duet, said she had the most natural jazz voice of her generation. But it was too late. The only English female to have won five Grammy awards, but it didn't matter.

This sophisticated, clever, funny young woman made herself a car crash of a life. Lady Gaga

Flowers and tributes outside the home of Amy Winehouse in London after the announcement of her death, aged 27.
Photograph: Stefan Wermuth/Reuters.

gets her grotesquerie made for her by *outré* costume designers. Amy Winehouse became the show. The press photographers followed her to the off-licence at night, when she was getting her booze and fags.

In fact, alcohol is probably much more of a key player in this tragedy than we, the faintly respectable, would like to admit. On her recent, abandoned, comeback tour, it was alcohol that her handlers were trying to keep her away from. To them she had become a nightmare, where once she was their dream. Yesterday her first manager, Nick Godwyn, with whom Winehouse signed when she was 16, told of how he had taken her to rehab for the first time because 'I couldn't watch'.

Yet Amy Winehouse's terrific charm flickers in and out of this story like a glow-worm. Perhaps the wisest words come from Mary Gallagher, a regular

at Winehouse's local pub in Camden, the Hawley Arms. Speaking to the BBC yesterday, Gallagher said: 'She was such a lovely person and, to be honest, I don't think fame agreed with her. She was an ordinary girl at heart.'

Perhaps this is the time to look at the added pressure that young females are put under in the entertainment industry. My blood runs cold when I hear of a 16-year-old going to an audition unaccompanied by an adult. (Godwyn was careful that Winehouse didn't release an album until she was 20.) Or when you see a young female vocalist getting plastered before she can sing with a band. This is not to say that young male performers aren't under comparable stresses, it's just that the girls have more of it to deal with.

The thing is, when you're old, you lose patience with the whole live fast, die young thing.

You're more in favour of the live slow, die at an extraordinarily advanced age whilst with your fifth husband approach. You're on the side not of Kurt Cobain, a rock singer who blew his brains out at the age of 27, but of Kurt Cobain's mother, who said: 'Now he's gone and joined that stupid club. I told him not to join that stupid club.'

The stupid club consists of rock stars with drug problems who have died, mostly accidentally, at the age of 27. The stupid club roll call includes Brian Jones, Jim Morrison, Janis Joplin and Jimi Hendrix. Amy Winehouse was 27. She looked like hell.

In Norway the bodies are still being counted. Anders Behring Breivik, who has admitted to the killings, is a fine, strapping, blond example of clean-cut Nordic manliness.

Unlike the 93 mostly very young people who were killed by Anders Behring Breivik, the death of Amy Winehouse was widely predicted. In some quarters it was greeted with a sort of weary contempt. The tributes to her include the faintly damning phrases such as 'tortured soul' and 'poor creature'. The poor child, so full of talent, has become a rock and roll cliché.

And there are some of us who are old enough to be very sorry indeed.

MONDAY, 1 AUGUST 2011

Norris Acted Wrongly But Should Not Be Scapegoat

Fintan O'Toole

There is a simple principle to be applied to the case of David Norris's pleas on behalf of a man convicted of having sex with a 15-year-old boy.

He should be treated exactly like any other politician caught doing the same thing. He should not be given a free pass because of his immense contribution to the cause of equality and decency in this society. Neither should his actions be used to vent the closet homophobia that lies behind so much of the antipathy to him. Let's try, rather, to be dispassionate and morally consistent.

Let's start with the obvious. Politicians should not be trying to influence sentences for those convicted of serious crimes. Full stop. No qualifications, no excuses. (Sexual crimes obviously have a particular emotional resonance, but the principle should be no different for any serious offence.) David Norris used his position as a member of the Oireachtas to try to influence a court.

His first letter was on Seanad notepaper and signed in his capacity as a member of the Oireachtas Committee on Foreign Affairs. His second, longer letter made extensive reference to his public positions and even to the possibility of him running for the presidency.

This is inexcusable. It is quite understandable (even admirable) at a human level that he would have wished to make a plea for mercy for someone he loved. But to do so in an official capacity is an abuse of public office. Public representatives must know how to distinguish the personal from the official. If he is ever to be president, David Norris has a big job to do in convincing the Irish people that he fully understands that distinction.

Given that Norris was completely wrong in this case, what are the consequences of treating him exactly the same as anyone else in his position? Let's look at the precedents.

My educated guess – based on the exceptional cases that have been exposed – is that, since 1997 when Norris wrote the Israeli letters, hundreds of similar letters have been written to Irish courts by other members of the Oireachtas.

In 2002, when it emerged that the then junior minister Bobby Molloy had intervened in a much more serious way on behalf of a child rapist, Patrick Naughton, the then taoiseach, Bertie Ahern, defended him on the basis that 'that's what politicians do. A Teachta Dála is a public representative

David Norris enters his house on Dublin's North Great George's Street after announcing his withdrawal from the presidential race. Photograph: Dara Mac Dónaill.

and you make representations'. There is nothing to suggest that Ahern was wrong about this. In relation to child rape alone, we know of three specific cases of TDs making pleas on their behalf. In 2007, it emerged that Fianna Fáil TD Tony Killeen had twice written to the minister for justice seeking early release for a heinous double rapist, Joseph Nugent. Fine Gael's Pat Breen went so far as to put down a parliamentary question about when Nugent would be released. The Cork Labour TD Kathleen Lynch wrote a letter to a judge in 2008 to tell him that a convicted rapist of two children came from 'a good family'.

What happened when these interventions came to public attention? Molloy eventually resigned – but that was because his office had gone even further and tried to contact the judge directly. The other three subsequently gained political promotion: Killeen to the cabinet as minister for defence; Breen to the chairmanship of the Oireachtas committee on foreign affairs; and Lynch to a junior ministry with responsibility for disability and older people. It is absolutely clear that the existing standard in Ireland is that making representations on behalf of a child rapist does not debar you from public office.

So, is Norris's offence worse than these others? Hardly. It relates to a crime that, while utterly inexcusable, is less violent and brutal than the others. And, on a human level, it is considerably less cynical. Killeen, Lynch and Breen made their interventions purely as part of the demented system of clientelism. They did it to get votes. Norris did it out of a misguided sense of loyalty to someone who had been the love of his life.

It is also relevant that a plea to a foreign court was much less likely to result in improper influence than an intervention by a TD in Ireland's intimate nexus of local and political connections.

So, we come to the key question: should David Norris be the one who takes the hit so that this kind of abuse is ended once and for all?

There is certainly a case to be made that he should be – sometimes a high-profile casualty is needed to scare other politicians into righteousness. But isn't it just a bit too convenient for our system that Fianna Fáil, Fine Gael and Labour TDs should get away with it while the Independent gets hammered? And shouldn't we feel uneasy at the notion that the gay man whose own sexuality was criminalised for so long is held to a higher standard than straight politicians?

David Norris has a lot of explaining to do, but he should be allowed to do it in a free electoral debate.

SATURDAY, 6 AUGUST 2011

Euro Dream Threatens to Become Nightmare

Dan O'Brien

Last weekend the world's attention was on Washington DC as America's politicians peered into the abyss of sovereign default. On Sunday they stepped back. This weekend attention is on Rome and Madrid. Politicians in those two capitals are sliding towards the same abyss.

But there is a big difference between the US and the Mediterranean countries. In America, that country's leaders walked voluntarily to the edge of the chasm for political reasons. They were not beaten to that point by the bond market.

Political leaders in Italy and Spain are in an altogether more difficult position. They are being propelled towards the precipice because confidence in their economies is draining away. They are clutching desperately for something to halt the slide. But it appears ever less likely that they can save themselves.

With each passing week it seems increasingly clear that Europe is coming to a fork in the road: one route leads to deeper integration, with very considerable political implications; the other leads

One of the last 13 red kites is released near Avoca in Co. Wicklow under a project to reintroduce the birds of prey into the wild. Thirty-nine red kites are also being released in Co. Dublin during 2011.
Photograph: Garry O'Neill.

down into the dark valley of disorderly disintegration. The decision on which way to go will be among the most important collective choices taken by Europeans in the post-Second World War era.

If a half century of integration ends in sudden disintegration, the European economic and political landscape will undergo huge upheaval. It is impossible to predict how it will look when the dust settles.

If, on the other hand, the eurozone countries bind themselves ever more closely together, the challenges facing the bloc will be enormous, but more predictable. For a closer union to succeed, a central issue – perhaps the central issue – will be whether the dangerous fault line that has opened up between the continent's north and south can be closed.

While Greece looks destined to remain subject to intensive and intrusive outside intervention for many years to come, and Ireland and Portugal face tough, if shorter, journeys back to sustainability, they may be too small to make a closer union unsustainable, whatever happens to them.

But what happens to peninsular Europe's big two – Italy and Spain – is different. If they cannot make themselves more like their northern neighbours, a closer union might not survive.

What are their prospects?

The Italian state marked the 150th anniversary of its creation earlier this year. Its people did so with little celebration. Apart from Italy's post-Second World War decades of successful modernisation, most of this history has been one of underachievement and worse.

The Italian state's first 50 years were marked by instability and weakness before two decades of fascist night descended over the country. Invasion, defeat and civil war in the 1940s left deep scars.

Now, the economy has been stagnating for almost two decades, with living standards barely rising and its once-vaunted industries – from textiles to autos – shrinking in the face of low-wage competition.

Italian entrepreneurialism and design flair succeeded in medium-tech industries when foreign competition was less intense, but success in high-tech sectors operating in a globalised context has been much harder to achieve.

One reason is schooling. Italy's education system is ever more inadequate in preparing its young for the modern world of work and many of those who manage to do well are stymied in one of Europe's least meritocratic societies.

Government influence on economies is often overstated, but it is important. Bad government in particular can have big negative effects on growth. The evidence that mismanaged public finances stifle growth is strong. And in this area Italy has long been a European leader – it is the only country to have a national debt bigger than its GDP uninterruptedly since the 1980s.

In the early 1990s the sweeping away of the Cold War political parties and the jailing of many of the most corrupt politicians brought hope of better and cleaner government. Those hopes have long since been dashed.

The country's long-time Prime Minister, Silvio Berlusconi, has dominated for most of that

Queen of Puck Muireann Arthurs (13) crowns a wild mountain goat as King Puck in Killorglin, Co. Kerry. Photograph: Don MacMonagle.

period. Even by the low standards of Italian politics, he has plumbed new depths. But however bad his actions, his inactions have been even more damaging.

Many of the reforms that could help spur the economy have gone unimplemented, despite his promises to shake up the country. Nor has he made much of a dent in Italy's public debt mountain. His main appeal – that he could bring to the business of government the same get-things-done approach that made him one of Europe's richest men – has proved baseless.

But Berlusconi will not lead Italy forever, and the country's political class has shown that it can push through painful reform. Perhaps ironically, its biggest achievement in recent times was ensuring that Italy squeezed into the euro as a founding member. There is no such prize for taking radical action now. Instead, incentive comes from the need to avoid disaster. Italy's politicians might yet rise to the challenge.

If Italy faces huge challenges, Spain's are no less daunting.

Unlike the plodding Italian economy, Spain enjoyed a decade-long boom from the late 1990s. But the Iberian tiger, like its Celtic cousin, became engorged on credit. Property prices soared, construction boomed and competitiveness evaporated.

When the bubble burst the public finances went into a tailspin, the banks teetered and unemployment soared. It has suffered a much bigger shock than Italy and its economy is still on the floor, with consumers and households pinned down by huge mortgage debts.

Spain's economy faces bigger challenges than Italy, with the exception of its government's indebtedness.

With debts of 60 per cent of GDP in 2010, Spain has some breathing space (in Italy the figure was 120 per cent and in Ireland almost 100 per cent).

With such a manageable debt burden Spain does not look close to being insolvent, as the bond market has been moving towards concluding in recent weeks. So why the panic?

One reason for the recent loss of confidence in the country has been because fears are rife that its banks are not coming clean on their property losses. So far, those admitted to have been a tiny fraction of Irish banks' losses, despite a property collapse there that is much more than a fraction the size of ours. Another suspicion is that the country's 17 big-spending regional governments are keeping liabilities hidden.

If either or both of these suspicions have some basis in truth, Spain's true debt levels are higher than officially stated.

But one reason to be optimistic about Spain relative to Italy over the long term is its more effective political system. This has been in evidence since the crisis erupted, with the government earning praise for undertaking some bold reforms and for reining in its budget deficit.

Although the Spanish are sometimes called the Germans of the south, the more likely explanation for their better governance is not cultural but institutional. Whereas in Italy the executive is weak and unstable – famously, the government has changed on average once a year since the Second World War – in Spain, since the return to democracy in the late 1970s, governments have been stable and more effective.

This did not happen by accident but by design, and was informed by the lessons the two countries learned from their respective decades of dictatorship. While Italy's 1948 constitution deliberately created a weak centre to avoid a repetition of the abuses in Mussolini's time when power was highly centralised, Spain's 1978 constitution created a strong and stable executive because weak government was seen to be a big factor in Franco's seizing power in the 1930s.

Spain's better political system gives reason to believe that it can manage its public debt problems, but no government can magic away a huge private debt burden or restore at a stroke chronic economy-wide uncompetitiveness. Even with lots of luck Spain faces a long and painful struggle.

Europe is in a bad place now. It looks increasingly likely that the eurozone countries will have to throw their fiscal lot in together in order to avoid cataclysm in the short term. But this brings its own risks.

Northerners will not like it. If they feel they will permanently foot the bill for southern profligacy they may rise up against it. That could get very ugly. The longer Italy and Spain remain in a slump, the greater the chances of that happening.

Southerners may not take their medicine lying down either. If their economies don't return to growth, their peoples may reach breaking point. If they come to believe that an uncaring and alien force is imposing its will on them, resentments could boil over.

The euro was designed to bring Europeans together and to crown decades of integration. It could end up causing deep divisions and, ultimately, disintegration.

WEDNESDAY, 10 AUGUST 2011

Extraordinary Scale of Destruction Wrought by Marauding Gangs

Ronan McGreevy in Croydon

There can be no more incongruous soundtrack to the riots that have convulsed Britain than John Lennon's 'Imagine'.

As a fire truck pumped water into the smouldering remains of what used to be a dry cleaners and launderette in London Road, Croydon, yesterday afternoon, somebody put the song, with its naive aspirations of universal peace, on the public address.

Either side of the dry cleaners, four shops and their upstairs apartments have been burned out. The front wall of one shop has collapsed, flattening a bus shelter.

Sailors from the Royal Alfred Yacht Club participating in the Flying Fifteen Liffey Challenge in the waters of Dublin's docklands. Photograph: Brenda Fitzsimons.

A riot police officer directs his colleagues to clear people away from a burning car on Clarence Road in Hackney, London. Photograph: Dan Istitene/Getty Images.

The scale of destruction wrought by marauding gangs on this dishevelled road, with its densely packed assortments of ethnic shops and high street chains, was quite extraordinary.

In their attempts to corral rioters and keep them away from the centre of Croydon with its two state-of-the-art shopping centres, the police action only served to drive the mob down London Road.

They burned a jewellery shop to the ground, a Ladbrokes bookie shop and a Pizza Hut. They smashed windows as they went along. Nothing was spared, not even an undertaker's windows.

It was not only their actions that were shocking, but the brazen manner in which they behaved that shocked locals.

'They were parking their motors up, filling them up and coming back for more in front of the police,' said Michael Cox, caretaker of a parade of shops all smashed and looted.

An Irish-owned pub, the Fox and Hound, provided a late-night shelter for the 16 occupants above the jewellery shop that was burned down. The foreign nationals included a Lithuanian couple with a six-month-old baby.

'They were well organised. They were coming out of eight- to ten-seater vans. What they did was mindless brutality, but it was organised,' said Alan McCabe (28) from Cavan, landlord of the pub that escaped the mob.

McCabe said the ethnic make-up of the gangs was clear. 'IC3s every single one of them,' he said, citing the police's ethnic classification for black.

Donovan Thomas, standing outside a club that caters for black people and is due to be closed by the police, said the violence was inexcusable. He described those involved as 'common thieves', but said those involved had trivialised the legitimate grievances held by black and ethnic groups.

He cited the example of reggae singer Smiley Culture who died during a police raid on his home allegedly from a self-inflicted knife wound earlier this year. 'We've been waiting four months and still we have no answers,' he said.

Most people had no truck though with excuses, surmising that to explain was to excuse.

Yesterday British Prime Minister David Cameron, Mayor of London Boris Johnson and his predecessor and rival Ken Livingstone visited Croydon and the ground zero of the rioting, the Reeves bed shop that burned to the ground live on television on Monday night.

It was noted that Cameron talked only to the emergency service personnel and not local people who had questions to ask about the police response.

The plaque that says the family-owned shop was established in 1867 remains on the wall. The shop survived Hitler's bombs, which pulverised Croydon in 1940, but it couldn't survive the two young thugs who went in and set fire to the building just as the owner was calling for help.

Annette Reeves, the wife of co-owner Trevor Reeves, watched from behind a police cordon yesterday as forensic officers searched through the charred remains. 'I'm sad that the people who did this have not been brought up properly to respect other people's properties, very sad,' she said. People had already pledged to pay for furniture they bought though it cannot now be delivered, she added.

Last night Croydon was enveloped by police smarting from being bested by rioters on Monday night. The rioting has claimed its first fatality: a 26-year-old man shot dead in Croydon on Monday night.

'We lost the battle, but we'll win the war,' said assistant chief police constable Bernard Hogan-Howe. 'Nobody could anticipate the violence we had here on Monday night.'

Remedial Plants Under Threat from EU Directive

Michael Viney

Wreathed so often in mists and drizzle this summer, the moister waysides of the west are billowing with creamy meadowsweet, the soporific strewing herb of medieval bedrooms (anything to soften the pong from the privy).

Like willow, it is rich in salicylic compounds, the herbal fount of aspirin. Once, in the feverish throes of a summer flu, I bade the kitchen maid prepare a draught of meadowsweet tea. The fever broken, and blinking through the sweat, I recognised the maid to be my own dear wife, Ethna.

The trouble with such self-medication is its guesswork, and one sees the point of regulating commercial herbal remedies for quality and safety. We are regular customers of the botanical shelves in shops that sell the right, unadulterated flour for our bread and have hitherto trusted the Swiss, among others in Europe, in their distillations of remedial herbs.

We wait to see which of the familiar potions on our kitchen-shelf pharmacy will survive the EU Directive on Traditional Herbal Medicinal Products, whose transitional grace for existing products expired at the end of April. Those left unregistered with the Irish Medicines Board, and unauthorised for sale, are already beginning to disappear from health food shops, robbed of their freelance existence as 'food supplements'.

The board has published two draft lists of herbal substances which may, and may not, be acceptable for inclusion in food supplements. Of those so far approved, most are ordinary vegetables, fruits and spices, together with herbs from the wayside (burdock, yarrow, hawthorn, goldenrod, agrimony and so on) that have survived pharmaceutical reports

Punjabi drummer Johnny Kalsi and traditional Irish harpist Seána Davey at a dress rehearsal for Globe, a fusion of global music, dance and percussion at Liberty Hall Theatre, Dublin. Photograph: Mark Stedman/Photocall Ireland.

and for which no specific medicinal claim is made on the packaging.

The list of herbs not permitted as 'supplements' include obvious poisons, such as deadly nightshade, and other plants containing toxic alkaloids. But here also are herbs excluded simply because their action is pharmaceutical and thus, like any synthetic medicine, will have side-effects, some of which, in some instances, may prove severe or harmful in the long term.

Rather than entrust the user with the same contraindications and warnings that come with any sheet of synthesised drugs, some herbal preparations have been abruptly curtailed. It is concerning to find that, along with echinacea, the cultivated

coneflower thousands have recruited to the benefit of their immune system, and St John's wort, that has relieved a legion of the mildly depressed, I find listed my own blessed herb serenoa repens, or saw palmetto.

This berry of a spiky palm that grows in subtropical America has, for some dozen years or more, subdued the efforts of my prostate gland to strangle my urethra, an affliction common to most ageing men and prompting frequent night-time trips to the loo.

Having found one prescribed drug too draining of energy, I discovered saw palmetto as a regular over-the-counter herbal remedy in Germany, and one that authoritative studies in

America have judged to be perfectly safe for most men.

Saw palmetto and its herbal kin now have a home in the chemist's shop in town. As a practising pharmacist when medicine's debt to plant life was still readily on view, Ethna can only approve (her venerable mortar and pestle now grinds coriander in the kitchen). But the EU directive can only regulate single herbs, while safe and successful blends evolved from generations of professional herbalism will be denied. The EU's insatiable drive for standardisation and control will mean, as herbalists argue, fewer, more costly, single herbs and a narrower spectrum of remedies.

Botany is no longer taught to medical students, but its links to drug discovery and development are still as strong as ever. It's simply that, rather than using the plants themselves when they offer novel chemicals, drug companies find ways of reproducing them synthetically on an industrial scale.

TCD's Dr Hazel Proctor explains this in her fascinating guide to Trinity's new Physic Garden, planted (behind the O'Reilly Building) to celebrate the college's 300 years of botany. The first botany professor, Henry Nicholson, catalogued almost 400 plants with promise of medicinal qualities. The new garden has more than 70, many of them still in use as herbal remedies, and others that are still under current research.

Almost 20, as it happens, are flourishing within our own acre, a few already tried to our benefit (comfrey root for bruises, yarrow tea for rheumatism, valerian for sleep) and others we'd never considered – guelder rose to prompt the immune system, sage for an ageing memory, angelica as a general feel-good tonic.

The old cottage of healer Biddy Early, in Co. Clare, is to be rescued again from the nettles: how many little blue bottles she'd have filled from stuff picked down our garden path . . .

Herbal remedies are already beginning to disappear from health food shops, robbed of their freelance existence as 'food supplements'.

'I've Had My Time'

Tara Brady

There is no training manual or official protocol to prepare for the moment one knocks on a door to find Harrison Ford standing on the other side. We know it's probably best not to stare at the earring. We know to be polite for, as the euphemism goes, he is said to 'suffer fools badly'. He shakes hands and exchanges pleasantries just like a regular mortal. Yes, we've just flown in from Dublin; weather not so bad this morning.

But it's Harrison Ford, dude. What can we possibly say to the man who has embodied Han Solo and Indiana Jones and Deckard?

His face and delivery stays deadpan and motionless, it's enough to signal that much of the star's perceived grumpiness is likely parch-dry midwestern wit. More than four decades have elapsed since Ford arrived in La La Land, hoping to find work as his mother once had, in radio voiceovers. But he retains a direct, succinct manner befitting the prairie state. It's not that he's cantankerous exactly – he leaves little room for horseshit to creep into a conversation.

Enquire about the genres that made him a household name: 'I don't know how to think about it because I just don't. I have no genre consciousness. I don't act in genre films; I just act. I try always to confine my work and my focus to character and how that character relates to the movie. I could care less if it's a western or sci-fi.'

Mention red carpets, premières and the blandishments of Hollywood: 'A nightmare. Never liked that stuff.' Talk about fans and adulation: 'I think of them as customers.' Ask him about himself: 'Nobody wants to see a romance with a 69-year-old man.'

He attributes this plain sensibility to his plain Illinois upbringing. 'We don't talk about religion or politics or how much money we make,' he says. 'We have no time for flattery. But what makes Chicago and Illinois interesting is the work ethic. It's a very practical, pragmatic, strong work-ethic-based mentality.' He says he approaches his glittering career accordingly. A former carpenter, he likes to think of his roles as 'piece work' to be undertaken with due care and pride. He 'works for wages' but only if a job is worth doing.

'What's consistent for me across disciplines is focus and work,' he says. 'How I organise it. What tools I need to bring. And you can always pick out the bits you wish you'd done better. You learn something every time that'll help you to train your energy and intelligence better in the future. I always thought when I was imagining what it would be like as an actor that that was a good point. You can keep working. You can keep learning. You don't have to stop as long as you're willing to play old farts.'

It is perhaps not the most nuanced description of *Cowboys & Aliens*' ruthless cattle baron Colonel Dolarhyde, but it is, nonetheless, accurate. Ford's latest movie assignment weds his sizeable box office clout ($3.6 billion and counting) to the popcorn might of Daniel Craig and *Iron Man* director Jon Favreau for a spectacular stand-off between an old west posse and marauding extra-terrestrials.

'The first time I read it I made it as far as 20–30 pages,' says Ford. 'It's not that I didn't get it. I thought "oh well, it's kind of jokey and it's from a comic book". But what I didn't know was that John (Favreau) had an intention of making a serious western. I was reading the same words and

Actor Harrison Ford as Dr Norman Spencer from the film **What Lies Beneath**. *Photograph: Francois Duhamel/Reuters.*

hearing different music. Tone is everything here. And then Daniel Craig – who had been attached to the movie for months – was very generous by allowing my character a bit more space and time.'

Is it weird finding himself second on the bill to James Bond?

'Well, I'm not a leading man anymore, I'm a character actor,' he shrugs. 'I've had my time. Some people realise they're old when they're 50 or 60, but at 69 you know it. So the leading man is Daniel Craig and I'm playing a character part and I'm happy to do it. I loved it. It was never my ambition to be on top of anything. It was

my ambition to do good work in whatever was available.'

Ford was born in Chicago in 1942 to Dorothy, a former radio actress of Jewish-German descent, and Christopher, an actor turned advertising executive with Irish Catholic origins. 'But there was never a clear path for me to go seeking relatives in Ireland,' says Ford. 'My father didn't seem to know too much about his Irish heritage or else he was pretty closed-mouthed about what he did know. There wasn't much dialogue about anything with my father. He was orphaned early. His father was a vaudevillian who fell backwards onto a New York

Five-year-old horseman Joseph McAleenan enjoying his big day at the Auld Lammas Fair in Ballycastle, Co. Antrim. Photograph: Margaret McLaughlin.

brownstone stoop right onto his head and died. As far as I knew he had no family left after that.' Mostly, the actor remembers the 'religious' instruction. Harrison and younger brother Terence were, Ford says, 'raised Democrat'.

'We had no catechism,' he says. 'Instead we were given Democrat instruction; to be liberals of every stripe. I don't judge what other people do. At least I try not to ever judge what other people do unless they do it in my face.' Does that creed come with a guilt complex? 'It does, thank you,' says Ford. 'I only got out of the instruction. Nobody escapes the residual Jewish-Catholic guilt.'

And did he ever receive a tap on the shoulder from meaningful party sources? He has, after all, played a US president in *Air Force One*. How hard could it be?

'I've never been that interested in politics,' he says. 'Contrary to mythology I've never been a backdoor visitor to the White House. It's too big a job. With politics there's always an agenda and I don't think that way. I'll support someone but I don't want to meet them.' Acting was already something of a family guild when, in 1964, young Ford made his way to Hollywood. Within two years Columbia Pictures came in with a $150 a week contract.

'I was extraordinarily lucky,' he recalls. 'I had a five-minute interview. "How tall are you? Do you speak Spanish? Can you ride a horse? We'll let you know." I went down to get the elevator, realised I had to take a pee and when I came back out the guy's assistant was gesturing me in. And the guy said, "Do you want to be under contract?" and I said, "What does that mean?" and he said, "$150 a week". It took me a while to register that I wasn't obliged to pay him $150 a week. So now I was an actor. You can't be much luckier than that.'

He was lucky but far from content. He earned a regular stream of income from TV horse operas *The Virginian*, *Gunsmoke* and *Kung Fu*. The work was dull and unchallenging and inspired Ford to retreat into professional carpentry for some seven

years. He built stages for The Doors and a recording studio for Brazilian jazz musician, Sérgio Mendes, until 1973 when a call brought him to George Lucas's house to build cabinets.

The director promptly cast him in *American Graffiti* and brought him to the attention of Francis Ford Coppola, who in turn used the actor in *The Conversation* and *Apocalypse Now*, a set where Ford would meet Melissa Mathison, the future screenwriter of *E.T.* and his domestic partner for the next 20 years. Between those gigs, Ford built Coppola an office.

The actor insists, nonetheless, that his place and affiliation with Hollywood's Brat Pack – that loose nexus comprising his former employers Steven Spielberg, George Lucas and Francis Ford Coppola – has been grossly exaggerated.

'The perception that I was knocking around with those guys was never correct,' he says. 'I just worked with them a few times. I've only ever spent very small, finite periods of time with any of the people I work with.'

It is, however, difficult to envisage the Brativerse without him. Would *Indiana Jones* have had the same resonance if Tom Selleck, director Lucas's first choice for the role, had been available? Would *Star Wars* have worked if Ford hadn't insisted that Han Solo say 'I know' instead of 'I love you, too' as the line appeared on the script?

'I can't take credit,' shrugs Ford. 'It's a collaborative business.'

He doesn't share his peers' enthusiasm for the medium. He likes movies when he sees them, he says, but that doesn't happen often. It runs in the family: Calista Flockhart, whom he married during the *Cowboys & Aliens* shoot following an eight-year relationship and 16-month engagement, claims to have never seen *Star Wars*.

'I was never a film buff,' says Ford. 'I went to Saturday matinees when I was a kid and I went to movies when I was at college because it was a good way of getting a girl to go to a dark room with me for a couple of hours and I could make pathetic

Ukrainian Cossacks performing on the opening day of the Dublin Horse Show in the RDS, Ballsbridge.
Photograph: Dara Mac Dónaill.

attempts to grope her. Once I started to act I didn't want to see movies because I was worried I'd start imitating somebody else. So I just got out of the habit. We have a 10-year-old at home so movies start when we're doing the dishes.'

The young lad is Liam, Flockhart's first child, but Ford's fifth. Is it more tiring than it used to be?

'Yes, but it's also an opportunity,' smiles Ford. 'I think it's something you have to learn as a man. I think mothers are more naturally gifted caregivers. They're better at it. They have that connection. I've always felt very connected to my kids but sometimes I was also very connected to my work and – when my first kids were born in particular – I wasn't there as much as I should have been. Now I have a little more experience under my belt.'

Between parental duties and his newfound success as a character actor, Ford collects and flies helicopters and fixed-wing aircraft. Is it a boyish collecting impulse or is it something bigger?

'There's so much I love about it. A lot of it has to do with the combination of the discipline and the freedom. Being responsible for yourself. Meeting certain standards.

'I love the opportunity to live in a three-dimensional world. When your feet are on the ground you're only living in two dimensions. I was 52 years old when I started flying. I didn't know if I could learn anything really. I wanted to be something other than an actor when they came to engrave something on my tombstone. And I love the mechanics.'

Hasn't his inner-geek ever considered the other side of the lens?

'It looked too much like a real job. I'd come in and work on a film for a period of time and leave but the director would be working for a year and a half on it. I never wanted to be in charge of something as big and bumptious as a movie. I love to collaborate. I love to make my case. I don't need to be in charge. I want to do the job and move along.' Spoken like a cowboy.

FRIDAY, 26 AUGUST 2011

Evidence Suggests Daughter Did Not Die in 1986 Bombing, as Claimed

Mary Fitzgerald in Tripoli

For decades her name was invoked by Muammar Gadafy and his apologists as proof of his personal suffering as a result of the US bombing of his Tripoli compound in 1986.

After US aircraft struck the Bab al-Azizia complex on 14 April that year, in revenge for the bombing of the La Belle nightclub in Berlin by Libyan agents, the regime announced that an adopted infant daughter of Col. Gadafy, named Hana, had died in the raid.

The news was carried on Libya's radio, TV and print media, despite claims that Col. Gadafy had moved his family to safety, having received prior warning of the strikes.

An American journalist at the time was shown the body of a baby and told it was Hana. Since then, Col. Gadafy has repeatedly referred to her supposed death to bolster the notion that he had been a victim of western military aggression.

On the 20th anniversary of the US attack, the Libyan regime organised the 'Hana Festival of Freedom and Peace' to commemorate the incident.

A passport photo of Hana Gadafy, the adopted daughter of Muammar Gadafy, which was among documents discovered by **The Irish Times** *in the Bab al-Azizia compound in Tripoli yesterday. Gadafy claimed she died as an infant in a 1986 US bombing. Photograph: Mary Fitzgerald.*

Hana's existence was debated by intelligence agencies in the aftermath of the bombing, which then US president Ronald Reagan ordered to strike back at what he called the 'mad dog of the Middle East'.

Many Libyans have long doubted the story. In the rebel stronghold of Benghazi earlier this year, I heard constant claims that Hana had studied medicine and was working as a doctor in Tripoli. 'The whole story that she was killed was just more of Gadafy's propaganda,' one man told me.

Libyan web forums have buzzed with allegations that Hana was still alive and living in the capital. 'When I asked who she was, I was told she was Hana Gadafy, Gadafy's adopted daughter who was supposedly killed in 1986,' wrote an anonymous online commentator who claimed to have studied

Snapshot of Hana Gadafy with a pet camel.
Photograph: Mary Fitzgerald.

medicine at Tripoli's main university at the same time. Diplomatic circles in Tripoli are said to have known about Hana's existence for several years.

Yesterday in the terracotta-coloured section of Bab al-Azizia where the Gadafy family lived, I came across a room which seemed to be part-study, part-lounge. Its contents – including a *Sex and the City* DVD box set; CDs of the Backstreet Boys; cellulite treatments; WellWoman vitamin supplements and stuffed toys – hinted that it belonged to a young woman.

Amid the bookshelves lined with medical textbooks and copies of Col. Gadafy's *Green Book*, I found passport photographs of a woman, dressed in medical garb, who appeared to be in her mid-twenties.

Some of the rebels sifting through the room's contents shouted excitedly: 'It's Hana, it's Hana, the daughter Gadafy lied about. This was her room.'

I found an examination paper from a Libyan university medical faculty which was signed 'Hana Muammar Gadafy' in Arabic. A photograph showed a woman who seemed to be Hana with a group of people, including Col. Gadafy's blood daughter Aisha.

A British Council certificate, dated 19 July 2007, showed that a Hana Muammar Gadafy had completed an English language course at its Libyan centre, achieving an A grade.

A small envelope marked 'Miss Hana Muammar, Room 510' contained undated notes from Mohamad Azwai, who referred to himself as Libya's ambassador to the UK, and his wife, wishing Hana a pleasant stay in London.

A postcard sent from a woman named Katia in Rome was addressed only to Room No. 140, Hotel President Wilson, Geneva.

In February, the German newspaper *Welt am Sonntag* obtained a copy of a document related to the freezing of Muammar Gadafy's assets in Switzerland after Libya's uprising began. The document listed 23 members of the Gadafy clan. The seventh name on the list is Hana Gadafy. A Swiss government spokesperson told *Welt am Sonntag*: 'There are reasons why the name is on the list, which we are not revealing publicly.'

Hana's date of birth is listed as 11 November 1985, which would have made her six months old at the time of the US air strike, which was carried out shortly after the Berlin bombing in which three people, including two American soldiers, were killed.

The newspaper reported that Hana was a doctor working for the country's health ministry. Libyan exiles said she was a powerful figure in the Libyan medical profession, who had used her status to hinder the promotions of colleagues.

'Several hospitals were under her guidance,' the newspaper said. 'No one could make a career within the ministry of health without her consent.'

Group photograph apparently showing Hana Gadafy (in black headscarf) with others including Gadafy's other daughter, Aisha (centre, in black-and-white patterned headscarf). Photograph: Mary Fitzgerald.

It reported that she was said to speak fluent English and that she had travelled frequently to London on shopping trips.

In 1999, the Chinese state news agency Xinhua reported that 'Gadafy's wife, Safia Farkash al-Barassi, and Gadafy's daughters Aisha and Hana' had had lunch with then South African president Nelson Mandela. Photographs showed a young girl with Mrs Gadafy and Aisha.

It now seems almost certain that Hana Muammar Gadafy did not die in the 1986 bombing of the Gadafy compound, but her current whereabouts, like those of her adoptive father, mother and siblings, remain a mystery.

SATURDAY, 27 AUGUST 2011

It's Time Again to Talk Up Derval's Chances

Ian O'Riordan

It used to be the most frequently played track on her iPod, and might still be, but anyway, here we go again – Derval O'Rourke looking to seize everything she ever wanted in one moment.

It feels a little unfair to be talking up the same athlete as our main medal hope every time a championships rolls around, but that's what happens when you've medalled in two of your last four so-called 'majors' – and finished fourth in the other two.

Plus it's not like we haven't had some practice: for years Sonia O'Sullivan carried the mantle, and then, as if on cue, up stepped O'Rourke. Just like O'Sullivan the expectations are inevitably and justifiably high, and O'Rourke has rarely disappointed.

Think Moscow and Gothenburg, Berlin and Barcelona, and now Daegu. Think go, go, go! Indeed, O'Rourke has now claimed four of the last six medals that Ireland has won in senior athletics championships – and when it comes to peaking when it truly counts, no Irish athlete has done it better, and more consistently, than O'Rourke.

'Well it's nice to think that,' she says, 'but at the same time I'm never comfortable with it. It means I'm very tetchy coming into these championships, knowing I have to fight all the way. It's not like just showing up and flicking a switch. I don't fear anyone, but at the same time I respect them, the same way I think they respect me.'

The only problem with having a great championship record in athletics is that the longer you extend it the more difficult it becomes. O'Rourke turned 30 at the start of the summer, which isn't exactly ancient by sprint hurdling standards, yet it means she's probably in or around her peak. She improved her Irish record to 12.67 seconds when finishing fourth at the World Championships in Berlin two years ago, before bettering that again to 12.65 to win the silver medal at the European Championships in Barcelona last summer. Now, Daegu may well prove exactly where she is; still capable of mixing it with the very best 100-metres hurdlers in the world, or else perhaps a little past her best.

Not for the first time her form coming into

Athlete Derval O'Rourke strikes a pose at Morton Stadium in Santry, Dublin. Photograph: Morgan Treacy/Inpho.

Tom Summers from Co. Wicklow climbing Croagh Patrick in Co. Mayo during the annual Reek Sunday pilgrimage. Photograph: Keith Heneghan/Phocus.

these World Championships is a little questionable, but in some ways that's all part of the process. 'Yeah, it would be unlike me to get everything right during the season, coming into a major championship, but it does mean I have to work very, very hard, in every session, coming into this. And you know I've never actually run quick in Asia? I didn't run well in Osaka in 2007, and didn't run well in Beijing either. That's another reason why I'm far from comfortable,' says O'Rourke.

'But this year has been different in that I haven't had any major injury problems, like I did last year, or even been a little sick, like 2009. Between indoors and outdoors everything has gone the way I'd hope, although it has been frustrating that I haven't been running as well in races as I have in training. But at the same time I know it's all about Daegu, and running well here.

Because there is still so much more I want to achieve. I want to run faster than 12.65, and fourth in the last World Championships was still fourth. But I know my biggest challenge will be getting into the final.

'I've been there before, and need to be there again. It's so important to me. Then, when you're in there, the hunger is what matters. But I wouldn't be here unless I thought I could make the final. I don't like long flights, for a start.'

If O'Rourke's championship record isn't impressive enough, consider her championship longevity: spring hurdling is notoriously demanding on the body, and there'll be several high-profile absentees from Daegu – including two of the three medallists from Berlin two years ago (Canada's Priscilla Lopes-Schliep and Jamaica's Dolloreen Ennis-London) and two of the three

The 2011 Rose of Tralee, Tara Talbot, from Queensland, Australia, sitting in Tralee Town Park the morning after her victory, with her mother, Carmencita Talbot.
Photograph: Domnick Walsh/Eye Focus.

medallists from the European Indoors in Paris earlier this year (Germany's Carolin Nytra and Norway's Christina Vukicevic), where O'Rourke finished fourth.

The typically fancied American Lolo Jones didn't even make her team – and then there's the strangely poor form of the Turkish athlete Nevin Yanit, who beat O'Rourke to the European title last summer (although the less said about that the better).

At the same time, Australia's Sally Pearson – who finished one place behind O'Rourke in Berlin – has emerged as the red-hot favourite: she's run 12.48 this summer, unbeaten all year, and at age 25 is still approaching her peak. Not that the Americans Danielle Carruthers and Kellie Wells will be thinking Pearson can't be beaten.

'You have six very good girls there,' says O'Rourke, 'all capable of 12.5, then another six who could make the final. Hopefully myself included. I sometimes look at times, analyse them, but you can't get hung up on them either. It's one of those events where everyone knows each other very well, and no one will really surprise anyone else.'

O'Rourke does have a few things in her favour, not just her vast experience: last month she ran 12.84, in Switzerland, which was actually her fastest time ever outside of a major championship – with the bonus of being under the A-standard for next year's London Olympics.

'Yeah, and some people laughed when I told them that, because it's so much slower than my championship best. Conditions were perfect. No wind, hot track. And you don't get many days like that. It's also given me a massive awareness of how hard it is to run 12.6. I know how fast that felt, and that I have to work for every inch of it, and if anything at all goes wrong in Daegu then I won't run 12.6. I know I'm capable of it, but it's so far from a foregone conclusion that I'm going to go out and run another PB.'

There is one additional challenge facing O'Rourke in Daegu: her 100m hurdles heats are scheduled for next Friday at 10.20 a.m. – which is of course 2.20 a.m. Irish time. She's worked out her own schedule of adjustment and deliberately didn't fly out to Daegu until last Wednesday, yet realises it will all feel somewhat alien.

'There are some things I just won't prepare for, like getting up to run at 2.20 in the morning. I also prefer to stay at home as long as possible, eat my own food, and play with my dog. But getting through the heats is already a danger, not knowing how the body will adjust, and how fast you can run at that hour. I'll just have to deal with it on the morning, drink a big cup of coffee, and get over it.'

TUESDAY, 30 AUGUST 2011

'It Has Changed Me . . . I Used to be a Normal Irish Guy'

Mary Fitzgerald in Tripoli

Hosam al-Najjair's jeep is one of the most battered vehicles in Tripoli. Every window bar the windscreen has been shot through, with only tiny shards of glass left clinging to the frames. Some of the rear seats were ripped out after his friend Atef, who was standing with his head through the sunroof, died from a sniper's bullet as their unit neared Tripoli just over a week ago.

The door on the driver's side is punctured with two bullet holes. 'This jeep is a mess but I just can't give it up. Too many memories,' says the 32-year-old building contractor from Dublin.

Those memories include being at the wheel of the first rebel vehicle to enter Tripoli's landmark Green Square, now renamed Martyrs' Square by the rebels. 'I arrived into the square and saw two policemen standing there, shocked at what was happening. They couldn't understand how we arrived so quickly. They dropped their guns but there was heavy artillery fire coming at us. I

Hosam al-Najjair from Dublin, who works as head of security for the Tripoli Revolutionary Brigade, which is led by his brother-in-law Mahdi al-Harati, Irish-Libyan deputy leader of Tripoli's military council. Photograph: Mary Fitzgerald.

reversed the jeep, jumped out, and then we moved in to clear the square.'

Najjair, his pale, freckled skin wrapped in a white headdress to protect against the searing sun of a Tripoli summer, is recounting the rebels' light-ning advance on the capital as we drive around the city, crossing checkpoints where fighters bedecked in the red, black and green of Libya's pre-Gadafy flag greet each other with loud exhortations and broad grins.

'I'll need a long holiday if I'm still alive after all this. We've been through a long, long journey. We went through hell,' he says.

Son of a Libyan father and Irish mother, Najjair spent most of his life in Ireland before returning to Libya for a wedding just before the

February uprising took place. He is now head of security for the Tripoli Revolutionary Brigade, one of the biggest rebel units from western Libya and the first to reach the capital. It is led by his brother-in-law Mahdi al-Harati, a teacher of Arabic who lives in Dublin's Firhouse with his wife and family.

'It was Mahdi's idea to form a brigade for Tripoli because at that time Benghazi and other cities had been liberated, and he thought Tripoli needed a brigade made up of people from Tripoli who would help liberate their hometown,' he says.

We arrive at the brigade's base, a tightly guarded former military airport where aircraft carrying VIP guests of Muammar Gadafy used to land. The arrivals lounge, lushly carpeted and stuffed with garishly ornate gilt chairs, is now strewn with guns, ammunition, and sleeping rebels spread out on the floor. Najjair cries out when he spots a friend across the room – a doctor, whom Najjair had heard had been killed on the frontline. They embrace with tears in their eyes.

There are several Irish-inflected accents in the room. The brigade includes men who have lived and worked in Dublin, among them a software engineer and a psychiatrist. An American-Libyan in a keffiyeh remarks on the disproportionate number of Libyans with Irish connections within the rebels' ranks. 'It's almost an Irish revolution,' he jokes.

In an adjoining room, Mahdi al-Harati is taking a break from hours of meetings. His brigade, which has grown to some 1,300 men from when they first began training in western Libya's Nafusa mountains, is busy sweeping the city, district by district, for any remaining pockets of resistance. Harati, who was last week appointed deputy of the rebels' Tripoli Military Council, says they have now secured 90 per cent of the capital, and esti-mates that it will take at least six weeks to ensure full control.

Softly spoken and in his late thirties, Harati has none of the overbearing swagger often seen among the younger fighters. He speaks wistfully of his family back in Dublin. He is thoughtful and considerate, and says he has two main worries about Libya's post-Gadafy future. 'One is the political struggle, the process of setting up the state. If it takes a long time to take shape, this could cause problems. The second issue on my mind is the widespread availability of weapons since the uprising began. We are working now to create a mechanism through which these weapons could be handed back or collected.'

Related to this is the concern that people may take the law into their own hands and seek revenge for the past. 'I don't think the revolutionary fighters themselves, as groups, are doing this but it may be an issue in communities and neighbourhoods with ordinary people,' says Harati. 'Because of the number of weapons around and because of the suffering of the past, people might want revenge.' Like most Libyans, he bristles at any comparison with post-Saddam Iraq. 'The two countries are very different on several different levels. We have no sectarian or ethnic divisions, plus the Libyans, as a population, have a tradition of being a peaceful people.'

He also plays down the issue of tribal fault lines. 'Until now, we don't have any problem arising from this, nothing that would be cause for fear or alarm.' Most of the men in Harati's brigade had never even picked up a gun before their country tipped into armed revolt earlier this year. They were doctors, engineers, lawyers, business people and students.

Najjair, who has tried to keep a diary over the past six months, mulls over how it has affected him. 'It has changed me as a person, this war. I've seen death in front of my eyes. I used to be a normal Irish guy who would give everyone the benefit of the doubt. Now I put a question mark over every person I see. I have to be like that because this is a dirty war – you're walking through the city trying to secure it and make the people feel safe, and a sniper could hit you from anywhere.

I'm hoping that attitude will disappear whenever I leave all this behind.' The rebels are all too aware that their war is not over yet.

'When we got here first, I thought the regime would have just crumbled but it hasn't,' says Najjair. 'Gadafy is going to fight to the end, but so are we. Wherever he goes, we'll be after him.'

FRIDAY, 2 SEPTEMBER 2011

Facing an Uncertain Future After Fall of Leader

Mary Fitzgerald in Tripoli

The sound of sing-song chanting carries from where children play on a balcony in Abu Salim, a rundown neighbourhood renowned as one of the most staunchly pro-Gadafy districts in Tripoli. *'Allah, Muammar, Libya wa bas* [That's all we need],' they trill, most likely in imitation of elders heard professing a once ubiquitous loyalist slogan.

The bleak, dun-coloured apartment blocks of Abu Salim, located a short distance from Gadafy's Bab al-Azizia compound, produced many of his most devoted supporters and fighters. It was one of the last areas of the capital to fall to the rebels, and only then after heavy fighting.

The ferocity of the battle is clear from the charred shell of the fire station opposite, which locals said had been used as a field hospital for Gadafy forces that retreated from Bab al-Azizia after it was overrun by rebel fighters. The residential blocks across the road are now pocked with bullet marks and holes gouged by artillery fire. The street is littered with shell casings and empty cartridges. In a room on the ground floor of one apartment building lie army boots and the remnants of green uniforms belonging to Gadafy

Men believed to be loyalists of Muammar Gadafy are detained in Zwara near al-Ymal and worried about the future as the former rebels tighten their hold on Libya. Photograph: Goran Tomasevic/Reuters.

forces who had fired at the advancing rebels from the windows.

In contrast to the watchful yet jubilant mood of opposition strongholds, the atmosphere here is subdued. Of those who have not fled, most are wary as they observe the changing order, and wonder where the man they looked up to for more than four decades has disappeared to. Their comments are guarded, and very often ambivalent. 'We are neither with Gadafy nor the revolution now,' says Khalifa, a shopkeeper transporting gallons of water in a wheelbarrow. 'We just want security.' He points out that, as a 30-year-old, he has known nothing but Libya under Gadafy. 'He has been with us for 42 years. How could we say that we didn't like him?' There are murmurs of agreement from the men around Khalifa when he says he is worried over what might come next. 'I'm not optimistic about the future. We don't know what

these rebels will bring. We have no water, power or security now. It is a chaotic situation already, and we are very, very afraid that a tribal war may break out.'

Far more forthcoming is the man who approaches and identifies himself as a former official in Gadafy's intelligence services. He claims that the loyalists that appear to have melted away in Tripoli and elsewhere are only biding their time. 'We are waiting for the end of NATO's intervention,' he says in English. 'When NATO finishes its mission, the *muqawama* [resistance] will rise up.'

He continues: 'If Muammar had no sons, it may have been different and everything would have been over by now, but since he has several sons, they will organise the *muqawama*.'

Similar rhetoric from Gadafy and his son Saif-ul-Islam in recent days has been largely dismissed by most Libyans, but anxiety over loyalist 'fifth columns' remains. There was some apprehension that they might choose yesterday's 42nd anniversary of the military coup that brought Gadafy to power to stage a counterattack – in a recent audio message Gadafy had promised a 'surprise' on 1 September – but the day passed off without incident.

Ridar Mohammed lives in an apartment facing the burnt-out fire station with his uncle, Farhat, an unemployed musician, and several cousins. All had escaped by the time the rebels reached Abu Salim. Ridar points out large holes ripped by artillery fire on the balcony and an exterior wall, but says he is not bitter or angry. One of his cousins flashes a victory sign at a rebel convoy passing on the street outside. 'Now we are with the revolution,' Farhat says. 'Gadafy's propaganda made us fear the revolutionaries. It turned people against the revolution but when they came here they didn't rape or pillage as we had been warned. They fought Gadafy's forces and went looking for arms in the area. What we had been told by state media was not true.'

Farhat and his nephews may have been won over to the rebels' cause but it will take time for others here, and in other pockets of Libya, to accept the new reality, if they ever do.

At a farmhouse across the city, I met one man who had worked on Saif-ul-Islam's youth programme when the regime was still in place. In a drab room, where a TV was tuned to the pro-Gadafy channel that broadcast an audio message by Saif-ul-Islam earlier this week, he complained about the rebels. 'They give the impression that anyone who is not with them is against them,' he claimed. 'This should not be about being pro-Gadafy or pro-revolution but patriotism. My greatest fear is that if civilised people don't come in swiftly to organise the country, there will be chaos and Libya will be a battlefield.' He questions how much the National Transitional Council, now considered Libya's interim government, will be prepared to accommodate people like him.

'A lot depends on how people like me are

treated. If they are badly treated, I'm sure there will be retaliation. I don't want to be humiliated. We all lived under Gadafy, we were working for our country,' he says.

'If [the NTC] is not able to bring such people on side, Gadafy could benefit. Will we be like the Iraqi people who were saying that life under Saddam was better than what they faced after he was toppled?'

SATURDAY, 3 SEPTEMBER 2011

No Class in RTÉ Establishment's Crass Attack

Keith Duggan

So if and when Pat Spillane or Joe Brolly or Colm O'Rourke or any of the voices of Establishment happen to bump into Jim McGuinness at some of the velvet-tie functions this autumn, will they have the good grace to apologise to him? Doubtful.

But that doesn't make the comments emanating from RTÉ on Sunday afternoon and Sunday evening any less disgraceful or insulting – not just to McGuinness but to the entire squad and, by extension, to the county.

The tone of disparagement set by Spillane after Donegal's championship opening-day victory over Antrim overflowed into naked contempt following their 0–8 to 0–6 All-Ireland semi-final loss to Dublin on Sunday night. In slagging off McGuinness and the Donegal side, the afternoon panellists positioned themselves as aesthetes, brimming with concern about the image of the game.

Funny, that. Maybe weird things happen to the memory when you enter the powder room at Montrose and get dolled up for the cameras.

But it might be worth recalling the reality of Gaelic football when they were playing the game. In 1987, Paddy Downey, the doyen of Gaelic games coverage, penned an article predicting that the upcoming All-Ireland final between the Meath team of Colm O'Rourke's vintage and Cork would be every bit as ugly as the 1967 showdown between the counties, which was remembered chiefly for providing the statistic of 51 frees in 60 minutes.

'The final of 20 years ago is far from the minds of the two squads of players who prepare for Sunday's encounter,' Downey wrote. 'Nor is either side concerned with critics' comments over the standard of the 1987 championship, nor the special pleading that they are obliged to redeem the game's tarnished image.'

That year's final marked the beginning of a four-year rivalry, in which the Meath and Cork players habitually assaulted each other in a series of games which saw private hatreds played out in a public arena. It was a dark and ugly rivalry. Both teams were ravenous for success and would stop at nothing to get it: this was the period of liberation just after the demise of the great Kerry team.

Two years earlier, Kerry and Monaghan met in the 1985 All-Ireland semi-final. Pat Spillane played that day. It was a novel pairing and yet it attracted a crowd of just 21,746 people.

Isn't it peculiar now to think that here were the gods of the modern game playing brand new Ulster champions and nobody bothered going? Maybe it was because they remembered the 1979 semi-final between the teams, when poor old Monaghan shipped a 5–14 to 0–7 hammering against the Kingdom (but the Monaghan men played in the spirit of the game!).

It has to be presumed that most of the attendance came from Kavanagh country in 1985. Nobody from Kerry or no neutrals could be bothered to go and see the greats, Pat! If the game that Spillane and Kerry espoused was so irresistible, then how come they weren't pouring through the turnstiles?

The answer, surely, is that by then, everyone was sick of Kerry; sick of their winning, sick of seeing the same old faces and listening to the same old schtick. Watching the same team win becomes monotonous. All those Kerry versus Dublin games – the Kingdom and the Power – was fine if you came from those two counties. But it didn't do much for Gaelic football around the country.

In the 1990s came the Ulster resurgence. Joe Brolly played on a tough and talented Derry team, whose lone All-Ireland success in 1993 revolved around that year's Ulster final against Donegal, the All-Ireland champions of the previous year. The teams disliked one another and it was a horrible game. And yes, it was played in a torrential downpour but you could have played it in Hawaii and the atmosphere would still have been poisonous.

You remember it, Joe. You remember the score. Look away because the sight of it might offend you these days. It was 0–8 to 0–6, the same as the score last Sunday. Did you worry about the entertainment value or the romance of the game that night, Joe? Doubtful.

So back to Dublin and Donegal last Sunday. Dublin's big misfortune was the sending off of Diarmuid Connolly and the incident was replayed and analysed at length.

Donegal's big misfortune was losing Karl Lacey. The Four Masters man is Donegal's most important player. It was notable that Barry Cahill's late 32nd-minute hit on Lacey was not replayed on the Sunday Game. It was notable that during the live broadcast, commentator Ger Canning and analyst Kevin McStay seemed determined to talk about anything other than the challenge as Lacey lay flat on his back.

It was interesting also that RTÉ made prominent use of a statistics icon noting (with due incredulity) the number of handpasses Donegal used in comparison to Dublin. And on the handpass issue, three of the Kerry goals in the celebrated Dublin–Kerry 1978 All-Ireland final were scored with the hands. It must make Pat Spillane ill to think about them now, given his aversion to that passing method.

And it was interesting that several of the frees Dublin were awarded were described on television as 'handy'. Does that mean that the referee whistled a few soft ones? If so, why not come out and say it? For there seemed to be no shyness about calling the Donegal team and tactics exactly as they saw it and the studio stars used language that must have stung the ears of those watching up in the Inishowen Peninsula.

The weird thing is that Spillane, O'Rourke and Brolly seemed sort of . . . aroused after the match. What other match has provoked the Kerry man to reference Marlon Brando and *Apocalypse Now*? Distasteful as they found the spectacle, it moved them to the use of flamboyant and excited language.

Maybe that was why Spillane felt emboldened enough to use terms like 'Shi'ite football' and to bring in The Hague and war crimes. How they must have laughed out in Srebrenica at that one. You can imagine the reaction if a term like that was ever applied to an establishment GAA county like Dublin, Kerry or Cork or to the hurling strongholds of Kilkenny or Tipperary. There would be outrage. But a nothing county like Donegal – 'up there' as it is often referred to – can shut up and take it. God knows what they would have said if Donegal had dared to actually win the game.

If Spillane and the others are going to take the grand-a-twist or whatever the Sunday Game fee is nowadays, they have to be more aware of their influence. So too should their employers.

They have to be aware of just how stinging those comments sound to the television licence-holders watching televisions in the bars of Glenties or Kilcar. They need to be aware of the weight of their reputations and of the weight that their words carry; they set the tone for the hysterical lynching that followed in the days afterwards.

There are people in Donegal dismayed by the way the team played against Dublin and who would dearly wish that the players might have expressed themselves a bit more openly when the game was in the balance.

However, they were entitled to set up that way. In most other field games in the world, from association football to baseball, the clean sheet or the shut-out is an acceptable – and lauded – element of the game. The Donegal team was guilty of nothing more than failing to enhance a clever and ferociously tough defensive strategy with a bit more attacking imagination.

They committed 22 fouls in the game – handy ones included. They scored two fewer points than Dublin. That was it. That failure did not merit the hostility and disdain which dripped from the state broadcaster on Sunday evening.

Anyhow, the Establishment has the All-Ireland final that it craved. The Kingdom and the Power, Alive-Alive-Oh and all of that. Meantime, the television stars might want to consider how they throw their words around.

If they do meet McGuinness and have the courage to look him in the eye, they will probably find the Glenties man will give them all the time in the world. They might learn from him something about that phrase which they like to confer on the gilded sons from the Establishment counties in the Montrose studio.

A bit of? What is it again? Oh, yeah. Class.

MONDAY, 5 SEPTEMBER 2011

It Takes 25 Pages and 11,000 Words to Say – 'Nothing to Do With Us'

Patsy McGarry

The Vatican's response to the Cloyne report, as well as to comments by Taoiseach Enda Kenny, Tánaiste Eamon Gilmore and motions passed by Dáil and Seanad, would have us believe that the clerical child sex abuse scandals in Ireland are an Irish problem, where Rome's only involvement has been in helping with a solution.

Vatican spokesman Fr Federico Lombardi repeatedly acknowledged the 'understandable outrage' of Irish public opinion. Photograph: Pier Paolo Cito/AP.

For this, it believes, it has received little or no acknowledgement in Ireland. For instance, Saturday's response noted that nowhere in his Dáil speech of 20 July last did Kenny recognise any of its efforts to improve matters in this context, and that Pope Benedict's Letter to the Catholics of Ireland in March last year didn't even merit a mention in the Cloyne report.

What happened in Ireland was because of local factors, the response indicates – helpfully quoting from the pope's letter of March last year to underline this.

There, addressing the Irish bishops directly, he said: 'Some of you and your predecessors failed, at times grievously, to apply the long-established norms of canon law to the crime of child abuse.'

That may well be so, but it is not the entire picture.

Selectively choosing what it wished to address, the Vatican response ignored completely its own treatment of the Murphy commission. It was set up by this State, yet it did not merit an acknowledgement from the Vatican when in September 2006 it wrote to the Congregation for the Doctrine of the Faith requesting information. Two further requests for information received no reply.

Nowhere in its response, which runs to 25 pages and almost 11,000 words, is any of this addressed by the Vatican. Rather it takes issue with certain findings of the Cloyne report which might have been clarified had it co-operated with the commission, whose remit was extended from the Dublin diocese to cover Cloyne in 2009. It can hardly complain if its non-cooperation backfired.

The response largely focused on the 1996 framework document on child protection, prepared

Aoife Cogan (left) and Bláthnaid McKenna model Coast's new collection in windswept Dublin.
Photograph: Bryan O'Brien.

for the Irish bishops, but shot down in a letter circulated to them by the Vatican in January 1997.

The response rejected, robustly, a finding of the Cloyne report that: 'There can be no doubt that this letter greatly strengthened the position of those in the church in Ireland who did not approve of the framework document as it effectively cautioned them against its implementation.'

The letter pointed out how the then prefect of that congregation, Cardinal Darío Castrillón Hoyos, had, at a meeting in November 1998 with the Irish bishops at Rosses Point in Sligo, 'unequivocally stated' that the church 'should not in any way put an obstacle in the legitimate path of civil justice' when it came to issues of clerical child abuse.

Nowhere does it quote from that 1997 letter, which said that, where the Congregation for Clergy was concerned, a framework document direction on mandatory reporting 'gives rise to serious reservations of both a moral and a canonical nature'.

The congregation also warned that procedures in the document appeared 'contrary to canonical discipline'. It also referred to it as 'merely a study document'.

This latter observation, it said at the weekend, was a reflection of the document's standing among the Irish bishops. The weekend response also emphasised that none of this meant the framework document guidelines could not be implemented in Irish dioceses and that 'each individual bishop was free to adopt it . . . provided these were not contrary to canon law'. The Vatican appears to be trying to have its cake and eat it, repeating what was said in the 1997 letter.

All of which is to ignore the frustration felt by the Irish bishops in dealing with Cardinal Hoyos over the abuse issue. In a comment to this newspaper last December, Archbishop Diarmuid Martin of Dublin said that in the past 'most of the Irish bishops felt that dealing with the Congregation for Clergy was disastrous'. It was understood he was referring to the period between 1996 and 2006, when Cardinal Hoyos was prefect at that congregation.

An Irish bishop confirmed, on condition of anonymity, that he made a note at the time of his receipt of that 1997 letter in which he described it as 'a mandate to conceal the crimes of a priest'.

At the same Rosses Point meeting in 1998, the then archbishop of Dublin Desmond Connell thumped a table in frustration as Cardinal Hoyos insisted it was Vatican policy to defend the rights of an accused priest above all.

In 2001 Cardinal Hoyos wrote a letter to French bishop Pierre Pican praising him for not passing information about an abuser priest to police. Bishop Pican received a suspended sentence for failing to report the priest who was sentenced to 18 years for the repeated sexual assault of boys over 20 years, and the rape of one of them.

Cardinal Hoyos wrote to Bishop Pican: 'I am pleased to have a colleague in the episcopate who, in the eyes of history and of all other bishops in the world, preferred prison to denouncing his son and priest.'

In the Murphy report, chancellor of the Dublin archdiocese Msgr John Dolan is reported as having said that the 1997 letter 'placed the [Irish] bishops in an invidious position'. It meant any priest against whom they took action 'had a right of appeal to Rome and was most likely to succeed'.

None of this is addressed in Rome's weekend response.

Cody's Driven Cohorts Reclaim Place at the Top

Seán Moran

Kilkenny 2–17 Tipperary 1–16

After a performance of feral intensity, Kilkenny are once more champions. Driven by the grievance of losing an exclusive place in history 12 months ago when Tipperary foiled the 'drive for five', Brian Cody's team hustled the holders into submission and were a little maligned by the tightness of the winning margin.

Just as Tipperary's aggression and desire proved too hot to handle in last season's final, the motivation of having lost the previous year again subdued the defending champions.

Tipperary went down with honour even though they were not allowed to play anywhere near their best. Pa Bourke's goal 15 minutes from time revealed glimpses of an attainable happy ending, but the efforts at recovery were too frantic and the Leinster champions never lost their nerve.

From the start, all of the early indicators fell Kilkenny's way. In a match which saw defences playing well, the winners' forwards were more clinical in the early stages, doing better under pressure and creating small openings as well as finishing enough of the chances that presented themselves to go 0–5 to 0–0 ahead after a quarter of an hour.

That was a conservative estimate of the damage and it required Paul Curran, who battled well for Tipperary at full back, to take the ball off the line in the 12th minute when Eoin Larkin looked to have finessed a goal.

Kilkenny's defence was magnificent. In the first 10 minutes both JJ Delaney and Tommy Walsh stamped their authority on the wings with super catches, characteristic of their best form.

Walsh was facing up to the opponent, Patrick

Tommy Walsh celebrates with manager Brian Cody after Kilkenny's triumph in the All-Ireland senior hurling final. Photograph: Alan Betson.

Maher, who had inhibited his influence a year ago but yesterday, and this time not labouring under the constraints of a shoulder injury, the Tullaroan wing back was like a hornet buzzing around, sweeping behind his line and placing some telling deliveries into the forwards.

Curiously he achieved this, although Maher came into the match in the second half and made an impact winning ball and drawings frees, but without quite turning the tide for the Tipperary attack.

The cockpit of the match had been expected to be in the full back line. Tipperary's devastating form in Munster and in the All-Ireland stages of the 2010 championship had been built on fluid interchange of forwards, luring defenders out of position – as in last year's final – to exploit the space, as Lar Corbett had been doing spectacularly with five goals in his past two matches.

There had been intimations of system breakdown in the semi-final when Dublin deployed an extra defender to cut down on the space available and make the attacking zone more crowded. Kilkenny were unlikely to drop a man back but how they guarded the approaches to goal would be critical.

With their full-back line looking far from impregnable at stages this year, Kilkenny had to tread carefully. In the event the defensive performance was integrated and exceptional.

Jackie Tyrrell, who hadn't been having the best of years, was assigned to track Corbett and although the Hurler of the Year probably saw more ball than in last year's final when he scored a hat-trick, none of his possessions came in situations where he had a clear sight at goal and Tyrrell kept him scoreless.

Tipperary's Lar Corbett chases Tommy Walsh of Kilkenny. Photograph: Lorraine O'Sullivan/Inpho.

The injury that kept Brian Hogan out of last year's final looked even more costly by the full-time whistle yesterday, as his presence intelligently maintained in the centre, played a key role in turning the avenues of 2010 into cul de sacs.

Effectively screened, Noel Hickey at full back wasn't exposed to the indignities of a year ago and formidably held his position. Rookie defender, Paul Murphy, thrived in such an efficient context and his dash and exuberance complemented the experienced strategists around him.

Eventually the champions got moving in the second quarter. Noel McGrath scored their first point in the 16th minute but that was the only score Tipp's forwards managed from play before half-time.

Eoin Kelly converted four frees – the award of which triggered a confrontation between the players during which Walsh's stick cracked referee Brian Gavin on the nose and necessitated some extensive running repairs – and Gearóid Ryan added another point from centrefield.

The critical score of the half – and arguably the match as it stripped bare Tipperary's growing confidence that they could get to the interval with a relatively small deficit despite having been distinctly second best – had its origins in carelessness.

Fatefully relaxing as Henry Shefflin addressed a line ball, the defence didn't react smartly enough when Shefflin quickly regained possession to find Richie Hogan. Hogan spotted Michael Fennelly surging through the middle and he hammered home the first goal for a 1–7 to 0–4 lead.

An illustration of the Kilkenny commitment came before half-time when Colin Fennelly, showing no ill effects of the hamstring injury that had threatened his participation, dived to block Corbett and sustained a nasty gash that required his temporary substitution.

Tipp brought Brendan Maher into the fray after half an hour and the 2010 All Star picked up the rhythm of the match to have a very productive second half.

At half-time Declan Ryan sent in Pa Bourke and Benny Dunne to replace Séamus Callanan and Shane McGrath, the latter a recognition of the problems Michael Fennelly and Michael Rice were causing at centrefield.

Despite Patrick Maher asserting himself (by the end earning four pointed frees, one converted 65 and making the first incision for the Tipp goal) Tipperary couldn't make huge inroads into the deficit and in the 44th minute Richie Power pointed to increase the half-time lead to six, 1–11 to 0–8.

Five minutes later the game was up. Eddie Brennan, deployed to complicate things for Pádraic Maher and with the help of his industrious teammates succeeding to the extent that the exceptional Tipp wing back was unable to reach the previous heights of earlier in the season, came onto a ball in space in the middle of the field.

Racing through the heart of the defence, he spotted Richie Hogan and set him up for a sweet finish. Hogan controlled the ball on his stick and fired his shot beyond Cummins for an eight-point lead. Bourke's goal, supplied by Corbett after work by Patrick Maher, raised hopes but the margin would never drop below a goal.

Like in 2006 when they last had a score to settle in an All-Ireland and thwarted Cork's three-in-a-row, Kilkenny ran on high-octane fuel. Cody, animated on the line by everything from sloppy wides to disputed refereeing decisions, eventually danced his victory jig as the team locked down his eighth All-Ireland in 13 years of management.

Brian Hogan made a very gracious victory speech and those who had speculated on the end of the line for this great team were left feeling pensive.

Memorials Salute Survival and Resilience

Lara Marlowe in New York

Ten years later, visiting the World Trade Center construction site is like receiving a jolt of high-voltage current.

In the streets surrounding the security enclosure, people and vehicles seem to converge from every direction. The noise of traffic, drills, hammers, diggers and clanging steel meld in an indescribable din. The earth rumbles each time a train passes beneath.

This is Manhattan at maximum sensory overload, deafening and smelling of hot dogs, pizza, mustard, sweat, dust, exhaust, singed rubber and soldered steel. Were it not for the solemnity of Michael Arad's monument to the 2,983 victims of 9/11 and the 1993 World Trade Center bombing, and the Tribute Center created by the families in a former deli outside the perimeter, you could almost forget the human cost of that day.

For two different stories co-exist here; one of heroism and loss, the other of renewal. Survival and resilience are the watchwords of the 9/11 commemorations, the essence of America's self-image. The 'survivor tree' has been replanted in the memorial plaza, after recovering in a botanical garden, a lone pear among a young forest of white swamp oaks. The 'survivor stairs', by which thousands of employees escaped from the north tower, are part of the unfinished National Memorial Museum.

'Three thousand of our loved ones and family members were taken from us,' says Bill Baroni, a dual citizen of Ireland and the US and deputy director of the Port Authority of New York and New Jersey, which has overall responsibility for the World Trade Center site.

'Yet we will remember those we lost with this stunning memorial. We will rebuild even higher.

The 9/11 memorial at the site of the World Trade Center in New York; one of two waterfalls, each designed by Michael Arad, that mark the footplate of the Twin Towers destroyed in the 2001 terrorist attack. Photograph: Joe Woolhead.

One World Trade Center is higher than the Twin Towers were. That's the message. You can attack us. We will remember with deep passion and sadness those we lost, but we will also rebuild, and we will be resilient. We're a tough lot.'

The 16 acres spread out before the observation deck where I stand with Baroni look like a cross between an archaeological dig and a science fiction film set. Two giant grey voids, entitled 'Reflecting Absence', fill the exact outline of the original Twin Towers, surrounded by an oasis of trees where presidents Barack Obama and George W. Bush will address the families next Sunday.

Construction workers in fluorescent vests, hard hats and boots – 3,500 men working 24/7 – teem over the other half of the site, to the north and east. Girders, pipes and concrete walls are layered below like lasagne. These are the foundations

for the new Port Authority Trans-Hudson (Path) railroad hub – designed by Spanish architect Santiago Calatrava, who created Dublin's Beckett Bridge – and World Trade Center towers two and three, which will be built when there is sufficient demand for office space.

When an Irish-American named Austin Tobin oversaw the building of the original World Trade Center in the late 1960s and early 1970s, it was vaunted as the greatest building project since the pyramids. Superlatives are a way of life in New York.

'This is certainly the biggest construction project in the US,' Baroni boasts. The waterfalls that form the pools of Arad's monument are 'the biggest man-made waterfalls in the world'. The $17 billion project is 'the most complex construction project on the planet', he continues, 'because we are building four office towers, a transportation hub, a shopping centre, museum and memorial on top of each other.'

To complicate matters, the old Path station, the terminus for trains to and from New Jersey, and the number one subway line, have been kept open through construction. Engineers enclosed the subway line in a $1 billion steel box. The Port Authority says 49,000 people travel through the construction site daily, and another 15,000 pass by on the street outside.

At the northwest and southeast corners, towers one and four rise almost before one's eyes, clad in mirror glass reflecting the clouds and sky. The elegant, twisting form of Number One World Trade Center has reached 80 floors and is adding another floor weekly. 'We never finish. Next floor. Next floor,' I hear a workman mutter in the lift when his shift ends.

Number One WTC will be the tallest building in the western hemisphere. 'It will rise to 1,776 ft (541 m), and from the top, from the 104th storey, you'll be able to see the curvature of the earth,' says Baroni.

The original name, 'Freedom Tower', was dropped because it was too political, too acute a reminder of the 9/11 attacks.

The walls of the rudimentary construction lift in number one are covered with decals, bumper stickers and pin-ups in bikinis. Support America against Terrorism. Teamsters. Semper Fi. A host of local union chapters. An Irish tricolour with the letters Irl.

The 71st floor is open to the elements, with only a thin veil of netting separating one from dizzying views of the Empire State Building, New Jersey, the Statue of Liberty and Brooklyn Bridge. From this height, Manhattan is so narrow one could reach out with both arms and embrace it. This was the view they had from the Twin Towers.

On the plaza below, workmen put the last granite blocks into place, in anticipation of the first visit from families of 9/11 victims.

A section of the bronze border around the pools is reserved for 'First Responders New York Fire Department'. So many Irish names . . . Hannafin, Corrigan, Keating, McGovern, Donnelly, McAvoy, Maloney, Coyle, McSweeney, Kennedy, Byrne, McShane, Ryan, O'Keeffe . . .

The museum, which will not open until September 2012, points like the prow of a ship at the diagonal between the two pools, the invisible line where Philippe Petit performed his high-wire walk between the Twin Towers on 7 August 1974.

A photograph in Colum McCann's award-winning novel *Let the Great World Spin* shows a plane flying past as Petit makes his crossing; it looks like it's going to crash into the tower. 'We wait for the explosion but it never occurs,' McCann writes. 'The plane passes, the tightrope walker gets to the end of the wire. Things don't fall apart.'

Arad, the architect who designed the monument, said he had wanted to place a stone inscribed with Petit's name beneath the place where the wire was stretched. In the simplicity of the plaza one senses, in McCann's words, 'the intrusion of time and history. The collision point of stories'.

In grey, ash-laden images of the collapsed World Trade Center, leaning high arches give an impression of cathedral fan vaulting. Two of the multistorey steel tridents that created the distinctive arches stand in the glass atrium of the unfinished museum, amid scaffolds and dust.

The escalators leading down to bedrock do not yet function. Descending the stairs, ever deeper, one reaches a cavernous, tomb-like hall enclosed on one side by the slurry wall, which oozes rusty water.

'The whole site is below the level of the Hudson River,' explains Baroni of the Port Authority. 'When the towers came down, they were afraid the slurry wall would collapse. Had that happened, it would have flooded lower Manhattan and the entire New York subway system. It held.'

A new slurry wall has been built for the site, but the old one is part of the museum. It dwarfs the fire trucks and a taxi damaged on 9/11, wrapped like Christmas toys in white plastic, waiting to go on display.

At the southernmost tip of the original Twin Towers, deep in the entrails of lower Manhattan, is the place the families call 'the true Ground Zero', the last vestige of the concrete foundations of the Twin Towers – huge, dust-covered blocks with an aura of ancient ruins.

The landmark continues to haunt New York. In the tourist trinket shops around the site you can buy pre-9/11 photographs sold as postcards and fridge magnets. One night a year, its forms are replicated by two powerful shafts of light sent heavenward. This is all that remains: the outline of two voids filled with water; two rusted steel tridents; a staircase and the unearthed fundaments of the world's most unfortunate building.

At the Tribute Center across the street from the construction site, New Yorkers grieve for the towers in a video testimonial. It was a city within the city, each floor a whole acre, they recall with affection. They're nostalgic for the betrothal and wedding parties at the Windows on the World, the way one looked down on the clouds, like a bed of cotton . . .

But it is another wall – not the slurry wall, not the 'true Ground zero' – that moves one most. The poster wall, covered with hundreds of photocopied A4 pieces of paper. 'Missing', they all say at the top. Photographs of smiling men and women, young and old, black and white, Asian and Hispanic, many in graduation or wedding garb. The physical description, what they were wearing that day, where they were last seen. The telephone number of a parent, spouse or sibling. Call if you've seen them.

One poster seems to acknowledge the futility of the exercise. 'Missing', it says above the face of a handsome young man. No name. No details. Just, 'Please Pray'. Until now, no trace has been found of 1,123 people – nearly 41 per cent of the 2,753 who died in the World Trade Center. (The

other victims were casualties of the planes that crashed into the Pentagon and in Shanksville, Pennsylvania, and six people killed in the 1993 bombing.)

For months, even years, grieving friends and relatives left these posters on the walls of lower Manhattan, the way one searches for a lost pet. They hung T-shirts with the names of the missing on the wrought iron gate at St Paul's Chapel, around the corner from the World Trade Center.

In every war, in every massacre, it is enough to enter into the individual lives of the victims for sorrow to engulf you. Orchestral music is piped into a back room of the Tribute Center. A wilted bouquet of red roses is propped against a wall bearing the names of all 2,983 victims. Photographs and mementos line the other three walls. Tourists sit staring, stunned, boxes of tissues pre-positioned on the benches beside them.

Lee Ielpi, a co-founder of the Tribute Center, tells how the 'band of dads' – eight retired firemen, including himself – returned to the smouldering ruins, day after day, searching for their sons. Jonathan Ielpi's helmet and torn fireman's coat are preserved in a glass case. 'I was the most fortunate of the bunch,' Ielpi says. 'I'm the only one who was able to bring his son's body home in one piece.'

Handwritten notes appear among the collage of photos. 'Mom', one starts, with a happy face drawn in the 'o' of 'Mom'. The borders of the white note card are filled with Xs and Os, hugs and kisses. 'I am going to wash the dishes tonight . . . Your loving, devoted, caring, thoughtful, sincere, kind kid Jody.'

In the very last room, where visitors sit around a large table, writing messages for the bulletin board, a group of Far East Asians huddle, weeping. I strike up a conversation with two Spanish cops and their wives. They're in New York for the 2011 World Police and Fire Games, and felt compelled to visit the centre, 'to touch history', says Jaime Curulla Sierra (33). He and his friend Raúl Cabrera

Alonso are drafting a note to pin on the wall, with the shoulder patch of the Barcelona constabulary.

'In Catalonia, 9/11 is our national day, so everyone was at home, watching TV,' Curulla Sierra remembers. 'It was lunchtime – around 3 p.m. In Spain we lunch late. I think nobody ate lunch that day.'

These 10 years later, Curulla Sierra says he is not angry, only sad. He feels solidarity with the victims and their families, 'not because they are American, but because they are human beings. Nationality isn't important'.

No man is an island . . . Any man's death diminishes me.

A few days earlier, Colum McCann said he didn't think of 9/11 as an Irish or even an American tragedy. 'I think of it as belonging to everybody,' he said. 'It was one of the first truly universal events. It's when the 21st century started.'

WEDNESDAY, 7 SEPTEMBER 2011

Indebted Fenians Flock to Land League

Newton Emerson

Far be it from me to suggest the mortgage forgiveness debate reveals the Irish to be a shadow of their former fighting selves. So instead let me retell the history of the Land League, as it might have been if led by today's bold Fenian men.

1873 The first Great Depression begins with the failure of an American investment bank, the collapse of a European property bubble and the new German Empire forcing everyone on to the gold standard. Uncanny, isn't it?

1876 As incomes slump across the world, Irish farmers are unable to pay the high rents they agreed during the previous agricultural boom. From his prison cell, Irish Republican Brotherhood leader Michael Davitt writes: 'Let's face it, we all partied.'

1877 Evictions leave estates across Ireland practically deserted, echoing only to the screams of abandoned women. Touring one such 'banshee estate', Home Rule MP Charles Stewart Parnell promises 'remedial landscaping and streetlights where possible to protect the value of your crofts until prices recover'.

1878 Poor harvests cause localised famine with many families forced to choose between eating or paying the rent. Davitt and Parnell meet to discuss the 'moral hazard' of helping those in need without helping those who can still eat and pay the rent.

1879 The Land League is launched with a 'monster rally' of 20,000 tenant farmers who march through Co. Mayo chanting: 'What do we want? Lower rents. When do we want them? Until the situation returns to exactly the way it was before, without any effect on the rents we charge our sub-tenants, which is a completely separate issue.'

1880 The league begins a tactic of boycotting landlords, then stops because it is 'unfair to scullery maids and other frontline domestic servants'.

1881 The league switches focus to resisting evictions, offering landlords an 'indentured servitude holiday' or a debt-for-equity swap of one guinea per tenant's daughter. Landlords are allowed to inspect the daughter for any signs of frivolous spending.

1882 Davitt, Parnell and the other league leaders are thrown in prison and tortured with a lesson on the Liberal party, including detailed descriptions of its internal rivalries and how they relate to its reform proposals. On their release, they are prepared to accept almost anything, including the argument that rent reductions would be 'socially divisive'.

1883 The league calls for a radical overhaul of Ireland's bankruptcy laws, so that people who want to walk away from their debts and emigrate to Australia will no longer be arrested and transported to Australia.

1885 The Government says a scheme for lower rents is impossible because, although Irish

Reflected in a work by Peruvian artist Jota Castro, Bob Geldof joins Castro's co-curator Christian Viveros-Fauné at the opening of the Dublin Contemporary exhibition at Earlsfort Terrace. Photograph: Dara Mac Dónaill.

landlords might co-operate, English landlords would have to be compensated. William Redmond says: 'Fair enough'.

1886 League secretary Timothy Harrington considers a plan for a general rent strike, forcing landlords to accept lower payments from those in financial difficulty. However, he decides a 'one-size-fits-all' approach is impractical and tenants will have to negotiate rent restructuring on a 'strictly case-by-case basis'.

1887 As the global economy starts to recover, everyone stops caring and goes back to exploiting their subtenants.

1889 Capt. William O'Shea names Parnell in his divorce, citing moral hazard.

WEDNESDAY, 14 SEPTEMBER 2011

My Manifesto for the Pork

Ross O'Carroll-Kelly

1. Forgive us, this day, our mortgage debt

During the years of the Celtic Tiger, Irish people were encouraged to buy things from maps – whether it was maps of muddy fields in makey-up places, such as Lucan and Tormonfeckin, or maps of Eastern Europe and makey-up countries, such as Bulgaria and Lithuania. They were assured by just about everyone that they'd be mad not to – in fact, the exact opposite was the case.

Ross O'Carroll-Kelly is in favour of mortgage

forgiveness for anyone who bought investment properties that they've never actually seen.

2. It's time to repopulate rural Ireland

Decentralisation is a thorny subject that successive governments have attempted to grasp but failed. Ross O'Carroll-Kelly is fully in favour of repopulating the south and west of Ireland. For a start, anyone who's from Leinster but supports the Munster rugby team should be forced to go and live there immediately.

3. Tough on England rugby captains, tough on the causes of England rugby captains

In 2003, Martin Johnson reduced President Mary McAleese – and millions of other Irish people – to tears when he forced her to walk on the grass at Lansdowne Road. As president, Ross O'Carroll-Kelly will take no shit from England rugby captains, especially those with faces like inside-out arses.

On official business, he will be accompanied by a new presidential guard, who will be authorised to Taser any English rugby player who refuses to move when he's told.

4. Save Superquinn in Blackrock and Ireland's other special heritage sites

Ross O'Carroll-Kelly recognises that there are landmarks of unique historical interest in Ireland that must be preserved as part of our rich cultural heritage. Renards, Superquinn in Blackrock and the Berkeley Court Hotel should be acquired by the Government and kept open to the public, with the same special heritage status as the Rock of Cashel, the passage tomb at Newgrange and the ancient stone fort of Dún Aengus. And the same with the corner of Croke Park where Shane Horgan scored against England in 2007.

5. My new underground plan for Dublin

Dublin is a city that has expanded at a rate of knots in recent years, often without the infrastructure to support that growth. Ross O'Carroll-Kelly is in favour of the underground plan for north Dublin. In fact, by the end of his presidency, he hopes that all of the northside of Dublin will be under the ground – bulldozing to commence in January 2012.

6. New national anthem – why Ireland needs to change its tune

Let's be honest, 'Amhrán na bhFiann' isn't doing it for us anymore – if it ever did! No one knows what a 'bearna baoil' even is. And the invention of the word 'sireland' just to find something to rhyme with 'Ireland' has made us a laughing stock around the world.

Ross O'Carroll-Kelly believes that 'Ireland's Call' should be the new national anthem and – as such – played at all official functions. The line at the end of each verse referring to the 'four proud provinces of Ireland' will be changed to 'three proud provinces of Ireland (plus Munster)'.

The presidential salute – played when the president arrives at an official engagement – will be changed to a simple high-five.

7. My solution to the housing crisis

Ireland's housing bubble, once the envy of the world, has burst. Shrewsbury Road – where once they complained that the billionaires were forcing out the millionaires – is now the country's most famous ghost estate.

Ross O'Carroll-Kelly is in favour of allowing people who are forced to trade downwards in the property market to bring their postcodes with them when they move.

8. Special Area Order for north Dublin's southsiders

Malahide, Howth, Clontarf and Portmarnock should be given the new postcode of Dublin 4N. Ringsend and Irishtown should be redesignated Dublin 4E. Or surrendered to the sea.

9. Gaelic football – what is it good for?

Ross O'Carroll-Kelly believes that Gaelic football is an integral part of Ireland's cultural identity and, as such, should be preserved – with certain refinements to the rules.

The existing round ball will be replaced by an oval-shaped one, which can only be passed backwards. The 'goal' will be replaced as a method of

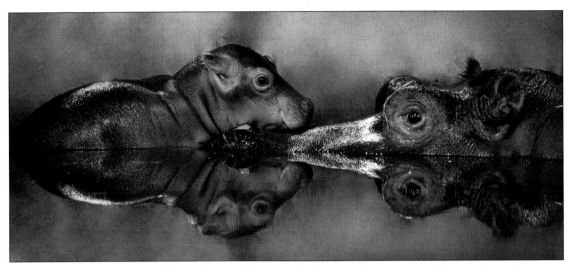

Dublin Zoo's newest arrival: Heidi the Hippo (right) gave birth to a 30 kg calf, the first born at the zoo in 10 years. Photograph: Patrick Bolger Photography.

point-scoring, the new objective being to place the ball within a squared-off, rectangular area behind the opponent's goal.

Teams will still be made up of 15 players but these will be divided into 'backs' and 'forwards'. When play is broken, the game will be restarted by a 'lineout' or 'scrum'. Further rule changes can be worked out later.

10. Rerouting the Liffey

Seismic activity within the earth's crust over the course of millions of years has resulted in a large number of Dubliners finding themselves marooned on the wrong side of the city's river. Ross O'Carroll-Kelly believes that the Liffey should be rerouted to place Tallaght, Crumlin and Westmoreland Street on the north side of the city.

11. Eradicate poverty – or at least the evidence of it

Ross O'Carroll-Kelly believes that certain shops and businesses that have proliferated in the years since the end of Ireland's economic boom have lowered the moral tone of the country – or at least that bit of the country that he's familiar with, between Leeson Street Bridge and Foxrock Church.

Ross O'Carroll-Kelly believes that cash-for-gold outlets – trading in everything from mismatched jewellery to gold fillings – as well as all-you-can-eat Chinese buffet restaurants prey on the unfortunate in our society and should be closed.

He is also in favour of the forced closure of all foreign discount supermarkets here and supports his mother's campaign group, Every Lidl Helps.

MONDAY, 19 SEPTEMBER 2011

This Really was Team Ireland in Eden

Gerry Thornley in Auckland, New Zealand

Ireland 15 Australia 6

Depending on which side of the world you were on Saturday, it either started in daylight and ended in darkness, or vice versa. Or something like that.

This was a great morning, day or night, and quite probably all three, to be Irish. We love a party, but as excuses for one go, heck, an epic 15–6 win over Australia, the Tri-Nations champions for heaven's sakes, was right up there.

Grit and determination etched on the faces of Irish forwards (from right to left) Jamie Heaslip, Donncha O'Callaghan, Paul O'Connell (partly hidden) and scrum half Eoin Reddan as Stephen Ferris locks arms around Australia's Will Genia on the way to Ireland's epic 15–6 World Cup win over the Wallabies. Photograph: Billy Stickland/Inpho.

There's something a little poignant, and even sad, about the way we've become more of a nation of ex-pats and grasp major sporting occasions such as these to find an outlet for our nationalistic pride.

But it makes nights such as these all the more special. This was more than a little patch of New Zealand green becoming Irish for the night. Auckland was a city invaded.

It appears half of the Irish diaspora are in the Antipodes, and as most of them are at least working can thus afford to reconnect with the old sod. It helps, mind, that New Zealanders don't exactly adore their neighbours, least of all when it comes to rugby and World Cups.

The sense of obligation to the fans was expressed by Gordon D'Arcy, who likened it to a home match. 'Look how far we are from Ireland and (how many) people are here. People living in New Zealand, Australia, Hong Kong and places like that, that are making the effort to come here. We get support no matter where we go in Europe or down in the Southern Hemisphere and it's great to be able to repay that intensity the fans gave us, and we gave it back to them today.'

As ever abroad (and Irish fans are not unique), they painted their faces and adorned themselves in riotous shades of green, and some gold and white, from head to toe.

They also fuelled their engines, as it were, well

in advance and sang their hearts out. Even 'Ireland's Call' had the hairs standing and in a barometer of what unfolded on the pitch, Australians were lustily out-sung and chanted.

Though not the finest of Irish ditties, on nights like these 'Olé, Olé, Olé' serves as a rallying call, but by midway through the second half, with Ireland in the ascendancy and the 25,000-plus in green becoming giddy with the real sense that they were witnessing a little piece of history, 'The Fields of Athenry' was echoing around the refurbished, 60,000-capacity World Cup final venue.

As many veterans of the press box and elsewhere confided, Eden Park, the ultimate All Blacks citadel, has never seen or heard or witnessed anything quite like it.

On New Zealand television news programmes yesterday, the lead item was of Irish fans celebrating on both sides of the globe, and added it was 'a trouble-free night' in Auckland. It also seemed to go down very well hereabouts.

In the process, Brian O'Driscoll et al have shaken the 2011 World Cup to its core. All pre-conceived notions have been shredded. As the odyssey continues to take in the length and breadth of New Zealand, the squad flew to Taupo yesterday for four nights.

Paul O'Connell's tight hamstring and Gordon D'Arcy's grade one hamstring strain were due to have scans today but neither appeared to be causing concern.

Now, victories over Russia and Italy over the next two Sundays in Rotorua and Dunedin would seal first place in Group C and a possible quarter-final against Wales in windy Wellington after the latter's win over Samoa yesterday.

Tom Court (centre) celebrates Ireland's victory with team mates Paul O'Connell (right) and Stephen Ferris (No. 6). Photograph: Sandra Mu/Getty Images.

Taoiseach Enda Kenny attracts attention as he greets Charlie Flanagan (9) at the Cannonball 2011 supercar event in aid of Barretstown, which he officially started in Merrion Square in Dublin. Photograph: Frank Miller.

It also opens up the distinct possibility of the Europeans being corralled into one half of the draw and the Tri-Nations heavyweights in the other – perhaps with Argentina.

This was also a vintage Irish rugby performance by, quite probably, Ireland's greatest generation of players. For how else do you rate this win, the first by an Irish team in the Southern Hemisphere since twice beating Australia, then the Bledisloe Cup winners, in 1979. It's certainly the best World Cup win ever and so it's right up there, even if they do drive you nuts by seemingly having to be blind-folded, handcuffed, put up against the wall and with the firing squad locked and loaded before they decide to come out and play as they can.

But then again, why should we expect a vintage crop of players – many with a couple of Heineken Cups and Grand Slams to their names –

to be at their best in non-competitive warm-up matches. At the outset of August we said this team (and all Irish supporters for that matter) would happily exchange four warm-up defeats for four Pool wins. Now, that is a very realistic possibility.

They sensed something special was brewing in the camp all week.

'Yeah, it's something hard to always read and predict,' admitted defensive coach Les Kiss, 'but there was certainly something about the guys taking control. We are the coaches but ultimately the players define what they are about, and this was one of those weeks. And I think that was borne of the fact that they knew they weren't too far away in a couple of things, I know we haven't been as good as we would have liked to have been but underneath it all, there was something sitting there nicely and bubbling away and we just had to bring it out of ourselves.'

Heroes abounded, the near demonic O'Connell and O'Driscoll – they say a bird never flew on one wing but he gave it everything with, it seemed, one arm – led the way.

You also suspected the silver fox himself, Kidney, would have it all pitched right, and according to Kiss, masterfully managed the mood all week.

It helps too when the Brains Trust has people like Kiss and Gert Smal, amongst the very best defensive and forwards coaches in the global game and who had been masterminding their defensive and pack plans for months, nay years.

This win was founded first and foremost on the Irish scrum, where Cian Healy especially did a number on Ben Alexander, and their collective aggression and accuracy at the breakdown, and in the tackle area. They ran hard and straight, and tackled hard, none more so than Stephen Ferris and Seán O'Brien, and Kiss would have been thrilled at keeping the potent Wallabies tryless and at the way they pushed hard on to the playmaker Will Genia, rarely drifting off him or allowing him space.

Vintage Irish performances also draw heavily on emotion, albeit mixed with intelligence. Controlled fury, as it were. All week the players had spoken of their obligation to reward their supporters and deliver a performance more befitting their ability.

As Kidney has long since noted, we can be our own harshest critics as a nation, and the harsh analysis often starts from within. But the sense of all-for-one, one-for-all had been established earlier in the week by experienced players outside the 22 match-day squad – Shane Jennings and Geordan Murphy.

The emotional intensity was pitched a little further by Jerry Flannery, whose World Cup had been cruelly cut short by another calf tear the previous Tuesday, handing out the jerseys at Friday's captain's meeting. There weren't many words said

then, but there followed some emotive words from O'Driscoll and O'Connell, who spoke of there being no separate provincial entities. This would be Team Ireland at Eden Park. This was Team Ireland at Eden Park.

MONDAY, 19 SEPTEMBER 2011

Out of the Blue, a Performance to Banish Long Years of Torture

Seán Moran

Dublin 1–12 Kerry 1–11

Out of the blue it erupted. Dublin, for so long exemplars of under-achievement or, more accurately, the perennial experts at disappointing exaggerated expectation, did what they weren't supposed to do.

History had taught them to expect little from championship encounters with Kerry. It had also encouraged people to disbelieve their survival instincts in a tight finish. Both of these rules of thumb went unobserved in the most extraordinary of finales in yesterday's GAA All-Ireland football final at a reverberating Croke Park.

Ironically for a team that has consciously under the management of Pat Gilroy eschewed melodrama in front of the Hill, Dublin couldn't have devised a more startling *coup de théâtre* at the northern end of the ground than to summon Stephen Cluxton from goal to address a free, 35 metres out, in the dying moments of injury-time with the All-Ireland final tied at 1–11 each.

Cluxton, having survived a determined attempt by Kerry to hack his kick-outs and delivered another accomplished display in goal – at one stage pulling down a free kick that looked like dropping over the bar – may have felt that he wasn't under pressure given that by the time he kicked, the highest price of missing would be a replay. But that wasn't the full picture.

He was kicking for his county to defeat Kerry in championship for the first time in 34 years and in a final for the first time in 35. He was kicking for Dublin's first Sam Maguire since 1995 and the redemption of a season which had concluded with four All-Ireland finals in two weeks, three of which had been lost by the time he flighted the ball over the bar.

Within seconds Joe McQuillan had whistled the end and Kerry, masters of September, were beaten and spent.

They'll puzzle and agonise over this one long into the cold, dark winter. Having absorbed Dublin's most determined challenge to their imperium in a long time, the Munster champions looked to have pulled clear when their captain Colm Cooper, with characteristic brilliance in the crucible, pointed from the left sideline to put his team four in front with seven minutes left to his becoming the first Dr Croke's man since the legendary Dick Fitzgerald to captain Kerry to All-Ireland success.

He wasn't alone in carrying the fight to Dublin. Kieran Donaghy gave his best display in the championship in a long while, switching out to the wing early on and getting involved in the game before reverting to more natural environs at full forward and posing a constant threat, whether drifting in to menacing positions or tussling for the ball, as when at one stage he hustled Cluxton into losing possession.

His point to equalise at the end of normal time was both brave and bravura and looked to have swollen Croke Park's coffers by delivering a replay for which people might well have killed to get tickets.

Dublin goalkeeper Stephen Cluxton takes the free kick that, in the dying seconds of the All-Ireland senior football final, won the match for his team. Photograph: Donall Farmer/Inpho.

Dublin manager Pat Gilroy celebrates Cluxton's and the team's achievement. Morgan Treacy/Inpho.

Maybe it was the way Dublin had to win – not nervously defending a shrinking lead but throwing caution to the wind and attacking the opposition regardless of reputation and the natural order.

There were reasons why Dublin went on to take their 23rd All-Ireland. First, their mentality, so often doubted even when after the current team had been re-forged in the hellfire of the 17-point beating Kerry gave them two short years ago, was resilient and honest.

It's an indicator that there was such debate over the Man of the Match award afterwards – as of course there should be in a team sport – but all 15 played well and no-one hid when the pressure intensified.

Secondly, Gilroy's specific project – the stiffening of the defensive capability – produced a back-six performance as good as Dublin had given

in years and against the attack with the highest quota of quality and class in modern football.

Michael Fitzsimons from Cuala, following in the footsteps of the late and great Mick Holden, was surprisingly put in charge of Cooper and did a good job, erring in judgement just once when trying to let a ball run over the end line under pressure from Cooper and conceding a converted 45.

Rory O'Carroll gave nothing to Declan O'Sullivan after a point in just the second minute and Cian O'Sullivan, his Kilmacud team-mate, led the charge that produced the vital 64th-minute goal.

It came when Declan O'Sullivan was harried out of possession and his namesake gathered and pumped the ball into Alan Brogan, whose well-judged pass placed replacement Kevin McManamon for a decisive finish.

Man of the match Richard Dunne (right) is congratulated by goalkeeping coach Alan Kelly after leading a remarkable display of defensive defiance in Moscow as the Republic of Ireland maintained their European Championship hopes with a fortuitous 0–0 draw against Russia at the Luzhniki Stadium. Photograph: Donall Farmer/Inpho.

Kevin Nolan, the other Kilmacud back, equalised to cap a display of quality football and preternaturally calm judgement on the ball, making him the go-to man in many relieving bouts of hand-passing at the back.

Ger Brennan was on the back foot against Darran O'Sullivan but used his strength on the ball to help organise the break-outs, even if he conceded a couple of silly frees. O'Sullivan's pace was instrumental in setting up Cooper for the Kerry goal in the 19th minute and the blue hordes must have felt the icy grip of fear that has haunted recent generations when in the heat of battle with their most traditional rivals.

Thirdly, the precepts of the modern team panel have been observed by Dublin, and Gilroy

was able to make effective substitutions. For the second day in succession McManamon came off the bench and survived an underwhelming acclimatisation period when he wasted some early possession to make a huge impact on the match.

Aside from the obvious contribution of a goal that changed the course of the whole championship, McManamon was hungry for ball and drove hard at Kerry as their defence was ever so slightly fraying.

Fourthly, the quality of the forwards mightn't be hallmarked to the same carat as Kerry's but neither is it counterfeit.

Alan Brogan gave another industrious display, fired over a couple of points and provided the goal assist, whereas his brother Bernard again confirmed his evolution from a firecracker individualist and reigning Footballer of the Year into a complete team player, making the runs – although not always rewarded with serviceable deliveries – and taking on his nonpareil marker Marc Ó Sé in a memorable tussle.

His six-point haul could have been greater but for an inexplicable miss before half-time from a free, mirroring Cooper's similar error at the other end moments previously.

The day didn't start well with the defeat of the well fancied city minors, who had twice previously played Tipperary in the curtain raiser to Dublin–Kerry senior finals. The county had won the minor on those occasions only to lose the main event.

Yesterday inverted that and in a further coincidence linked the day to 1934 when Tipp last won the minor All-Ireland and Dublin defeated Kerry in a senior semi-final.

Injury failed to have its anticipated effect with both Kerry's Eoin Brosnan and Dublin's Paul Flynn starting and playing for most of the match, even if both were replaced before the end.

Flynn, Barry Cahill and captain Bryan Cullen worked extraordinarily hard in the winners' half-forward line and Dublin maintained a threatening tempo, apart from a period in the second half when it looked as if the match might be slipping away.

That coincided with a temporary waning in the influence of Dublin's centrefield. Denis Bastick worked himself to a standstill, enlivening the afternoon with an acrobatic back-flip on half an hour to raise himself off the ground, and kicking a point just after the break to keep Dublin's momentum going. His partner Michael Darragh Macauley was superb, getting onto the ball either fielding or making himself available and using his strength to break tackles.

Fianna Fáil deputy leader Éamon Ó Cuív (right) looks less than enthusiastic as party leader Micheál Martin seeks to explain why there will be no FF candidate for the presidential election in 2011, against Ó Cuív's wishes. Photograph: Bryan O'Brien.

If there was a slight dip in the second half, Macauley came roaring back into the match in the crucial endgame.

For Kerry, Bryan Sheehan was the cause of the recession in Dublin's fortunes in the sector and his second-half display was a huge factor in Kerry's apparently decisive break for victory.

It was also fitting that the Brogans – genetically engineered for this day, with their father who sealed Dublin's last win over Kerry in the August of 1977 and maternal bloodlines in the Kingdom – should play such a significant role not just in yesterday's gripping finale, but throughout a season that has restored the glow of confidence to the county whose proud reputation had been shot through with self-doubt in the years since last keeping Sam Maguire in the city.

Free at last. Those family holidays will be a riot over the next 12 months.

Index

Page numbers set in *italic* indicate a picture.